W9-ABP-330

OPERA MEDIAGRAPHY

Recent Titles in the Music Reference Collection

The Classical Reproducing Piano Roll: A Catalogue-Index
Volume I: Composers
Larry Sitsky, compiler

The Classical Reproducing Piano Roll: A Catalogue-Index
Volume II: Pianists
Larry Sitsky, compiler

An Eighteenth-Century Musical Chronicle: Events 1750-1799
Charles J. Hall, compiler

Jazz Performers: An Annotated Bibliography of Biographical Materials
Gary Carner, compiler

Music History during the Renaissance Period, 1425-1520: A Documented Chronology
Blanche M. Gangwere

Music for Two or More Players at Clavichord, Harpsichord, Organ: An Annotated Bibliography
Sally Jo Sloane, compiler

Fire Music: A Bibliography of the New Jazz, 1959-1990
John Gray, compiler

String Music of Black Composers: A Bibliography
Aaron Horne, compiler

The American Wind Symphony Commissioning Project: A Descriptive Catalog of Published Editions, 1957-1991
Jeffrey H. Renshaw

Piano Music by Black Women Composers: A Catalog of Solo and Ensemble Works
Helen Walker-Hill

Keyboard Music of Black Composers: A Bibliography
Aaron Horne, compiler

A Conductor's Repertory of Chamber Music: Compositions for Nine to Fifteen Solo Instruments
William Scott, compiler

OPERA MEDIAGRAPHY

Video Recordings and Motion Pictures

Compiled by
Sharon G. Almquist

Music Reference Collection, Number 40

Greenwood Press
Westport, Connecticut • London

Library of Congress Cataloging-in-Publication Data

Opera mediagraphy : video recordings and motion pictures / compiled by
Sharon G. Almquist.
p. cm.—(Music reference collection, ISSN 0736-7740 ; no.
40)
Includes index.
ISBN 0-313-28490-3 (alk. paper)
1. Operas—Film and video adaptations—Catalogs. I. Almquist,
Sharon G. II. Series.
ML158.6.06064 1993
016.7821'0267—dc20 93-28491

British Library Cataloguing in Publication Data is available.

Library of Congress Catalog Card Number: 93-28491
ISBN: 0-313-28490-3
ISSN: 0736-7740

First published in 1993

Greenwood Press, 88 Post Road West, Westport, CT 06881
An imprint of Greenwood Publishing Group, Inc.

Printed in the United States of America

The paper used in this book complies with the
Permanent Paper Standard issued by the National
Information Standards Organization (Z39.48-1984).

10 9 8 7 6 5 4 3 2 1

For Arne

Contents

Acknowledgments

This work could not have been completed without the special help of the following people.

Kathleen A. Abromeit, Oberlin Conservatory, Oberlin, Ohio
Marvin W. Andrews, Head, Reynolds Audio Visual Department, Rochester Public Library, Rochester, New York
Dana Hendrix Barnekow, Southwestern University, Georgetown, Texas
Suzanne Byron, Head, User Education, University of North Texas, Denton, Texas
Keith D. Eiten, Central College, Pella, Iowa
Michael Fling, Music Library, Indiana University, Bloomington, Indiana
Greg S. Greary, Music Librarian, University of Hawaii at Manoa, Honolulu, Hawaii
Iva Helen Gross, Amarillo Public Library, Amarillo, Texas
Scott Hawkins, Music Librarian, Dayton and Montgomery County Library, Dayton, Ohio
Ellen Hines, Arlington Heights Memorial Library, Arlington Heights, Illinois
Jennifer Hood and Phil Simms, Music Library, Southwestern Baptist Theological Seminary, Ft. Worth, Texas
Jim Kroll, Manager, Humanities Department, Denver Public Library, Denver, Colorado
Walter R. Laude, Indiana University of Pennsylvania, Indiana, Pennsylvania
Kenneth Lavender, Rare Books Curator, University of North Texas, Denton, Texas
Rachel Opheim Lohafer, Iowa State University Film & Video Library, Ames, Iowa
Alice N. Loranth, Cleveland Public Library, Cleveland, Ohio
Morris Martin, Music Librarian, University of North Texas, Denton, Texas
Paula D. Matthews, Media Librarian, Bates College, Lewiston, Maine
Jerry McBride, Music Librarian, Middlebury College, Middlebury, Vermont
Ruth Ann Mctyre, Music Librarian, Beth Tice, and the staff of the Music Library, Baylor University, Waco, Texas

Pat Means, Media Specialist, Austin College, Sherman, Texas
Philip Myette, Educational Media Center, Greenville College, Greenville, Illinois
Holly Oberle, Music/Dance Librarian, Ohio University, Athens, Ohio
Dennis G. Odom, Music Library, Texas Christian University, Fort Worth, Texas
Kathryn Olsen, Head, Film/Video Services, Broward County Main Library, Fort Lauderdale, Florida
Barbara Pfahl, Wadsworth Public Library, Wadsworth, Ohio
Rick Provine, Media Library, University of Virginia, Charlottesville, Virginia
Ruth R. Rains, University of Illinois Film Center, Champaign, Illinois
Don Richter, Stephen F. Austin State University, Nacogdoches, Texas
Darlene Scifres, Media Services, Sul Ross State University, Alpine, Texas
Corinne Smith, Audio-Visual Services, Pennsylvania State University, University Park, Pennsylvania
Ruth Southard, Media Services, University of Texas at Dallas, Dallas, Texas
Beverly Teach, Center for Media and Teaching Resources, Indiana University, Bloomington, Indiana
Trinity University, the staff of Instructional Media Services, San Antonio, Texas
David Truesdale, Recorded Sound Collection, University of Missouri at Columbia, Columbia, Missouri
Jean Weaver, Instructional Media, Dickinson College, Carlisle, Pennsylvania
Marta Wodnicka, Technical Services, University of North Texas, Denton, Texas
Marge Wood, Audiovisual Supervisor, Abilene Christian University, Abilene, Texas

Introduction

Scope

This opera mediagraphy lists operas released as motion pictures, both as theatrical feature films on 35mm film and educational films on 16mm film, and videorecordings, including the VHS videotape format and optical video laser disc. The final date for adding newly released videorecordings was March 1, 1993.

Operas issued on video (either videotape or video laser disc) are restricted to those that have been released in the United States in the American television standard for video called NTSC (National Television Standards Committee). Operas that were recorded and released solely in formats not compatible with NTSC, such as PAL (Phase Alternate Line, used in England) and SECAM (Sequential Color And Memory), are not included. Many operas are, of course, issued in multiple formats, but inclusion here is dependent upon a video's release in the United States in NTSC format. No such restriction has been placed on feature or educational films because of the universal nature of the film format.

Most of the operas are available for purchase on VHS video and/or laser disc or rental on film; check with individual distributors for availability of titles on Beta and 8mm videocassette. Several titles that were out-of-print at the time of publication are included because they were once available and, with the video revolution still continuing, may well be available again in the near future. It is not uncommon to see films and videos which were withdrawn from distribution reappear years later.

Unfortunately, while new titles continue to be released on video and old ones are reissued, many film rental centers are closing. One major loss is the University of Illinois Film Center (1325 S. Oak Street, Champaign, IL 61820; 800-367-3456), which shut down operations in June of 1993. Several opera films that were available solely from Illinois must now be considered unavailable.

Almost all of the operas listed herein are complete works; a few abridgements are included for their historical or entertainment value. Musicals are not included although operettas by Gilbert and Sullivan and Lehár are included. (The Laurel and Hardy operettas, such as *The Devil's Brother* and *The Bohemian Girl*, are also excluded.) Full cast credits are provided for each opera. The opera character names are followed by the name of the singer/performer of the role. Character names are based upon those found in *Kobbé's Complete Opera Book* and from published libretti. Purely descriptive character names such as "a messenger" or "a servant" are translated into English. In most instances, the singer/performer credits were obtained by viewing the title and/or examining the accompanying information and container. For out-of-print motion pictures, credit information was derived from published guides, press notices, and distributors' catalogs. Archival film credits were provided by the caretakers of the collections in which they are housed.

Standard Titles

Entry of operas is by the standard or uniform title of the work. By using standard titles, the same operas can be listed together regardless of the language or grammatical format of their title. Standard titles are created in the language of the original except in a few instances in order to avoid confusion, such as in using *Xerxes* instead of *Serse*. For works in Russian, Hungarian, and Polish, the equivalent English title is used. Throughout there are *SEE* references from variant titles to the standard title. Initial articles in the language of the standard title are included in the *Listing of Operas by Title* section of the mediagraphy but are not included in any of the indices. The alphabetical arrangement ignores initial articles.

Indices

Since entry is by title, three indices are provided: singers and conductors, which includes all singers listed in an entry (Actors, actresses, and dancers are not indexed.); composer; and production types, such as feature film, film or television version, and stage production. The term "feature film" refers to theatrically produced films that are often free adaptations of the opera with spoken dialogue and selected musical excerpts. A "film version" or "television production" is a film or television production of the opera that may be abridged but is a true performance of the opera and is not an adaptation. The majority of operas listed are stage productions; that is, actual recorded productions documenting an evening at the opera with a live audience. The term stage production is not used in the index. Instead, these productions are indexed by the opera company or festival that produced them such as the Metropolitan Opera (New York City) or the Bayreuth Festival.

Distributors

As for distributors of audiovisual opera titles, not every conceivable distributor of a video or film is listed. Instead, only the primary distributor is provided. For example, Home Vision not only distributes titles under its name, but distributes HBO Video and Kultur releases as well. Home Vision is not, however, the primary distributor for these titles; HBO and Kultur are. In this instance, Home Vision would be considered a secondary distributor. A primary distributor is defined as the distributor that puts its name on the video.

Primary distributors do, of course, change periodically and without much notice or are absorbed by other distributors. They also change their names frequently. One prime example of this is the variation of the name of Thorn/EMI Video. In short, Thorn/EMI Video became Thorn EMI/HBO Video, and finally Thorn disappeared to be replaced by HBO Video. Even though originally issued with the Thorn/EMI label, these titles now fall under the HBO Video umbrella. It is also interesting to note that many of the initial releases by Thorn were issued without English subtitles; later releases often included subtitles. It is a good idea always to verify that a specific release comes with subtitles.

Another interesting mutation is the distributor Magnetic Video, which existed in the late 1970s as a distribution arm of 20th Century Fox. Magnetic Video was dissolved by Fox when the video market skyrocketed, and Fox then issued videos directly under its name, 20th Century Fox Video. Later, Fox was absorbed by CBS, and releases are now labelled CBS/FOX Video. Many of the Magnetic Video releases subsequently went out-of-print.

Optical Laser Discs

Please note that with very few exceptions, most notably Voyager's *Criterion Collection*, opera on optical laser disc is released in the CLV (constant linear velocity) format. CLV holds up to sixty minutes per side and permits chapter searching and pause but does not allow the user to freeze frame or use other special effects on most machines. (There are some expensive laser disc players that can do special effects with CLV discs.) Occasionally, the final side of a three- or four-disc opera will be recorded in the CAV (constant angular velocity) format that allows all special effects but is limited to thirty minutes per side. CAV format laser discs require more disc space than those recorded in CLV and are consequently more expensive.

Sound Tracks

Each entry includes information on the technical aspects of the sound track by specifying stereo, mono, hi-fi. Most of the operas recorded on laser disc have digitally recorded or digitally remastered sound tracks. Many of the most recent releases on videotape also feature digitally recorded or remastered sound tracks.

"Private" Sources

Most of the distributors of videorecordings listed herein are commercial suppliers. A few "private" releases by Lyric Distribution and Bel Canto, to name just two, are included since many times it is only through these "private" sources that operatic motion pictures or television productions are available. "Private" distributors also offer a wide variety of stage productions not available elsewhere. It is not the intent of this mediagraphy to list all titles available privately even though many are television productions. Lyric's catalog alone lists over five hundred titles with new additions appearing regularly. There is a caveat on "private" sources. Just as with their audio equivalents, the quality of the reproduction can vary greatly.

Running Times

The running times of the operas are based first upon viewing and second upon distributors' catalogs. In some instances there may be as much as fifteen minutes of commercials included. Interviews with performers, introductions by singers, and other documentary materials also add to the overall timing. Depending on the distributor, it may be this inclusive timing that is listed in catalogs as the actual running time of the opera. Wherever possible, these additional materials and their timings are so noted in the body of the entry.

Furthermore, it is quite common to see a one-to-three minute, sometimes more, difference in running times for what is, in fact, the same release. The following example not only illustrates the timing disparities but shows the concept of primary and secondary distributors as well. Movies Unlimited is a secondary distributor and lists a timing of 125 minutes for a particular work in its catalog. The primary distributor, Home Vision, lists a timing of 129 minutes for the same work in its catalog. To make matters even more confusing, the actual viewing time of the piece from first to final content frame is 131 minutes. Nothing has been deleted from or added to the opera proper. Differences in timings are just one of the vagaries of the video/film world.

Order Numbers

It is also important to note that both primary and secondary distributors use their own order number system in their catalogs and that these numbers are almost always different. Indeed, within a single distribution company numbers may differ depending on which catalog is consulted. Because there is not a consistent numbering system for media materials and because numbers can cause confusion when attempting to order a title, order numbers are not included in this mediagraphy.

Appendices

Appendix A contains an abbreviated listing of motion pictures and television productions that are worthy of mention but because of their relative inaccessibility are not included in the main body of the mediagraphy and are not indexed in any of the indices.

Appendix B contains a list of distributors with addresses and phone numbers. These are primary and secondary distributors that can supply opera titles on videocassette or laser disc, or are rental institutions for 16mm films. For sole source distributors or libraries holding an otherwise out-of-print title, the address is given with the specific entry.

Filmstrips

Outside of the scope of this work, but of interest historically, are the many opera filmstrips that were issued with accompanying phonodiscs or audiocassette tapes as well as those that were issued without any accompanying sound. These filmstrips appeared in the late 1950s and continued to be issued through the 1980s. In fact, many are still available from the Clearvue/EAV Corporation (6465 North Avondale, Chicago, IL 60631; 800-431-2196). Clearvue purchased the EAV (Educational Audio Visual) company, a distributor of many filmstrip sets in a series called the *Music Appreciation Series*. Other filmstrip distributors were: Brunswick Productions (the *Great Opera Series*); the Metropolitan Opera Guild; The Society for Visual Education, Division of The Singer Company (*Great Opera Stories* series); and the Jam Handy Organization (*Opera and Ballet Stories* series).

Many of these releases contained visuals from performances and rehearsals at a variety of opera houses, such as the Metropolitan Opera or the New York City Opera. Others used art work and text to illustrate an abridged version of the opera. The filmstrips ran from a single filmstrip reel of 40 frames to multiple filmstrip reels totalling over 180 frames. Sound accompaniment ranged from the principal arias of the opera with narration and thematic music to abridged performances ranging from 20 to 40 minutes.

Before the mid-1980s video releases were rare and expensive and 16mm films cost hundreds of dollars. At that time less expensive filmstrip sets were a good solution for schools. They served, and still can serve, to introduce the plots and principal arias from the operas.

Review Sources and Ratings

Citations to reviews of opera videorecordings, motion pictures, and laser discs are included from over twenty-two sources. The sources range from opera journals to video review periodicals to general publications. The reviewer is listed after each citation.

Each review is given a rating based on the mediagrapher's reading and interpretation of the reviewer's intent. Please note that ratings should never be used as the sole basis for purchasing, and should not be viewed as value judgments expressed or implied by the mediagrapher toward the works being reviewed or the reviewer.

Review Sources

Classical, premiere issue in December 1989, title change to *Classic CD* in March 1991. The US edition is published in Rahway, NJ.

EFLA, Educational Film Library Association, *Film Evaluation Guide, 1946-1964*, New York: EFLA, 1965. Abbreviated *EFLA* (1965). Reviews of non-theatrical 16mm films. The Association changed its name to AFVA, American Film and Video Association, in 1988 and continues to publish reviews as the ***AFVA Evaluations***.

Fanfare, "The magazine for serious record collectors," began publication in 1977. Later issues include a laser disc review section by James Reel.

Landers Film Reviews. *Landers* first started service in 1956 and changed its name to ***Landers Film and Video Reviews*** in Fall 1989. It ceased publication with the Winter 1992 issue.

Levine, Robert. *Guide to Opera and Dance on Videocassette.* Mount Vernon, NY: Consumers Union, 1989. Abbreviated *Levine*. A book of reviews written and compiled by music critic Robert Levine.

Library Journal, a journal devoted to librarianship that also includes reviews of print and non-print materials.

Motion Picture Guide, a multi-volume publication (also available on CD ROM) covering films released 1927-1983. Entries are alphabetical by title so this multi-volume work is simply cited as *Motion Picture Guide*.

Beginning with the 1986 issue, volumes are released annually. Each annual volume covers films released the previous year and are cited as *Motion Picture Guide, 1990*, etc. It is published in Chicago by Cinebooks.

Musical America, began publication in 1898. It ceased publication with the January/February 1992 issue.

New York, began publication in 1968. General publication with occasional reviews of opera videos.

Opera Canada, began publication in 1960, published in Toronto by the Canadian Opera Association.

Opera (England), began publication in 1950, published in London.

Opera Monthly, began publication in New York in May 1988.

Opera News, began publication in December 1936, published by the Metropolitan Opera Guild.

Opera Now, began publication in 1989, published in London by Opera Now Enterprises.

Opera Quarterly, began publication in Spring 1983. Chapel Hill, NC: University of North Carolina Press.

Opern Welt, "Die Internationale Opernzeitschrift," began publication in October 1960. A German language periodical devoted to opera.

Ovation, published by Ovation Magazine Associates in New York from 1980 through 1989.

Variety, began publication in 1905. Film reviews.

Video Librarian, began publication in 1986. Publisher/Editor, Randy Pitman. Box 2725, Bremerton, WA 98310.

Video Magazine, New York: Reese Communications. Began publication as *Video* in 1978 and changed its name to *Video Magazine* in September 1987.

Video Rating Guide for Libraries, began publication with the winter 1990 issue. Santa Barbara, CA: ABC-CLIO. A source for non-theatrical/educational videocassette reviews. It is cited as *Video Rating Guide*.

Video Review, began publication in April 1980, ceased publication, 1992.

Ratings

++ Highly recommended. The title is well done in all areas: singing, staging, and technical aspects.

+ Good. The title is recommended although the reviewer may have expressed reservations. If, for example, the technical aspects are bad but the singing and staging are exceptional, the citation will show where important: +–, with a notation, e.g., "– technical aspects."

- Acceptable. The title is average in all aspects. If one aspect or individual of the title is recommended, the citation will show where important, e.g., "+ technical aspects" or "+ Pavarotti."

– Poor quality. The title is not recommended. Again, as in the good and acceptable ranges, if one aspect or individual is recommended, the citation will usually reflect that recommendation.

Explanation of Entries

Titles are numbered sequentially with decimal numerals used to break down multiple entries under the same title. To alleviate confusing numbering, the first entry under an entry number, such as 5, is 5.1., the second is 5.2., and so on.

Titles in Appendix A, *Motion Pictures and Television Productions: Abbreviated Listing,* are entered in the same manner as the titles in the *Listing of Operas by Title* section or main body of the mediagraphy. Entry numbers for titles in Appendix A are prefixed by "A."

Multiple entries under the same title are arranged chronologically from the earliest to the most current date. The date is the year the opera was produced or performed not the date it was released, although these dates frequently do coincide. For entries under the same title and date, arrangement is further broken down by place of performance, e.g., Arena di Verona, Vienna State Opera.

Please note that the term "filmed" is used throughout in the generic sense, e.g., to capture a performance on a visual medium, and refers to both filmed and videotaped productions. The term "videotaped" is used in the specific sense and in conjunction with specific recording dates.

Not every entry, either in the main body of the mediagraphy or in Appendix A, will contain all of the elements shown in the explanatory sample entry below.

Sample Entry

Number. **TITLE** composer.
Date of production/performance. Primary distributor

Type of work (stage production, feature film, film version or television production), place of performance (opera house or festival; filmed at Glyndebourne), specific dates of performance (e.g., videotaped on March 26, 1989), running time in minutes, audio characteristics (stereo or mono, hi-fi), color or black and white, language of production with or without subtitles.

Producer; director; sets (e.g., set designer); costumes (e.g., costume designer); video/television director; other credits pertinent to the production.
Additional information on the production and performance, such as, Actors and actresses lip sync to a prerecorded sound track. Filmed on location in Mantua.

CAST:

Character Name . . . . Singer/Performer Name

Conductor, orchestra, chorus, ballet.

Reviews.

Rating. *Name of the review source* volume, issue number (date): page number(s), reviewer's name.

Listing of Operas by Title

Abduction from the Seraglio

SEE Die Entführung aus dem Serail, 40.1.—40.4.

1. **THE ABDUCTION OF FIGARO**: A Simply Grand Opera in Three Acts by P.D.Q. Bach.
1984. Video Artists International

Stage production, Minnesota Opera, Orpheum Theater, Minneapolis, videotaped on April 27 and 28, 1984, 114 min., stereo hi-fi, color, sung in the original English.

Producer, Stephen Schmidt; director, Michael Montel; sets, John Lee Beatty; television director, Kay S. Lavine. World premiere performance. Introduction to the life and works of P.D.Q. Bach by Prof. Peter Schickele, about 6 min., at the beginning of the video.

CAST:

Donna Donna	Marilyn Brustadt
Blondie	Lisbeth Lloyd
Donald Giovanni	Michael Burt
Al Donfonso	LeRoy Lehr
Pasha Shaboom	LeRoy Lehr
Papa Geno	LeRoy Lehr
Susanna Susannadanna	Dana Krueger
Mama Geno	Dana Krueger
Pecadillo	Bruce Edwin Ford
Schlepporello	Jack Walsh
Captain Kadd	Will Roy
Opec	John Ferrante
Figaro (actor)	Arthur Kraemmer

Professor Peter Schickele, Orchestra and Chorus of the Minnesota Opera, the Minnesota Ballet.

+ *Opera News* 50, 16 (May 1986): 46, by Richard Hornak.
+– *Ovation* 7, 5 (June 1986): 43-44, by Nancy Malitz.
  + cast, – length

2.1. ADRIANA LECOUVREUR by Francesco Cilèa.
1984. SVS, Inc. (SONY)

Stage production, Australian Opera, Sydney, videotaped on February 18, 1984, 135 min., stereo hi-fi, color, sung in Italian with English subtitles.
Production, John Copley; sets, Allan Lees; costumes, Michael Stennett.

CAST:

Adriana Lecouvreur	Joan Sutherland
Princesse de Bouillon	Heather Begg
Michonnet	John Shaw
Maurizio	Anson Austin
L'Abate di Chazeuil	Graeme Ewer
Prince de Bouillon	John Wegner
Mlle. Jouvenot	Judith Saliba
Mlle. Dangeville	Jennifer Bermingham
Poisson	Christopher Dawes
Quinault	Jeffrey Black
Major-domo	Robert Mitchell
Adriana's Maid	Marie Driscoll

Richard Bonynge, Elizabethan Sydney Orchestra, Australian Opera Chorus.

– *Levine*, p. 10-11.
+ *Opera Canada* 29, 1 (Spring 1988): 52, by Ruby Mercer.
– *Opera News* 51, 4 (October 1986): 50, by Richard Hornak.
– *Ovation* 10, 7 (August 1989): 57, 60, by Robert Levine.

2.2. ADRIANA LECOUVREUR by Francesco Cilèa.
1989. Home Vision

Stage production, Teatro alla Scala, Milan, Italy, 157 min., stereo hi-fi, color, sung in Italian with English subtitles.
Director, Lamberto Puggelli; sets, Paolo Bregni; video director, Brian Large.

CAST:

Adriana Lecouvreur	Mirella Freni
Princesse de Bouillon	Fiorenza Cossotto
Michonnet	Alessandro Cassis
Maurizio	Peter Dvorský
L'Abate di Chazeuil	Ernesto Gavazzi
Prince de Bouillon	Ivo Vinco

Mlle. Jouvenot . . . . Patrizia Dordi
Mlle. Dangeville . . . . Sara Mingardo
Poisson . . . . Oslavio Di Credico
Quinault . . . . Giuseppe Riva
Major-domo . . . . Saverio Porzano
Dancers:
Paris . . . . Francisco Sedeno
Juno . . . . Vera Karpenko
Pallas . . . . Anita Magyari
Venus . . . . Adriana Scameroni

Gianandrea Gavazzeni, Orchestra and Chorus of Teatro alla Scala.

\+ *Landers Film and Video Reviews* 36, 1 (Fall 1991): 1.
\+ *Opera News* 56, 8 (January 4, 1992): 48, by Harvey E. Phillips.
++ *Video Librarian* 6, 3 (May 1991): 15.
\+ *Video Review* 11, 11 (February 1991): 71, by Roy Hemming.

3. **L'AFRICAINE** by Giacomo Meyerbeer.
1988. Home Vision

Stage production, San Francisco Opera, California, 191 min., stereo hi-fi, color, sung in French with English subtitles.
Production, Lotfi Mansouri; sets, Wolfram Skalicki; video director, Brian Large.

CAST:
Sélika . . . . Shirley Verrett
Vasco da Gama . . . . Plácido Domingo
Ines . . . . Ruth Ann Swenson
Nelusko . . . . Justino Díaz
Don Pedro . . . . Michael Devlin
Don Diego . . . . Philip Skinner
Grand Inquisitor . . . . Joseph Rouleau
Don Alvar . . . . Kevin Anderson
Anna . . . . Patricia Spence
High Priest of Brahma . . . . Mark Delavan
Priest . . . . Sigmund Seigel
Sailors . . . . James Croom
Valery Portnov
Alex Guerrero
Lawrence Rush
Frederick Matthews
Raymond Murcell

Maurizio Arena, Orchestra, Chorus, and Ballet of the San Francisco Opera.

\+ *Opera Canada* 31, 3 (Fall 1990): 59, by Ruby Mercer.
\+ *Opera Monthly* 3, 1 (May 1990): 46-47, by Keith Sherburne.

4. **AGRIPPINA** by George Frideric Handel.
1985. Home Vision

Stage production, Schwetzinger Festival, performed at the Rococo Theater at the Schwetzinger Palace in the small town of Schwetzingen near Heidelberg, the Cologne Opera, 160 min., stereo hi-fi, color, sung in Italian with English subtitles.
Producer and director, Michael Hampe; sets, Mauro Pagano; television director, Thomas Olofsson. Orchestra performs on period instruments. The opera is staged with early 1800s, Napoleonic era, costume.

CAST:
Agrippina .... Barbara Daniels
Nerone .... David Kuebler
Claudius .... Günther von Kannen
Poppea .... Janice Hall
Ottone .... Claudio Nicolai
Lesbo .... Carlos Feller
Pallante .... Ulrich Hielscher
Narcisco .... Eberhard Katz
Two Praetorians ...... Thomas Bremser, Michael Erb

Arnold Östman, London Baroque Players.

+ *Classical* 2, 8 (August 1990): 30-31, by Robert Levine.
+ *Levine*, p. 9-10.

5.1. **AÏDA** by Giuseppe Verdi.
1949. BMG Classics Video; RCA Gold Seal

Concert performance, originally broadcast on NBC from Studio 8-H in New York City on March 26 and April 2, 1949, 149 min., black and white, sung in Italian.
Producer, Don Gillis; director, Doug Rodgers.

CAST:
Aïda .... Herva Nelli
Amneris .... Eva Gustavson
Radames .... Richard Tucker
King of Egypt .... Dennis Harbour
Amonasro, King of Ethiopia ...... Giuseppe Valdengo
Ramphis .... Norman Scott
A Messenger .... Virginio Assandri
Priestess .... Teresa Stich-Randall

Arturo Toscanini, NBC Symphony Orchestra, Robert Shaw Chorale.

+ *Classical* 2, 7 (July 1990): 36-37, by Dick Adler.
+ *Musical America* 110, 5 (July 1990): 47, by Terry Teachout.
++ *Opera Monthly* 3, 2 (June 1990): 46-48, by Keith Sherburne.

5.2. **AÏDA** by Giuseppe Verdi.
1951. Lyric Distribution, Inc.; Bel Canto Society

Feature film, 96 min., abridged, mono, black and white, sung in Italian with English narration, no subtitles.
Producers, Ferruccio De Martino, Federico Teti; director, Clemente Fracassi; sets, Flavio Mogherini. Actors and actresses lip sync to a prerecorded sound track.

CAST:
Singers are listed first; actors and actresses are listed second.

Aïda . . . . Renata Tebaldi/Sophia Loren
Amneris . . . . Ebbe Stignani/Lois Maxwell
Radames . . . . Giuseppe Campora/Luciano Della Marra
King of Egypt . . . . Enrico Formichi
Amonasro, King of Ethiopia . . . . . Gino Bechi/Afro Poli
Ramphis . . . . Giulio Neri/Antonio Cassinelli

Music director, Renzo Rosselin with the Orchestra e Coro di Roma della Radio Italiana.

– *Motion Picture Guide*.

5.3. **AÏDA** by Giuseppe Verdi.
1981. HBO Video

Stage production, Arena di Verona, Italy, 150 min., stereo hi-fi, color, sung in Italian. This video was initially released without English subtitles; later issues may have subtitles.
Director, Giancarlo Sbragia; designer and costumes, Vittorio Rossi; video director, Brian Large.

CAST:
Aïda . . . . Maria Chiara
Amneris . . . . Fiorenza Cossotto
Radames . . . . Nicola Martinucci
King of Egypt . . . . Alfredo Zanazzo
Amonasro, King of Ethiopia . . . . Giuseppe Scandola
Ramphis . . . . Carlo Zardo
A Messenger . . . . Gian Paolo Corradi
Priestess . . . . Maria Gabriella Onesti

Anton Guadagno, Orchestra and Chorus of the Arena di Verona.

– *High Fidelity* 33, 7 (July 1983): 56-58, by Allan Kozinn.
+ *Levine*, p. 11-12.
+ *Opera News* 49, 14 (March 30, 1985): 25, by Richard Hornak.
+ *Opera Quarterly* 5, 2-3 (Summer/Autumn 1987): 157, by Robert Levine.

5.4. **AÏDA** by Giuseppe Verdi.
1986. Home Vision

Stage production, Teatro alla Scala, Milan, Italy, 160 min., stereo hi-fi, color, sung in Italian with English subtitles.
Producer, Luca Ronconi; sets, Mauro Pagano; costumes, Vera Marzot; video director, Derek Bailey.

CAST:
Aïda .... Maria Chiara
Amneris .... Gena Macheva Dimitrova
Radames .... Luciano Pavarotti
King of Egypt .... Paata Burchuladze
Amonasro, King of Ethiopia .... Juan Pons
Ramphis .... Nicolai Ghiaurov
A Messenger .... Ernesto Gavazzi
Priestess .... Francesca Garbi

Lorin Maazel, Orchestra and Chorus of Teatro alla Scala.

+ *Landers Film Reviews* 32, 3 (Spring 1988): 101-102.
+– *Levine*, 12-13. + singing, – sets and costumes
+ *Opera Canada* 30, 4 (Winter 1989): 52, by Ruby Mercer.
– *Opera News* 53, 13 (March 18, 1989): 45, by C.J. Luten.
+– *Opera Quarterly* 5, 2-3 (Summer/Autumn 1987): 157-159, by Robert Levine. + singing, – sets and costumes
+ *Ovation* 9, 1 (February 1988):46, by Robert Levine.
+– *Ovation* 9, 12 (January 1989): 47, by Dick Adler. + Pavarotti

5.5. **AÏDA** by Giuseppe Verdi.
1989. Deutsche Grammophon (PolyGram)

Stage production, Metropolitan Opera, New York City, videotaped on October 7, 1989, 158 min., stereo hi-fi, color, sung in Italian with English subtitles.
Production, Sonja Frisell; sets, Gianni Quaranta; video director, Brian Large.

CAST:
Aïda .... Aprile Millo
Amneris .... Dolora Zajic
Radames .... Plácido Domingo
King of Egypt .... Dimitri Kavrakos
Amonasro, King of Ethiopia .... Sherrill Milnes
Ramphis .... Paata Burchuladze
A Messenger .... Mark Baker
Priestess .... Margaret Jane Wray

James Levine, Orchestra and Chorus of the Metropolitan Opera.

6. ALBERT HERRING by Benjamin Britten.
1985. Home Vision

Stage production without an audience, Glyndebourne Festival, England, 147 min., stereo hi-fi, color, sung in the original English.
Producer for television and video, Robin Lough; director for stage and television, Peter Hall; designs, John Gunter.

CAST:

Albert Herring	John Graham-Hall
Sid	Alan Opie
Police Superintendent Budd	Richard Van Allan
Lady Billows	Patricia Johnson
Miss Wordsworth	Elizabeth Gale
Florence, Lady Billows's maid	Felicity Palmer
Nancy	Jean Rigby
Mr. Gedge, the Vicar	Derek Hammond-Stroud
Mr. Upfold, the Mayor	Alexander Oliver
Mrs. Herring	Patricia Kern
Emmie	Maria Bovino
Cis	Bernadette Lord
Harry	Richard Peachey

Bernard Haitink, London Philharmonic Orchestra, Glyndebourne Festival Chorus.

+ *Classical* 2, 4 (April 1990): 34, by Robert Levine.
++ *Levine*, p. 15-16.
+ *Opera News*, 56, 2 (August 1991): 44-45, "The Basics," by Harvey E. Phillips.

7. AMAHL AND THE NIGHT VISITORS by Gian Carlo Menotti.
1978. Video Artists International

Film version, 52 min., mono hi-fi, color, sung in the original English.
Producers, Alvin Cooperman, Judith De Paul; director, Arvin Brown; costumes, Ivy Baker Jones; photography, John Coquillon. Filmed on location in the Holy Land with interiors filmed at the EMI Elstreet Studios in Herts, England.

CAST:

The Mother	Teresa Stratas
Amahl	Robert Sapolsky
King Melchior	Giorgio Tozzi
King Balthazar	Willard White
King Kaspar	Nico Castel
The Page	Michael Lewis
Peasant Dancers	Kate Castle Peter Walker John Terry Bates

Jesús López Cobos, Ambrosian Opera Chorus and Philharmonia.

+– *Levine*, p. 84-85. – sound
+– *Opera News*, 51, 9 (January 17, 1987): 42, by Thor Eckert, Jr.
+ singing, – sound and picture
+– *Opera Quarterly* 5, 1 (Spring 1987): 123-125, by Roger Pines.
+ singing, – sound
+ *Ovation* 7, 12 (January 1987): 30, by Richard Hornak.
+ *Video Review* 9, 9 (December 1988): 62, by Roy Hemming.

8.1. ANDREA CHÉNIER by Umberto Giordano.
1958. Lyric Distribution, Inc.; Bel Canto Society

Television production, 116 min., mono, black and white, sung in Italian, no subtitles.
The singers lip sync to a prerecorded sound track of their own voices.

CAST:

Andrea Chénier	Mario Del Monaco
Maddalena di Coigny	Antonietta Stella
Carlo Gérard	Giuseppe Taddei
Bersi	Luisa Mandelli
Countess di Coigny	Maria Amadini
Madelon	Ortensia Beggiato
Roucher	Franco Calabrese
Sans-Culotte Mathieu	Leo Pudis
Novelist Pietro Fléville	Antonio Sacchetti
Fouquier-Tinville	Leonard Monreal
Abbé	Salvatore de Tommaso
Spy (L'Incroyable)	Athos Cesarini
Major-domo	Egidio Casolar
Dumas	Arigo Cattelani
Schmidt (Jailer)	Eruno Cion

Angelo Questa, Orchestra sinfonica di Milano.

+ *Levine*, p. 15.
+– *Opera News* 51, 12 (February 28, 1987): 44, by Thor Eckert, Jr.
+ singing, – technical aspects

8.2. ANDREA CHÉNIER by Umberto Giordano.
1985. Home Vision

Stage production, Royal Opera House, Covent Garden, London, England, 118 min., stereo hi-fi, color, sung in Italian with English subtitles.
Producer, Michael Hampe; designs by William Orlandi after a concept by Ezio Frigerio; costumes, Franca Squariapino; video director, Humphrey Burton.

Cast:

Andrea Chénier	Plácido Domingo
Maddalena di Coigny	Anna Tomowa-Sintow
Carlo Gérard	Giorgio Zancanaro
Bersi	Cynthia Buchan
Countess di Coigny	Patricia Johnson
Madelon	Anny Schlemm
Roucher	Jonathan Summers
Sans-Culotte Mathieu	Rodney Macann
Novelist Pietro Fléville	Gordon Sandison
Fouquier-Tinville	John Gibbs
Abbé	Alexander Oliver
Spy (L'Incroyable)	John Dobson
Major-domo	John Gibbs
Dumas	Roderick Earle
Schmidt (Jailer)	Eric Garrett

Julius Rudel, Orchestra and Chorus of the Royal Opera House, Covent Garden.

\+ *Landers Film Reviews* 32, 2 (Winter 1987): 52.
++ *Opera (England)* 41, 1 (January 1990): 120-121, by Max Loppert.

8.3. ANDREA CHÉNIER by Umberto Giordano.
1985. Home Vision

Stage production, Teatro alla Scala, Milan, Italy, 128 min., stereo hi-fi, color, sung in Italian with English subtitles.
Director, Lamberto Puggelli; video director, Brian Large.

CAST:

Andrea Chénier	José Carreras
Maddalena di Coigny	Eva Marton
Carlo Gérard	Piero Cappuccilli
Bersi	Silvana Mazzieri
Countess di Coigny	Nella Verri
Madelon	Rosa Laghezza
Roucher	Franco Frederici
Sans-Culotte Mathieu	Silvestro Sammaritano
Novelist Pietro Fléville	Giuseppe Riva
Fouquier-Tinville	Angelo Nosotti
Abbé	Carlo Gaifa
Spy (L'Incroyable)	Bruno Lazzaretti
Major-domo	Claudio Lobbia
Dumas	Ivan Del Manto
Schmidt (Jailer)	Sergio Fontana
Footman	Giuseppe Zecchillo

Riccardo Chailly, Orchestra and Chorus of Teatro alla Scala.

\+ *Opera News* 52, 5 (November 1987): 74, by Thor Eckert, Jr. + Marton, – Carreras
\+ *Opera Quarterly* 5, 4 (Winter 1987/88): 108-110, by Thor Eckert, Jr. – Carreras.
\+ *Ovation* 8, 5 (June 1987): 46, by Robert Levine.

9.1. ARABELLA by Richard Strauss.
1977. London (PolyGram)

Film version, 149 min., stereo hi-fi, color, sung in German with English subtitles.
Production, Otto Schenk; designer, Jan Schlubach; costumes, Bernd Müller, Jörg Neumann; photography, Wolfgang Treu. Singers lip sync to a prerecorded sound track of their own voices.

CAST:

Arabella	Gundula Janowitz
Mandryka	Bernd Weikl
Matteo	René Kollo
Zdenka	Sona Ghazarian
Adelaide	Margarita Lilova
Graf Waldner	Hans Kraemmer
The *Fiakermilli*	Edita Gruberova
A Fortuneteller	Martha Mödl
Graf Elemer	Göran Fransson
Graf Dominik	Hans Helm
Graf Lamoral	Kurt Rydl

Sir Georg Solti, Vienna Philharmonic Orchestra.

\+ *Opera Canada* 33, 2 (Summer 1992): 47, by Neil Crory.
\+ *Opera (England)* 44, 1 (January 1993): 120, by Charles Osborne.
\+ *Opera Monthly* 5, 12 (May/June 1993): 38, by William H. Wells.
•– *Opera News* 56, 8 (January 4, 1992): 48, by Harvey E. Phillips. – production

9.2. ARABELLA by Richard Strauss.
1984. HBO Video

Stage production, Glyndebourne Festival, England, 154 min., stereo hi-fi, color, sung in German with English subtitles.
Director, John Cox; sets and costumes, Julia Trevelyan Oman; television director, John Vernon.

CAST:

Arabella	Ashley Putnam
Mandryka	John Bröcheler
Matteo	Keith Lewis
Zdenka	Gianna Rolandi
Adelaide	Regina Sarfaty

Graf Waldner . . . . Arthur Korn
The *Fiakermilli* . . . . Gwendolyn Bradley
A Fortuneteller . . . . Enid Hartle
Graf Elemer . . . . Glenn Winslade
Graf Dominik . . . . Jeremy Munro
Graf Lamoral . . . . Geoffrey Moses
Welko . . . . John Hall
Waiter . . . . John Oakman
Djura . . . . Timothy Evans-Jones
Jankel . . . . Peter Coleman-Wright

Bernard Haitink, London Philharmonic Orchestra, Glyndebourne Festival Chorus.

+– *Levine*, p. 15-16. + conductor, orchestra, and production, – singing
– *Opera News* 52, 10 (January 30, 1988): 40, by Thor Eckert, Jr.

10. ARIADNE AUF NAXOS by Richard Strauss.
1988. Deutsche Grammophon (PolyGram)

Stage production, Metropolitan Opera, New York City, videotaped in March 1988, 148 min., stereo hi-fi, color, sung in German with English subtitles.
Producer, Samuel J. Paul; director, Bodo Igesz; video director, Brian Large. Includes *Ariadne auf Naxos in Rehearsal* a film by Susan Froemke, Peter Gelb, and Pat Jaffe, at end.

CAST:
Primadonna/Ariadne . . . . Jessye Norman
Zerbinetta . . . . Kathleen Battle
The Composer . . . . Tatiana Troyanos
Tenor/Bacchus . . . . James King
Music Master . . . . Franz Ferdinand Nentwig
Harlequin . . . . Stephen Dickson
Brighella . . . . Anthony Laciura
Scaramuccio . . . . Allan Glassman
Truffaldino . . . . Arthur Korn
Dancing Master . . . . Joseph Frank
Naiade . . . . Barbara Bonney
Dryade . . . . Gweneth Bean
Echo . . . . Dawn Upshaw
Major-domo . . . . Nico Castel
Wig-Maker . . . . Russell Christopher
A Lackey . . . . James Courtney
An Officer . . . . Charles Anthony

James Levine, Orchestra and Chorus of the Metropolitan Opera.

++ *Classical* 2, 6 (June 1990): 36-37, by Robert Levine.
• *New York* 22, 39 (October 2, 1989): 80-81, by Peter G. Davis.
+ *Opera News* 56, 13 (March 14, 1992): 37, by Harvey E. Phillips.

11.1. ATTILA by Giuseppe Verdi.
1985. Home Vision

Stage production, Arena di Verona, Italy, 120 min., stereo hi-fi, color, sung in Italian with English subtitles.
Producer and director, Giuliano Montaldo; sets, Luciano Ricceri; costumes, Nana Cecchi; video director, Brian Large. Performed complete with all repeats.

CAST:

Attila	Evgeny Nesterenko
Ezio	Silvano Carroli
Odabella	Maria Chiara
Foresto	Veriano Luchetti
Leone	Gianni Brunelli
Uldino	Mario Ferrara

Nello Santi, Orchestra and Chorus of the Arena di Verona.

\+ *Levine*, p. 16-17.
\+ *Opera News* 52, 10 (January 30, 1988): 41, by Harvey E. Phillips.
\+ *Opera Quarterly* 5, 2-3 (Summer/Autumn 1987): 149-150, by Robert Levine.

11.2. ATTILA by Giuseppe Verdi.
1991. Home Vision

Stage production, Teatro alla Scala, Milan, Italy, videotaped on June 25, 1991, 115 min., stereo hi-fi, color, sung in Italian with English subtitles.
Director, Jerome Savary; sets, Michel Lebois; costumes, Jacques Schmidt; video director, Christopher Swann.

CAST:

Attila	Samuel Ramey
Ezio	Giorgio Zancanaro
Odabella	Cheryl Studer
Foresto	Kaludi Kaludov
Leone	Mario Luperi
Uldino	Ernesto Gavazzi

Riccardo Muti, Orchestra and Chorus of Teatro alla Scala.

- *Opera News* 57, 9 (January 16, 1993): 44, by Harvey E. Phillips.
  \+ Ramey, technical aspects

12.1. UN BALLO IN MASCHERA by Giuseppe Verdi.
1980. Bel Canto/Paramount Home Video

Stage production (uses the Boston locale), Metropolitan Opera, New York City, videotaped on February 16, 1980, 150 min., stereo hi-fi, color, sung in Italian with English subtitles.
Production, Elijah Moshinsky; sets, Peter Wexler; costumes, Peter J. Hall; video director, Brian Large.

CAST:
Amelia . . . . Katia Ricciarelli
Riccardo . . . . Luciano Pavarotti
Renato . . . . Louis Quilico
Ulrica . . . . Bianca Berini
Oscar . . . . Judith Blegen
Samuele . . . . William Wildermann
Tomaso . . . . Julien Robbins
Silvano . . . . John Darrenkamp
A Judge . . . . Charles Anthony
Amelia's servant . . . . Paul Franke

Giuseppe Patanè, Orchestra and Chorus of the Metropolitan Opera.

\+ *Levine*, p. 17-18.
\+ *Opera News* 50, 3 (September 1985): 68, by John W. Freeman.
+– *Opera News* 50, 13 (March 15, 1986): 41, by Richard Hornak.
+ singing, – sets
\+ *Opera Quarterly* 5, 2-3 (Summer/Autumn 1987): 154-155, by Robert Levine.

12.2. UN BALLO IN MASCHERA by Giuseppe Verdi.
1991. Deutsche Grammophon (PolyGram)

Stage production (uses the Swedish locale), Metropolitan Opera, New York City, 137 min., stereo hi-fi, color, sung in Italian with English subtitles.
Production, set, costume designer, Piero Faggioni; video director, Brian Large.

CAST:
Amelia . . . . Aprile Millo
Gustavus III . . . . Luciano Pavarotti
Anckarstroem . . . . Leo Nucci
Arvidson . . . . Florence Quivar
Oscar . . . . Harolyn Blackwell
Christian . . . . Gordon Hawkins
Count Horn . . . . Terry Cook
Count Ribbing . . . . Jeffrey Wells
A Judge . . . . Charles Anthony
Amelia's servant . . . . Richard Fracker

James Levine, Orchestra and Chorus of the Metropolitan Opera.

13.1. IL BARBIERE DI SIVIGLIA by Gioacchino Rossini.
1947. Lyric Distribution, Inc.

Feature film, 110 min., mono, black and white, sung in Italian with a commentator explaining the plot in English, no subtitles.
Producers, Marie and Ugo Trombetti; director, Mario Costa; written by Deems Taylor and based on the opera by Rossini; costumes, Giorgio Foeldes; photography, Massimo Terano. Originally released as a motion picture in Italy by Excelsior. Also known as *Figaro*.

CAST:

Rosina .... Nelly Corradi
Count Almaviva .... Ferruccio Tagliavini
Figaro .... Tito Gobbi
Doctor Bartolo .... Vito De Taranto
Basilio .... Italo Tajo
Fiorello .... Nino Mazziotti
Berta .... Natalia Nicolini

Giuseppe Morelli, Orchestra and Chorus of the Rome Opera House.

- *Motion Picture Guide*.
+ *Opera (England)* 39, 11 (November 1988): 1386-1387, by Max Loppert.

13.2. IL BARBIERE DI SIVIGLIA by Gioacchino Rossini.
1948. 16mm film rental available prior to June 1993 from the University of Illinois Film Center

Film version, 23 min., abridged, mono, black and white, sung in Italian with a commentator explaining the plot in English, no subtitles.
Producer, George Richfield; musical arrangement and script, Raffaele Gervasio. Filmed on stage at the Rome Opera House, Italy. Part of the *First Opera Film Festival* series. Giulio Tomei and Gino Conti are singers who also appear as actors.

CAST:
Singers are listed first; actors and actresses are listed second.

Rosina .... Angelica Tuccari/Pina Malgharini
Count Almaviva .... Cesare Valletti/Mino Russo
Figaro .... Tito Gobbi
Doctor Bartolo .... Giulio Tomei/Gino Conti
Basilio .... Luciano Neroni/Giulio Tomei
Fiorello .... Gino Conti/Filiberto Picozzi
Berta .... Anna Marcangeli

Angelo Questa, Orchestra and Chorus of the Rome Opera House.

- *EFLA* (1965), p. 35 [No. 1949, 564]

13.3. IL BARBIERE DI SIVIGLIA by Gioacchino Rossini.
1973. Deutsche Grammophon (PolyGram)

Film version, 142 min., stereo hi-fi, color, sung in Italian with English subtitles.
Production, Jean-Pierre Ponnelle; director and photographer, Ernst Wild.

CAST:

Rosina .... Teresa Berganza
Count Almaviva .... Luigi Alva
Figaro .... Hermann Prey
Doctor Bartolo .... Enzo Dara
Basilio .... Paolo Montarsolo
Fiorello .... Renato Cesari
Berta .... Stefania Malagù
An Officer .... Luigi Roni
A Notary .... Karl Schaidler
Ambrogio .... Hans Kraemmer

Claudio Abbado, Orchestra and Chorus of Teatro alla Scala.

\+ *Motion Picture Guide.*

13.4. IL BARBIERE DI SIVIGLIA by Gioacchino Rossini.
1975. 16mm rental, Iowa State University

Film version, 54 min., abridged, mono, color, sung in English.
Translation and musical direction, Peter Murray. Filmed at Knebworth House, Hertfordshire, England. Part of the *Focus on Opera* series directed by Peter Seabourne. Originally released by Chatsworth Film Distributors; U.S. distributor, Centron Educational Films.

CAST:

Rosina .... Margaret Eels
Count Almaviva .... Edmund Bohan
Figaro .... Michael Wakeham
Doctor Bartolo .... Malcolm Rivers
Basilio .... Philip Summerscales

John J. Davies, the Classical Orchestra.

\+ *Landers Film Reviews* 26, 2 (November/December 1981): 48.

13.5. IL BARBIERE DI SIVIGLIA by Gioacchino Rossini.
1976. Bel Canto/Paramount Home Video

Stage production, New York City Opera, New York State Theater, live from Lincoln Center, New York City, videotaped on November 3, 1976, 156 min., stereo hi-fi, color, sung in Italian with English subtitles.
Production devised and directed by Sarah Caldwell; sets, Helen Pond and Herbert Senn; costumes, Jan Skalicky; video director, Kirk Browning.

CAST:

Rosina . . . . Beverly Sills
Count Almaviva . . . . Henry Price
Figaro . . . . Alan Titus
Doctor Bartolo . . . . Donald Gramm
Basilio . . . . Samuel Ramey
Fiorello . . . . William Ledbetter
Berta . . . . Caroll Wood
An Officer . . . . Don Yule
A Notary . . . . Michael Rubino
Ambrogio . . . . Nicholas Muni

Sarah Caldwell, Orchestra and Chorus of the New York City Opera.

13.6. IL BARBIERE DI SIVIGLIA by Gioacchino Rossini.
1982. Home Vision

Stage production, Glyndebourne Festival, England, 155 min., stereo hi-fi, color, sung in Italian with English subtitles.
Director, John Cox; video director, Dave Heather.

CAST:

Rosina . . . . Maria Ewing
Count Almaviva . . . . Max René Cosotti
Figaro . . . . John Rawnsley
Doctor Bartolo . . . . Claudio Desderi
Basilio . . . . Ferruccio Furlanetto
Fiorello . . . . Robert Dean
Berta . . . . Catherine McCord
An Officer . . . . Hugh Davies

Sylvain Cambreling, London Philharmonic Orchestra, Glyndebourne Festival Chorus.

- • *Levine*, p. 18-19. + Ewing
- \+ *Opera Canada* 29, 2 (Summer 1988): 52, by Ruby Mercer.
- \+ *Opera News* 53, 3 (September 1988): 58, by Harvey E. Phillips.
- – *Opera Quarterly* 7, 1 (Spring 1990): 199-200, by Thor Eckert, Jr.
- \+ *Ovation* 9, 8 (September 1988): 44, by Dick Adler.
  ++ Ewing, Furlanetto

13.7. IL BARBIERE DI SIVIGLIA by Gioacchino Rossini.
1988. Deutsche Grammophon (PolyGram)

Stage production, Metropolitan Opera, New York City, videotaped on December 3, 1988, 161 min., stereo hi-fi, color, sung in Italian with English subtitles.
Producer, John Cox; sets, Robin Wagner; video director, Brian Large. Includes "Cessa di più resistere," sung by Rockwell Blake (Count Almaviva).

CAST:

Rosina .... Kathleen Battle
Count Almaviva .... Rockwell Blake
Figaro .... Leo Nucci
Doctor Bartolo .... Enzo Dara
Basilio .... Ferruccio Furlanetto
Fiorello .... David Hamilton
Berta .... Loretta Di Franco
An Officer .... Charles Anthony
Ambrogio .... Edward Ghazal

Ralf Weikert, Orchestra and Chorus of the Metropolitan Opera.

\+ *Opera (England)* 43, 12 (December 1992): 1447-1448, by Noël Goodwin.

The Bat
SEE Die Fledermaus, 48.1.—48.4.

The Beggar Student
SEE Der Bettelstudent, 15.

14. THE BEGGAR'S OPERA by John Gay.
1983. Home Vision; Philips (PolyGram)

Film version, BBC studio production, 138 min., stereo hi-fi, color, sung in English. Music arranged by Jeremy Barlow, John Eliot Gardiner.
Director, Jonathan Miller. Includes the sixty-nine ballads.

CAST:

Macheath .... Roger Daltrey
Beggar .... Bob Hoskins
Peachum .... Stratford Johns
Mrs. Peachum .... Patricia Routledge
Polly Peachum .... Carol Hall
Player .... Graham Crowden
Filch .... Gary Tibbs
Ben Budge .... Gawn Grainger
Matt of the Mint .... Anthony Pedley
Crook-fingered Jack .... Don Estelle
Jemmy Twitcher .... Ken Stott
Wat Dreary .... Richard Suart
Robin of Bagshot .... Tim Brown

Nimming Ned . . . . Leslie Sarony
Harry Paddington . . . . Peter Spraggon
Drawer . . . . Derek Deadman
Mrs. Coaxer . . . . Jeannie Crowther
Dolly Trull . . . . Elayne Sharling
Mrs. Vixen . . . . Kay Stonham
Betty Doxy . . . . Iris Saunders
Jenny Diver . . . . Isla Blair
Mrs. Slammekin . . . . Lucie Skeaping
Suky Tawdry . . . . Paddy Navin
Molly Brazen . . . . Jacqueline Davis
Lockit . . . . Peter Bayliss
Lucy Lockit . . . . Rosemary Ashe
Jailer . . . . John Benfield
Mrs. Trapes . . . . Gaye Brown

John Eliot Gardiner, English Baroque Soloists.

+ *Fanfare* 16, 2 (November/December 1992): 482, by James Reel.
• *Levine*, p. 19-20.
+ *Opera News* 57, 2 (August 1992): 53, by Shirley Fleming.
+ *Video Review* 9, 2 (May 1988): 76, by Christie Barter.

15. DER BETTELSTUDENT by Carl Millöcker.
1980s. European Video Distributors

Film version, 90 min., stereo hi-fi, color, sung in Hungarian with English subtitles.
Director, László Seregi.

CAST:
Simon, the Beggar Student . . . . Tivadar Horváth
and:
Marika Németh, Zsuzsa Domonkos, József Kovács, Mária Zempléni, József Virágh

16. BILLY BUDD by Benjamin Britten.
1988. Home Vision

Stage production without an audience, English National Opera at the London Coliseum, England, 157 min., stereo hi-fi, color, sung in the original English.
Director, Tim Albery; designers, Tom Cairns, Antony McDonald; video director, Barrie Gavin.

CAST:
Billy Budd . . . . Thomas Allen
Captain Vere . . . . Philip Langridge
John Claggart . . . . Richard Van Allan
Mr. Redburn . . . . Neil Howlett

Mr. Flint	Phillip Guy-Bromley
Lieutenant Ratcliffe	Clive Bayley
Red Whiskers	Edward Byles
Donald	Mark Richardson
Dansker	John Connell
Novice	Barry Banks
Squeak	Howard Milner
Novice's Friend	Christopher Booth-Jones
Bosun	Malcolm Rivers
First Mate	Anthony Cunningham
Second Mate	Christopher Ross
Arthur Jones	Richard Reaville
Cabin Boy	Oscar Ces
Maintop	Richard Reaville

David Atherton, Orchestra and Chorus of the English National Opera.

+ *Opera Canada* 31, 1 (Spring 1990): 68, by Ruby Mercer.
+ *Opera Quarterly* 8, 1 (Spring 1991): 112-114, by David McKee.
+ *Video Librarian* 5, 6 (September 1990): 15.

17. BLUEBEARD'S CASTLE by Béla Bartók.
1981. London (PolyGram)

Film version, 59 min., stereo hi-fi, color, sung in Hungarian with English subtitles.
Producers, Anikó Kovács, Lásló Steiner; director, Miklós Szinetár.

CAST:

Duke Bluebeard	Kolos Kováts
Judith, his wife	Sylvia Sass

Sir Georg Solti, London Philharmonic Orchestra.

+ *Fanfare* 16, 5 (May/June 1993): 437, by James Reel.

18.1. LA BOHÈME by Giacomo Puccini.
1953. Video Yesteryear

Television production, originally broadcast on the television series *Omnibus*, February 23, 1953, the Metropolitan Opera, 81 min., mono, black and white, sung in English, English text by Howard Dietz.
Director, Bob Banner; costumes and scenery, Rolf Gerard; television script, John Gutman. Host, Alistair Cooke. Sponsored by AMF Bowling Pinspotters (other commercials deleted). For other *Omnibus* titles, see Appendix A. Conducted by Alberto Erede.

CAST:

Mimi	Nadine Conner
Rodolfo	Brian Sullivan

Marcello .... Frank Guarrera
Musetta .... Brenda Lewis
Colline .... Norman Scott
Schaunard .... Clifford Harvuot
Alcindoro .... Alessio De Paolis

18.2. LA BOHÈME by Giacomo Puccini.
1965. Deutsche Grammophon (PolyGram)

Film version, Teatro alla Scala, Milan, Italy, 104 min., stereo hi-fi, color, sung in Italian with English subtitles.
Production, Franco Zeffirelli; photographer, Werner Krein; video director, Wilhelm Semmelroth. Singers lip sync to prerecorded sound track of their own voices.

CAST:
Mimi .... Mirella Freni
Rodolfo .... Gianni Raimondi
Marcello .... Rolando Panerai
Musetta .... Adriana Martino
Colline .... Ivo Vinco
Schaunard .... Gianni Maffeo
Benoit .... Carlo Badioli
Alcindoro .... Virgilio Carbonari
Parpignol .... Franco Ricciardi
Customs Official .... Carlo Forti
A Sergeant .... Giuseppe Morresi
A Salesman .... Angelo Mercuriali

Herbert von Karajan, Orchestra and Chorus of Teatro alla Scala.

++ *Motion Picture Guide*.
+ *New York* 21, 38 (September 26, 1988): 126, by Peter G. Davis.
+ *Opera Quarterly* 6, 3 (Spring 1989): 120-124, by Thor Eckert, Jr.
+ *Ovation* 9, 10 (November 1988): 44, by David Hurwitz.

18.3. LA BOHÈME by Giacomo Puccini.
1982. Bel Canto/Paramount Home Video

Stage production, Metropolitan Opera, New York City, videotaped on Saturday afternoon, January 16, 1982, 141 min. (inclusive of additional materials), stereo hi-fi, color, sung in Italian with English subtitles.
Production, Franco Zeffirelli; costume designer, Peter J. Hall; video director, Kirk Browning. Includes *Behind the scenes of La Bohème with Franco Zeffirelli*, produced by Equinox Films, a film by Gene Searchinger, in English, about 20 min.

CAST:
Mimi .... Teresa Stratas
Rodolfo .... José Carreras

Marcello .... Richard Stilwell
Musetta .... Renata Scotto
Colline .... James Morris
Schaunard .... Allan Monk
Benoit .... Italo Tajo
Alcindoro .... Italo Tajo
Parpignol .... Dale Caldwell
Customs Official .... James Brewer
A Sergeant .... Glen Bater

James Levine, Orchestra and Chorus of the Metropolitan Opera.

++ *Levine*, p. 21-23.
\+ *Library Journal* 111, 20 (December 1986): 88, 90, by Jerome Earley.
\+ *Opera News* 50, 9 (January 18, 1986): 45, by John W. Freeman.
+– *Opera News* 50, 11 (February 15, 1986): 34-35, by Richard Hornak.
– Scotto
\+ *Opera News* 56, 2 (August 1991): 44-45, "The Basics," by Harvey E. Phillips.

18.4. LA BOHÈME by Giacomo Puccini.
1982. HBO Video

Stage production, Royal Opera House, Covent Garden, London, England, videotaped on February 16, 1982, 115 min., stereo hi-fi, color, sung in Italian. This video was initially released without English subtitles; later issues may have subtitles.
Producer, John Copley; sets, Julia Trevelyan Oman; video director, Brian Large.

CAST:
Mimi .... Ileana Cotrubas
Rodolfo .... Neil Schicoff
Marcello .... Thomas Allen
Musetta .... Marilyn Zschau
Colline .... Gwynne Howell
Schaunard .... John Rawnsley
Benoit .... Brian Donlan
Alcindoro .... John Gibbs
Parpignol .... Daniel McCoshan
Customs Official .... Richard Hazell
A Sergeant .... David Whelan

Lamberto Gardelli, Orchestra and Chorus of the Royal Opera House, Covent Garden.

\+ *High Fidelity* 33, 7 (July 1983): 56-58, by Allan Kozinn.
• *Levine*, p. 21.
\+ *Opera News* 50, 2 (August 1985): 37, by Richard Hornak.

18.5. LA BOHÈME by Giacomo Puccini.
1986. Kultur

Stage production, Municipal Opera Theatre of Genoa on tour in Beijing, China, 120 min., stereo hi-fi, color, sung in Italian with English subtitles.
Director, Gian Carlo Menotti. Filmed at the Tianquiao Theatre in Beijing.

CAST:

Mimi . . . . Fiamma Izzo d'Amico
Rodolfo . . . . Luciano Pavarotti
Marcello . . . . Roberto Servile
Musetta . . . . Madelyn Renée
Colline . . . . Francesco Ellero D'Artegna
Schaunard . . . . Jeffrey Mattsey
Benoit . . . . Roberto Scaltriti
Alcindoro . . . . Guido Pasella
Parpignol . . . . Fernando Pavarotti
A Sergeant . . . . Enrico Fibrini

Leone Magiera, Orchestra and Chorus of the Municipal Opera Theatre of Genoa.

\+ *Video Rating Guide* 1, 4 (Fall 1990): 1695, by F.W. Lancaster.

18.6. LA BOHÈME by Giacomo Puccini.
1988. Erato (Italy); film rental available from: New Yorker Films, 16 West 61st St. New York, NY 10023 212-247-6110, fax 212-307-7855

Feature film, 106 min., stereo hi-fi, color, sung in Italian with English subtitles.
Producers, Claude Abeille, Massimo Patrizi, Daniel Toscan du Plantier; director, Luigi Comencini; photography, Armando Nannuzzi. The sound track features the voice of Carreras as Rodolfo; Rodolfo was acted on screen by Luca Canonici. The opera is re-set in the Paris of 1910.

CAST:

Mimi . . . . Barbara Hendricks
Rodolfo . . . . José Carreras/Luca Canonici (actor)
Marcello . . . . Gino Quilico
Musetta . . . . Angela Maria Blasi
Colline . . . . Francesco Ellero D'Artegna
Schaunard . . . . Richard Cowan
and Federico Davià.

James Conlon, National Orchestra of France.

- *Motion Picture Guide, 1990*, p. 129.
- *New York Times Film Reviews, 1989-90*, p. 87, by Vincent Canby.

– *Variety* (February 24, 1988): 467, by Len.

18.7. LA BOHÈME by Giacomo Puccini.
1989. Home Vision

Stage production, San Francisco Opera, California, 111 min., stereo hi-fi, color, sung in Italian with English subtitles.
Director, Francesca Zambello; sets, David Mitchell; Miss Freni's costumes and chorus costumes designed by Peter J. Hall; other costumes, Jeanne Button; television director, Brian Large; television producer, Judy Flannery.

CAST:

Mimi .... Mirella Freni
Rodolfo .... Luciano Pavarotti
Marcello .... Gino Quilico
Musetta .... Sandra Pacetti
Colline .... Nicolai Ghiaurov
Schaunard .... Stephen Dickson
Benoit .... Italo Tajo
Alcindoro .... Italo Tajo
Parpignol .... Daniel Harper
Customs Official .... Cameron Henley
A Sergeant .... Mark Coles
A Boy .... John Wheeler-Rappe

Tiziano Severini, Orchestra and Chorus of the San Francisco Opera.

19.1. BORIS GODUNOV by Modest Petrovich Mussorgsky.
1954. Corinth Video; Corinth/Image Entertainment

Film version (Rimsky-Korsakov version), Bolshoi Theatre, Russia/Soviet Union, 105 min., mono, color, sung in Russian with English subtitles.
Producer, director, screenplay, Vera Stroyeva; photographer, V. Nikolaev. This film was originally released in the Soviet Union by Mosfilm/Artkino. The opera is severely cut and the role of Rangoni is eliminated. The role of Fyodor, Boris's son, is acted on stage by a man but is sung by a woman.

CAST:

Boris Godunov .... Aleksandr Pirogov
Grigory, The Pretender Dimitri ....
Georgy Mikhailovich Nėllep
Pimen .... Maksim Mikhailov
Varlaam .... Aleksei Krivchenya
The Fool .... Ivan Kozlovsky
Marina .... Larissa Avdeeva
Xenia, Boris's Daughter .... N. Kayagina
Prince Shuisky .... Nikandr Khanaev
Fyodor, Boris's Son ..... G. Allaxverdov/I. Zmelnishky
Xenia's Nurse ...... Evgenia Matseevna Verbitskaya
Andrei Shchelkalov .... I. Bogdanov

Nikitich . . . . S. Krasovsky
Boyar-in-Attendance . . . . Fedor Godovkin
Missail . . . . V. Shovchov

Vasily Nebolsin, Orchestra and Chorus of the Bolshoi Theatre.

++ *Motion Picture Guide.*
\+ *Opera News* 49, 14 (March 30, 1985): 25, by Richard Hornak.
\+ *Opera Quarterly* 3, 2 (Summer 1985): 139-141, by Christopher J. Thomas.
– *Variety* 323, 4 (May 21, 1986): 28, by Kell.

19.2. BORIS GODUNOV by Modest Petrovich Mussorgsky.
1978. Kultur

Stage production (Rimsky-Korsakov version), Bolshoi Theatre, Russia/Soviet Union, 180 min., stereo hi-fi, color, sung in Russian with English subtitles.
The final two scenes are reversed. The Rimsky-Korsakov version is used with Ippolitov-Ivanov orchestration of St. Basil's scene. Cuts include: half of the *Polish Act*, the role of Rangoni.

CAST:
Boris Godunov . . . . Evgeny Nesterenko
Grigory, The Pretender Dimitri . . . . . Vladislav Piavko
Pimen . . . . Valeri Yaroslavtsev
Varlaam . . . . Artur Eizen
The Fool . . . . Aleksei Maslennikov
Marina . . . . Irina Konstantinovna Arkhipova
Andrei Shchelkalov . . . . Vladimir Malchenko
Xenia, Boris's Daughter . . . . Galina Kalinina
Fyodor, Boris's Son . . . . Glafira Koroleva
Prince Shuisky . . . . Andrei Sokolov
Missail . . . . Vitaly Vlasov
Hostess of the Inn . . . . Larissa Nikitina

Boris Ėmmanuilovich Khaikin, Orchestra and Chorus of the Bolshoi Theatre.

++ *Levine*, p. 23-24.
\+ *Opera News* 51, 13 (March 14, 1987): 49, by Thor Eckert, Jr.
\+ *Variety* 325, 6 (December 3, 1986): 40, by Tyl.

19.3. BORIS GODUNOV by Modest Petrovich Mussorgsky.
1987. Home Vision

Stage production (Rimsky-Korsakov version), Bolshoi Theatre, Russia/Soviet Union, 171 min., stereo hi-fi, color, sung in Russian with English subtitles.
Producer, Irina Morozova; original production, Leonid Baratov; designer, Fyodor Federovsky; video director, Derek Bailey. The Rimsky-Korsakov version is used with Ippolitov-Ivanov orchestration of St. Basil's scene. Cuts include: half of the *Polish Act*, the role of Rangoni.

CAST:

Boris Godunov . . . . Evgeny Nesterenko
Grigory, The Pretender Dimitri . . . . . Vladislav Piavko
Pimen . . . . Aleksandr Vedernikov
Varlaam . . . . Artur Eizen
The Fool . . . . Alexander Fedin
Marina . . . . Tamara Sinyavskaya
Andrei Shchelkalov . . . . Yuri Mazurok
Xenia, Boris's Daughter . . . . Nelya Lebedeva
Fyodor, Boris's Son . . . . Tatiana Yerastova
Prince Shuisky . . . . Vladimir Kudryashov
Xenia's Nurse . . . . Raisa Kotova
Missail . . . . Alexander Arkhipov
Hostess of the Inn . . . . Larissa Nikitina
Nikitich . . . . Vyacheslav Pochapsky

Alexander Lazarev, Orchestra and Chorus of the Bolshoi Theatre.

+ *Classical* 14, 4 (September 1991): 34, by Neil Crory.
+ *Opera (England)* 40, 3 (March 1989): 370-371, by Noël Goodwin.
• *Opera News* 53, 1 (July 1988): 45, by Harvey E. Phillips.
+ *Opera News* 53, 13 (March 18, 1989): 44, by C.J. Luten.
• *Opera Quarterly* 7, 1 (Spring 1990): 196-198, by Thor Eckert, Jr.
+ *Ovation* 9, 9 (October 1988): 45, by Dick Adler. ++ Nesterenko

20. LA CAMBIALE DI MATRIMONIO by Gioacchino Rossini.
1989. Teldec

Stage production, Schwetzinger Festival, performed at the Rococo Theater at the Schwetzinger Palace in the small town of Schwetzingen near Heidelberg, the Cologne Opera, 85 min., stereo hi-fi, color, sung in Italian with English subtitles.
Director, Michael Hampe; sets, Carlo Tommasi; costumes, Carlo Diappi; video director, Claus Viller. Includes a six minute talk at the end of the performance by Hampe about Rossini and his short operas. The opera is re-set in Victorian England.

CAST:

Sir Tobias Mill . . . . John Del Carlo
Fanny . . . . Janice Hall

Edoardo Milfort	David Kuebler
Slook	Alberto Rinaldi
The Maid (Clarina)	Amelia Felle
Norton	Carlos Feller

Gianluigi Gelmetti, Stuttgart Radio Symphony Orchestra.

+ *Fanfare* 15, 3 (January/February 1992): 455, by James Reel.
+ *Musical America* 112, 1 (January/February 1992): 54-55, by Robert Levine.
+ *Opera (England)* 42, 9 (September 1991): 1111-1112, by Arthur Jacobs.
+ *Opera News* 56, 7 (December 21, 1991): 52, by Shirley Fleming.
+ *Opera Now* (December 1991): 56-57, by Richard Fawkes.

21. **CANDIDE** by Leonard Bernstein.
1989. Deutsche Grammophon (PolyGram)

Concert performance, Barbican Center, London, December 13, 1989, 147 min., stereo hi-fi, color, sung in the original English.
Video director, Humphrey Burton. This is a performance of Bernstein's final revised version (1989) of *Candide*.

CAST:

Candide	Jerry Hadley
Cunegonde	June Anderson
Dr. Pangloss/Martin	Martin Adolph Green
Old Lady	Christa Ludwig
Governor/Vanderdendur/Ragotski	Nicolai Gedda
Paquette	Della Jones
Maximilian/Captain	Kurt Ollmann
Bear-keeper/Inquisitor/Tsar Ivan	Clive Bayley
Cosmetic Merchant/Inquisitor	Neil Jenkins
Prince Charles Edward	Neil Jenkins
Doctor/Inquisitor	Lindsay Benson
King Stanislaus	Lindsay Benson
Junkman/Inquisitor	Richard Suart
King Herman Augustus	Richard Suart
Alchemist/Inquisitor	John Treleaven
Sultan Achmet/Crook	John Treleaven

Leonard Bernstein, London Symphony Orchestra and Chorus.

• *Fanfare* 15, 4 (March/April 1992): 452, by James Reel.
• *Musical America* 112, 1 (January/February 1992): 55-56, by Charles Passy.
+ *Opera Now* (January 1992): 57, by Richard Fawkes.
+ *Wall Street Journal* (February 11, 1992): A14, by Mark Swed.

22.1. CARMEN by Georges Bizet.
1948. 16mm rental, Budget Films; Archival film, Indiana University

Film version, about 25 min., abridged, mono, black and white, sung in Italian with English narration by Olin Downes, no subtitles.
Produced by George Richfield; stage director, E. Fulchignoni; musical arrangement and script, Raffaele Gervasio; film director, E. Cancelleri. Filmed on stage at the Rome Opera House, Italy. Part of the *First Opera Film Festival* series.

CAST:
Singers are listed first; actors and actresses are listed second.

Carmen . . . . Cleo Elmo/Fernanda Cadoni
Don José . . . . Giancinto Prandelli/Zwonko Gluk
Micaela . . . . Pina Malgharini
Escamillo . . . . Tito Gobbi
Zuniga . . . . Giulio Tomei

Angelo Questa, Orchestra and Chorus of the Rome Opera House.

- *EFLA* (1965), p. 64 [EFLA No. 1949.603]

22.2. CARMEN by Georges Bizet.
1984. RCA/Columbia Pictures Home Video

Film version (uses the Oeser edition), 152 min., stereo hi-fi, color, sung and spoken in French with English subtitles.
Producer, Patrice Ledoux; director, Francesco Rosi; sets and costumes, Enrico Job. Cuts the Smuggler's Chorus in Act III.

CAST:
Carmen . . . . Julia Migenes-Johnson
Don José . . . . Plácido Domingo
Micaela . . . . Faith Esham
Escamillo . . . . Ruggero Raimondi
Frasquita . . . . Lillian Watson
Mercédès . . . . Susan Daniel
El Dancairo . . . . Jean-Philippe Lafont
El Remendado . . . . Gérard Garino
Zuniga . . . . John Paul Bogart
Morales . . . . François Le Roux
Lillas Pastia . . . . Julien Guiomar
The Guide . . . . Accursio di Leo
La Manuelita (non-singing) . . . . Maria Campano
Dancers . . . . Cristina Hayos
Juan Antonio Jimenez

Lorin Maazel, National Orchestra and Chorus of France and the Children's Chorus of Radio-France.

++ *Levine*, p. 85-86.
+ *Opera (England)* 36, 5 (May 1985): 582-583, by Max Loppert.
– *Opera News* 51, 12 (February 28, 1987): 44, by Thor Eckert, Jr.
+ *Opera News* 56, 2 (August 1991): 44-45, "The Basics," by Harvey E. Phillips
• *Opern Welt* 27, 3 (März 1986): 67, by Gerhard Persché.

22.3. CARMEN by Georges Bizet.
1985. Home Vision

Stage production, Glyndebourne Festival, England, 175 min., stereo hi-fi, color, sung in French with English subtitles.
Director, Sir Peter Hall; sets, John Bury.

CAST:

Carmen .... Maria Ewing
Don José .... Barry McCauley
Micaela .... Marie McLaughlin
Escamillo .... David Holloway
Frasquita .... Elizabeth Collier
Mercédès .... Jean Rigby
El Dancairo .... Gordon Sandison
El Remendado .... Petros Evangelides
Zuniga .... Xavier Depraz
Morales .... Malcolm Walker
Lillas Pastia .... Frederico Davià
The Guide .... Robert Kingham

Bernard Haitink, London Philharmonic Orchestra, Glyndebourne Festival Chorus.

– *Opera News* 52, 10 (January 30, 1988): 40-41, by Thor Eckert, Jr.

22.4. CARMEN by Georges Bizet.
1987. Deutsche Grammophon (PolyGram)

Stage production, Metropolitan Opera, New York City, 172 min., stereo hi-fi, color, sung in French with English subtitles.
Director, Paul Mills; sets and costumes, John Bury; video director, Brian Large.

CAST:

Carmen .... Agnes Baltsa
Don José .... José Carreras
Micaela .... Leona Mitchell
Escamillo .... Samuel Ramey
Frasquita .... Myra Merritt
Mercédès .... Diane Kesling
El Dancairo .... Bruce Hubbard
El Remendado .... Anthony Laciura
Zuniga .... Ara Berberian

Morales .... Vernon Hartman
Lillas Pasta .... Nico Castel
The Guide .... Charles Duval

James Levine, Orchestra and Chorus of the Metropolitan Opera.

– *New York* 22, 39 (October 2, 1989): 80, by Peter G. Davis.

22.5. CARMEN by Georges Bizet.
1991. Home Vision

Stage production (uses the Oeser edition), Royal Opera House, Covent Garden, London, England, 180 min., stereo hi-fi, color, sung in French with English subtitles.
Producer, Nuria Espert; video director, Barrie Gavin.

CAST:
Carmen .... Maria Ewing
Don José .... Luis Lima
Micaela .... Leontina Vaduva
Escamillo .... Gino Quilico
Frasquita .... Judith Howarth
Mercédès .... Jean Rigby
El Dancairo .... Bruno Caproni
El Remendado .... Francis Egerton
Zuniga .... Roderick Earle
Morales .... Christopher Booth-Jones

Zubin Mehta, Orchestra and Chorus of the Royal Opera House, Covent Garden.

+ *Opera (England)* 43, 1 (January 1992): 117-118, by Noël Goodwin.
+ *Opera News* 57, 9 (January 16, 1993): 44, by Harvey E. Phillips.
  ++ Ewing
•– *Opera Now* (December 1991): 56-57, by Richard Fawkes.
  – stage production

23.1. CAVALLERIA RUSTICANA by Pietro Mascagni.
1952. Lyric Distribution, Inc. issued with *Pagliacci*, 107.3.; Bel Canto Society; 16mm rental, Budget Films

Film version, 45 min., mono, black and white, sung in Italian, no subtitles.

CAST:
Santuzza .... Rina Telli
Turiddu .... Mario Del Monaco
Alfio .... Richard Torigi

23.2. CAVALLERIA RUSTICANA by Pietro Mascagni.
1982. Philips (PolyGram)

Film version, 70 min., stereo hi-fi, color, sung in Italian with English subtitles.
Director, Franco Zeffirelli; sets, Gianni Quaranta; costumes, Anna Anni. Filmed on location in Vinnini, Sicily.

CAST:

Santuzza	Elena Obrazstova
Turiddu	Plácido Domingo
Alfio	Renato Bruson
Mamma Lucia	Fedora Barbieri
Lola	Axelle Gall

Georges Prêtre, Orchestra and Chorus of Teatro alla Scala.

+ *New York* 22, 15 (April 10, 1989): 108-109, by Peter G. Davis.
• *Opera News* 53, 13 (March 28, 1989): 44, by C.J. Luten.

23.3. CAVALLERIA RUSTICANA by Pietro Mascagni.
1990. Video Artists International

Stage production, Teatro comunale dei Rinnovati, Siena, Italy, 87 min., stereo hi-fi, color, sung in Italian, no subtitles.
Director, Mario Monicelli; television director, Peter Goldfarb. With an short introduction by Shirley Verrett.

CAST:

Santuzza	Shirley Verrett
Turiddu	Kristjan Johannsson
Alfio	Ettore Nova
Mamma Lucia	Ambra Vespasiani
Lola	Rosy Orani

Baldo Podic, Philharmonic Orchestra of Russe.

– *Opera News* 56, 2 (August 1991): 45, by Harvey E. Phillips.

24.1. LA CENERENTOLA by Gioacchino Rossini.
1948. V.I.E.W. Video

Film version, 94 min., abridged, mono hi-fi, black and white, sung in Italian with English narration between arias, no subtitles.
Director, Fernando Cerchio; photographer, Mario Albertelli. Filmed on location in palaces in Italy.

CAST:

Singers are listed first; actors and actresses are listed second.

La Cenerentola . . . . Fedora Barbieri/Lori Randi
Don Ramiro . . . . Gino Del Signore
Dandini . . . . Afro Poli
Alidoro . . . . Enrico Formichi
Don Magnifico . . . . Vito De Taranto
Clorinda . . . . Fiorella Carmen Forte
Tisbe . . . . Fernanda Cadoni/Franca Tamantini

Oliviero De Fabritiis, Orchestra and Chorus of the Rome Opera House.

+ *Opera News* 55, 3 (September 1990): 50-51, by Harvey E. Phillips.

24.2. LA CENERENTOLA by Gioacchino Rossini.
1981. Deutsche Grammophon (PolyGram)

Television production, filmed on the stage of the Teatro alla Scala, Milan, Italy, 152 min., stereo hi-fi, color, sung in Italian with English subtitles.
Production, Jean-Pierre Ponnelle.

CAST:

La Cenerentola . . . . Frederica Von Stade
Don Ramiro . . . . Francisco Araiza
Dandini . . . . Claudio Desderi
Alidoro . . . . Paul Plishka
Don Magnifico . . . . Paolo Montarsolo
Clorinda . . . . Margherita Guglielmi
Tisbe . . . . Laura Zannini

Claudio Abbado, Orchestra and Chorus of Teatro alla Scala.

24.3. LA CENERENTOLA by Gioacchino Rossini.
1983. HBO Video

Stage production, Glyndebourne Festival, England, 152 min., stereo hi-fi, color, sung in Italian. This video was initially released without English subtitles; later issues may have subtitles.
Director, John Cox; designer, Allen Charles Klein; video director, John Vernon.

CAST:

La Cenerentola . . . . Kathleen Kuhlmann
Don Ramiro . . . . Laurence Dale
Dandini . . . . Alberto Rinaldi
Alidoro . . . . Roderick Kennedy
Don Magnifico . . . . Claudio Desderi
Clorinda . . . . Marta Taddei
Tisbe . . . . Laura Zannini

Donato Renzetti, London Philharmonic Orchestra, Glyndebourne Festival Chorus.

+ *Levine*, p. 24-25.
+ *Opera (England)* 41, 2 (February 1990): 245, by Noël Goodwin.
+ *Ovation* 10, 1 (February 1989): 53, by Robert Levine.

24.4. LA CENERENTOLA by Gioacchino Rossini.
1988. Home Vision

Stage production, Salzburg Festival, Vienna State Opera, Austria, 160 min., stereo hi-fi, color, sung in Italian with English subtitles.
Production, Michael Hampe; director, Mauro Pagano; video director, Claus Viller. Filmed in the Kleines Festspielhaus with a live audience. Does not use the Agolini additions. Alidoro sings "La del ciel" added by Rossini in 1820.

CAST:

La Cenerentola	Ann Murray
Don Ramiro	Francisco Araiza
Dandini	Gino Quilico
Alidoro	Wolfgang Schöne
Don Magnifico	Walter Berry
Clorinda	Angela Denning
Tisbe	Daphne Evangelatos

Riccardo Chailly, Vienna Philharmonic Orchestra.

- *Opera (England)* 41, 6 (June 1990): 747, by Noël Goodwin.

Cinderella
SEE La Cenerentola, 24.1.—24.4.

25. LE CINESI by Christoph Willibald Gluck.
1987. Home Vision, issued with *Echo et Narcisse* as *L'Innocenza ed il Piacer*

Stage production, Schwetzinger Festival, performed at the Rococo Theater at the Schwetzinger Palace in the small town of Schwetzingen near Heidelburg, 69 min. (total timing, 168 min.), stereo hi-fi, color, sung in Italian with English subtitles.
Producer, costumes, and sets, Herbert Wernicke; video director, Claus Viller.

CAST:

Silango	Kurt Streit
Sivene	Sophie Boulin
Lisinga	Christina Högman
Tangia	Eva Maria Tersson

René Jacobs, Concerto Köln.

26.1. LA CLEMENZA DI TITO by Wolfgang Amadeus Mozart.
1980. Deutsche Grammophon (PolyGram)

Film version, Vienna State Opera, Austria, 135 min., stereo hi-fi, color, sung in Italian with English subtitles.
Director, Jean-Pierre Ponnelle; designers, Giovanni Agostinucci, Pet Halmen; harpsichord, Philip Eisenberg. Filmed on location in Rome, at the Baths of Caracalla, Arch of Titus, and Hadrian's Villa in Tivoli. Singers lip sync to prerecorded sound track of their own voices.

CAST:
Tito Vespasiano .... Eric Tappy
Sesto .... Tatiana Troyanos
Vitellia .... Carol Neblett
Annio .... Anne Howells
Servilia .... Catherine Malfitano
Publio .... Kurt Rydl

James Levine, Vienna Philharmonic Orchestra, Concert Association of the Vienna State Opera Chorus.

- *Opera Quarterly* 8, 3 (Autumn 1991): 144-146, by Christopher Hunt.

26.2. LA CLEMENZA DI TITO by Wolfgang Amadeus Mozart.
1991. Home Vision

Stage production, Glyndebourne Festival, England, 150 min., stereo hi-fi, color, sung in Italian with English subtitles.
Director, Nicholas Hytner; sets, David Fielding. Newly composed recitatives by Stephen Oliver.

CAST:
Tito Vespasiano .... Philip Langridge
Sesto .... Diana Montague
Vitellia .... Ashley Putnam
Annio .... Martine Mahé
Servilia .... Elzbieta Szmytka
Publio .... Peter Rose

Andrew Davis, London Philharmonic Orchestra and Glyndebourne Festival Chorus.

\+ *Opera News* 57, 13 (March 13, 1993): 44, by Harvey E. Phillips.

The Cloak
SEE Il Tabarro, 132.

Clown Must Laugh
SEE Il Pagliacci, 107.1.

27.1. LES CONTES D'HOFFMANN by Jacques Offenbach.
1951. Home Vision; Voyager the *Criterion Collection*; 16mm rental, Budget Films

Feature film, 127 min., mono hi-fi, color, sung in English.
Writers, producers, and directors, Michael Powell and Emeric Pressburger; produced by The Archers for London Film Productions; design, Hein Heckroth; art director, Arthur Lawson; screenplay, Dennis Arundell; choreography, Sir Frederick Ashton. The final act was cut in the initial British release. Originally issued as a motion picture.

CAST:
Singers are listed first; dancers, actors, and actresses are listed second.

Hoffmann .... Robert Rounseville
Olympia .... Dorothy Bond/Moira Shearer
Giulietta ...... Margherita Grandi/Ludmilla Tcherina
Antonia .... Ann Ayars
Coppelius .... Bruce Dargavel/Robert Helpmann
Dapertutto .... Bruce Dargavel/Robert Helpmann
Doctor Miracle ..... Bruce Dargavel/Robert Helpmann
Lindorf .... Bruce Dargavel/Robert Helpmann
Nicklausse .... Monica Sinclair/Pamela Brown
Spalanzani ...... Grahame Clifford/Leonide Massine
Frantz .... Grahame Clifford/Leonide Massine
Schlemil .... Owen Brannigan/Leonide Massine
Crespel .... Owen Brannigan/Mogens Wieth
Hermann .... Owen Brannigan/Richard Golding
Cochenille .... Murray Dickie/Frederick Ashton
Pittichinaccio .... Murray Dickie/Lionel Harris
Luther .... Fisher Morgan/Meinhart Maur
Nathaniel .... Rene Soames/John Ford
Antonia's Mother .... Jean Alexander
Dancers (non-singing roles):
Stella .... Moira Shearer
Cancer .... Edmund Audran
Andreas .... Philip Leaver
Kleinzack .... Sir Frederick Ashton
Bank Clerk .... Alan Carter

Sir Thomas Beecham, Royal Philharmonic Orchestra, Sadler's Wells Chorus.

- *Motion Picture Guide.*
\+ *Video Magazine* 16, 8 (November 1992): 74-75, by Glenn Kenny.

27.2. LES CONTES D'HOFFMANN by Jacques Offenbach.
1974. 16mm rental, Iowa State University

Film version, 56 min., abridged, mono, color, sung in English.
Translation and musical direction, Peter Murray. Filmed at Knebworth House, Hertfordshire, England. Part of the *Focus on Opera* series directed by Peter Seabourne. Originally released by Chatsworth Film Distributors; U.S. distributor, Centron Educational Films.

CAST:

Hoffmann	Kenneth Woollam
Olympia	Susan Maisey
Giulietta	Janette Kearns
Antonia	Valerie Masterson
Coppelius	Malcolm Rivers
Dapertutto	Malcolm Rivers
Doctor Miracle	Malcolm Rivers
Nicklausse	Ann Hood
Spalanzani	Graham Allum
Crespel	Michael Wakeham
Lindorf	Malcolm Rivers
Antonia's Mother	Elizabeth Mynett
Luther (non-singing)	Paul Eddington
The Student (non-singing)	David Fennell

John J. Davies, the Classical Orchestra.

+ *Landers Film Reviews* 26, 3 (January/February 1982): 124.

27.3. LES CONTES D'HOFFMANN by Jacques Offenbach.
1981. HBO Video

Stage production, Royal Opera House, Covent Garden, London, England, 149 min., stereo hi-fi, color, sung in French. This video was initially released without English subtitles; later issues may have subtitles.
Producer, John Schlesinger; sets, William Dudley; costumes, Maria Bjoernson; video director, Brian Large.

Hoffmann	Plácido Domingo
Olympia	Luciana Serra
Giulietta	Agnes Baltsa
Antonia	Ileana Cotrubas
Coppelius	Sir Geraint Evans
Dapertutto	Siegmund Nimsgern
Doctor Miracle	Nicola Ghiuselev
Nicklausse	Claire Powell
Spalanzani	Robert Tear
Frantz	Bernard Dickerson
Schlemil	Philip Gelling

Crespel . . . . Gwynne Howell
Hermann . . . . John Rawnsley
Cochenille . . . . Paul Crook
Pittichinaccio . . . . Francis Egerton
Luther . . . . Eric Garrett
Nathaniel . . . . Robin Leggate
Andres . . . . Paul Crook
Lindorf . . . . Robert Lloyd
Antonia's Mother . . . . Phyllis Cannan
The Muse of Poetry . . . . Claire Powell
Stella . . . . Deanne Bergsma

Georges Prêtre, Orchestra and Chorus of the Royal Opera House, Covent Garden.

\+ *Opera News* 50, 2 (August 1985): 37, by Richard Hornak.

The Coronation of Poppea
SEE L'Incoronazione d'Poppea, 72.1.—72.2.

28.1. COSÌ FAN TUTTE by Wolfgang Amadeus Mozart.
1975. Video Artists International

Stage production, Glyndebourne Festival, England, 150 min., stereo hi-fi, color, sung in Italian with English subtitles.
Director, Adrian Slack; designer, Emanuele Luzzati.

CAST:

Fiordiligi . . . . Helena Döse
Dorabella . . . . Sylvia Lindenstrand
Ferrando . . . . Anson Austin
Guglielmo . . . . Thomas Allen
Don Alfonso . . . . Franz Petri
Despina . . . . Danièle Perriers

John Pritchard, London Philharmonic Orchestra and Glyndebourne Festival Chorus.

• *Levine*, p. 26-27.
• *Opera Monthly* 1, 1 (May 1988): 61-63, by Robert Levine.
+– *Opera Quarterly* 8, 3 (Autumn 1991): 137-141, by Roger Pines.
\+ Allen, Döse

28.2. COSÌ FAN TUTTE by Wolfgang Amadeus Mozart.
1984. HBO Video

Stage production, Drottningholm Theatre, Stockholm, Sweden, 141 min., stereo hi-fi, color, sung in Italian. This video was initially released without English subtitles; later issues may have subtitles.
Director, Willy Decker; designer, Tobias Hoheisel; video director, Thomas Olofsson. The orchestra performs on period instruments

CAST:

Fiordiligi . . . . Ann Christine Biel
Dorabella . . . . Maria Höglind
Ferrando . . . . Lars Tibell
Guglielmo . . . . Magnus Lindén
Don Alfonso . . . . Enzo Florimo
Despina . . . . Ulla Severin

Arnold Östman, Orchestra and Chorus of the Drottningholm Theatre.

+ *Levine*, p. 25-26.
• *Opera (England)* 40, 6 (June 1989): 749-750, by Noël Goodwin.
+ *Opera Monthly* 1, 1 (May 1988): 61-63, by Robert Levine.
– *Opera Quarterly* 8, 3 (Autumn 1991): 137-141, by Roger Pines.

28.3. COSÌ FAN TUTTE by Wolfgang Amadeus Mozart.
1989. Home Vision

Stage production, Teatro alla Scala, Milan, Italy, 186 min., stereo hi-fi, color, sung in Italian with English subtitles.
Production, Michael Hampe; director, Iliv Catani; sets and costumes, Mauro Pagano.

CAST:

Fiordiligi . . . . Daniela Dessì
Dorabella . . . . Delores Ziegler
Ferrando . . . . Josef Kundlak
Guglielmo . . . . Allessandro Corbelli
Don Alfonso . . . . Claudio Desderi
Despina . . . . Adelina Scarabelli

Riccardo Muti, Orchestra and Chorus of Teatro alla Scala.

+ *Landers Film and Video Reviews* 36, 1 (Fall 1991): 8.
+ *Opera Canada* 32, 3 (Fall 1991): 59, by Ruby Mercer.
• *Opera News* 56, 10 (February 1, 1992): 33, by Harvey E. Phillips.
+ Muti

28.4. COSÌ FAN TUTTE by Wolfgang Amadeus Mozart.
1990. London (PolyGram)

Film version, 199 min., stereo hi-fi, color, sung in Italian with English subtitles.
Director, Peter Sellars; sets, Adrianne Lobel; costumes, Dunya Ramicova; continuo: Myron Lutzke, cello, Suzanne Cleverdon, fortepiano. Action takes place in a seaside diner frequented by Vietnam veterans. Dorabella sings "Vado, ma Dove?" instead of "E Amore un Landroncello."

CAST:

Fiordiligi . . . . Susan Larson
Dorabella . . . . Janice Felty
Ferrando . . . . Frank Kelly
Guglielmo . . . . James Maddalena
Don Alfonso . . . . Sanford Sylvan
Despina . . . . Sue Ellen Kuzma

Craig Smith, Vienna Symphonic Orchestra, Arnold-Schoenberg-Choir.

+ *Fanfare* 16, 2 (November/December 1992): 482-485, by James Reel.
+– *New York* 25, 22 (June 1, 1992): 62-63, by Peter G. Davis.
+ direction, – singing
– *Opera News* 56, 1 (July 1991): 42-43, by Patrick J. Smith.
+ *Video Magazine* 16, 5 (August 1992): 41, "Editor's Choice," by Kenneth Korman.

29. LA DAMNATION DE FAUST by Hector Berlioz.
1989. London (PolyGram)

Concert performance, London Proms concert at the Royal Albert Hall, August 28, 1989, 134 min., stereo hi-fi, color, sung in French.

CAST:

Faust . . . . Keith Lewis
Marguerite . . . . Anne Sofie von Otter
Méphistophélès . . . . José van Dam
Brander . . . . Peter Rose

Sir Georg Solti, Chicago Symphony Orchestra.

+ *Fanfare* 16, 1 (September/October 1992): 469-470, by James Reel.

Daughter of the Regiment
SEE La Fille du Régiment, 47.1.—47.2.

30. DEATH IN VENICE by Benjamin Britten.
1990. Pioneer

Stage production, Glyndebourne Touring Opera Company, England, 137 min., stereo hi-fi, color, sung in the original English.
Production, Stephen Lawless, Martha Clarke; sets, Tobias Hoheisel; video director, Robin Lough.

CAST:

Gustav von Aschenbach . . . . Robert Tear
Traveller/Old Gondolier/Hotel Manager . . . . Alan Opie
Apollo . . . . Michael Chance
Beggar Woman . . . . Alison Hudson
1st Gondolier/Strolling Player . . . . Gordon Wilson
2nd Gondolier/Priest . . . . Aneirin Huws
3rd Gondolier/Hotel Porter . . . . . . Christopher Ventris
English Clerk . . . . Gerald Finley
Strawberry Seller . . . . Linda Clemens
Tadzio (non-singing) . . . . Paul Zeplichal
Tadzio's Mother (non-singing) . . . . Cathryn Pope

Graeme Jenkins, London Sinfonietta, Glyndebourne Festival Chorus.

- *Opera (England)* 42, 9 (September 1991): 1110-1111, by Noël Goodwin. + Tear
- *Opera News* 57, 13 (March 13, 1993): 44, by Harvey E. Phillips.

31. DIALOGUES DES CARMELITES by Francis Poulenc.
1985. SVS, Inc. (SONY)

Stage production, Australian Opera, Sydney, 155 min., stereo hi-fi, color, sung in English.
Producer, Elijah Moshinsky; television producer, Brian Adams; director, Henry Prokop; designer, John Bury.

CAST:

Madame Lidoine, 2nd Prioress . . . . . . Joan Sutherland
Mother Marie of the Incarnation . . . . . . Heather Begg
Blanche de la Force . . . . Isobel Buchanan
Madame de Croissy, 1st Prioress . . . . Lone Koppel
Marquis de la Force . . . . Geoffrey Chard
The Chevalier, His Son . . . . Paul Ferris
Sister Constance . . . . Ann-Marie MacDonald
M. Javelinot . . . . John Germain
Mother Jeanne . . . . Patricia Price
Sister Mathilde . . . . Cynthia Johnston
Sister Anne of the Cross . . . . Frances Chambers
Sister Gerald . . . . Judith Saliba
Sister Claire . . . . Olga Sanderson-Smith

Sister Antoine .... Marie Driscoll
Sister Catherine .... Helen Adams
Sister Alice .... Beryl Furlan
Sister Gertrude .... Luise Napier
Sister Felicity .... Helen Borthwick
Sister Valentine .... Hellen O'Rourke
Sister Martha .... Deborah Riedel
Sister St. Charles .... Dorothy Robertson-O'Brien
Father Confessor .... Richard Greager
First Commissary .... Gordon Wilcock
Second Commissary .... John Wegner
Officer .... Pieter van der Stolk
Goaler .... John Fulford
Thiery .... Anthony Warlow

Richard Bonynge, Elizabethan Sydney Orchestra, Australian Opera Chorus.

+ *Opera Canada* 28, 4 (Winter 1987): 52, by Ruby Mercer.
+ *Opera News* 51, 12 (February 28, 1987): 44, by Thor Eckert, Jr.

32.1. DON CARLO by Giuseppe Verdi.
1983. Bel Canto/Paramount Home Video

Stage production, Metropolitan Opera, New York City, videotaped on March 26, 1983, 214 min., stereo hi-fi, color, sung in Italian with English subtitles.

Production, John Dexter; sets, David Reppa; costumes, Ray Diffen; video director, Brian Large. Includes the *Fontainebleau* scene. Includes at end *Verdi at Sant'Agata,* an eight minute program originally broadcast during intermission in which host Francis Robinson describes Verdi's villa. The video was named *Stereo Review*'s Record of the Year for 1984.

CAST:

Don Carlo .... Plácido Domingo
Elisabetta di Valois .... Mirella Freni
Princess Eboli .... Grace Bumbry
Don Rodrigo, Marquis of Posa ...... Louis Quilico
Tebaldo .... Betsy Norden
Philip II, King of Spain .... Nicolai Ghiaurov
Grand Inquisitor .... Ferruccio Furlanetto
Count of Lerma .... John Gilmore
A Monk .... Julien Robbins
A Voice from Heaven .... Marvis Martin
A Royal Herald .... Charles Anthony
Countess of Aremberg .... Barbara Greene
A Forester .... Peter Sliker

James Levine, Orchestra and Chorus of the Metropolitan Opera.

+ *Levine*, p. 28-29. • Ghiaurov, Furlanetto
+ *Opera News* 49, 4 (October 1984): 59, by John W. Freeman.
+ *Opera Quarterly* 5, 2-3 (Summer/Autumn 1987): 155-157, by Robert Levine.

32.2. DON CARLO by Giuseppe Verdi.
1985. Home Vision

Stage production, Royal Opera House, Covent Garden, London, England, videotaped on April 17, 1985, 208 min., stereo hi-fi, color, sung in Italian with English subtitles.
Staged by Christopher Renshaw; design, Luchino Visconti; video director, Brian Large.

CAST:

Don Carlo	Luis Lima
Elisabetta di Valois	Ileana Cotrubas
Princess Eboli	Bruna Baglioni
Don Rodrigo, Marquis of Posa	Giorgio Zancanaro
Tebaldo	Patricia Parker
Philip II, King of Spain	Robert Lloyd
Grand Inquisitor	Joseph Rouleau
Count of Lerma	John Dobson
A Monk	Matthew Best
A Voice from Heaven	Lola Biagioni
A Royal Herald	Alan Jones
Countess of Aremberg	Romayne Grigorova
Flemish Deputies	Ian Comboy
	Brian Donlan
	Henry Herford
	Martin McEvoy
	Julian Moyle
	Stephen Rhys-Williams

Bernard Haitink, Orchestra and Chorus of the Royal Opera House, Covent Garden.

+ *Landers Film Reviews* 32, 2 (Winter 1987): 61.
• *Levine*, p. 27-28. – Baglioni, the chorus
– *Opera News* 52, 10 (January 30, 1988): 40, by Thor Eckert, Jr.
• *Opera Quarterly* 5, 2-3 (Summer/Autumn 1987): 155-157, by Robert Levine. – Baglioni, the chorus
• *Ovation* 8, 4 (May 1987): 46, by Robert Levine. – Baglioni, the chorus

33.1. DON GIOVANNI by Wolfgang Amadeus Mozart.
1954. Video Artists International

Stage production, Salzburg Festival, Austria, 129 min., mono, color, sung in Italian, no subtitles.
Producers, Paul Czinner, Fred Swann; directors, Paul Czinner, Alfred Travers. Performed in the Felsenreitschule, an open-air stage. "Dalla sua pace" is cut. Originally released as a motion picture in 1955 by Harmony/Maxwell (Britain).

CAST:

Don Giovanni	Cesare Siepi
Donna Anna	Elisabeth Grümmer
Donna Elvira	Lisa Della Casa
Zerlina	Erna Berger
Don Ottavio	Anton Dermota
Leporello	Otto Edelmann
Masetto	Walter Berry
The Commendatore	Dezsö Ernster

Wilhelm Furtwängler, Vienna Philharmonic Orchestra and Chorus of the Vienna State Opera.

- • *Motion Picture Guide*.
- • *Musical America* 111, 5 (September/October 1991): 58-59, by Robert Levine. ++ Siepi
- \+ *Opera News* 56, 5 (November 1991): 36, by Harvey E. Phillips.
- \+ *Opera Quarterly* 8, 3 (Autumn 1991): 131-132, by Bruce Burroughs.

33.2. DON GIOVANNI by Wolfgang Amadeus Mozart.
1956.

Feature film, 89 min., mono, color, sung in German with English subtitles.
Director, H.W. Kolm-Veltee; costumes, Hill Reihs-Oromes; photography, Willy Sohm-Hannes Fuchs. Actors and actresses lip sync to a prerecorded sound track. Originally issued as a motion picture titled *Don Juan* by Akkrod Film/Times Films (Austria).

CAST:
Singers are listed first; actors and actresses are listed second

Don Giovanni	Alfred Poell/Cesare Danova
Donna Anna	Anny Felbermayer/ Marianne Schoenauer
Donna Elvira	Hanna Loeser/Lotte Tobisch
Zerlina	Anny Felbermayer/Evelyne Cormand
Don Ottavio	Hugo Meyer-Welfing/Jean Vinci
Leporello	Harald Progelhof/Joseph Meinrad
Masetto	Walter Berry/Hans von Vorsody

The Commendatore ..... Gottlob Frick/Fred Hennings
Elvira's Maid (non-singing) .... Senta Wengraf

Music director, Professor Birkmeyer, Vienna Symphony Orchestra; danced by the Ballet Corps of the Vienna State Opera.

- *Motion Picture Guide.*

33.3. DON GIOVANNI by Wolfgang Amadeus Mozart.
1977. Video Artists International

Stage production, Glyndebourne Festival, England, 173 min., mono hi-fi, color, sung in Italian with English subtitles.
Producer, Peter Hall; designer, John Bury; television producer and director, Dave Heather. The opera is re-set in the Victorian era.

CAST:
Don Giovanni .... Benjamin Luxon
Donna Anna .... Horiana Branisteanu
Donna Elvira .... Rachel Yakar
Zerlina .... Elizabeth Gale
Don Ottavio .... Leo Goeke
Leporello .... Stafford Dean
Masetto .... John Rawnsley
The Commendatore .... Pierre Thau

Bernard Haitink, London Philharmonic Orchestra, Glyndebourne Festival Chorus.

+– *Levine*, p. 29-30. + Gale, Rawnsley
• *Opera (England)* 39, 8 (August 1988): 1016-1017, by Richard Law.
+ *Opera News* 50, 2 (August 1985): 36, by Richard Hornak.
– *Opera Quarterly* 3, 4 (Winter 1985/86): 122-125, by William Huck.
• *Opera Quarterly* 8, 3 (Autumn 1991): 132-135, by John Schauer.

33.4. DON GIOVANNI by Wolfgang Amadeus Mozart.
1978. Video purchase, Kultur; film rental, New Yorker Films, 16 West 61st St. New York, NY 10023 212-247-6110, fax 212-307-7855

Film version, 177 min., stereo hi-fi, color, sung in Italian with English subtitles.
Director, Joseph Losey; production by Janus Films and Antenne 2 with the Paris Opera; costumes, Martha Mikon; harpsichordist, Janine Reiss. Originally issued as a motion picture.

CAST:
Don Giovanni .... Ruggero Raimondi
Donna Anna .... Edda Moser
Donna Elvira .... Kiri Te Kanawa
Zerlina .... Teresa Berganza

Don Ottavio .... Kenneth Riegel
Leporello .... José van Dam
Masetto .... Malcolm King
The Commendatore .... John Macurdy
A Valet in Black (non-singing) .... Eric Adjani

Lorin Maazel, Orchestra and Chorus of the Paris Opera.

+ *Levine*, p. 86-87.
• *Motion Picture Guide*.
+ *Opera Canada* 30, 2 (Summer 1989): 52, by Ruby Mercer.
+ *Opera (England)* 31, 12 (December 1980): 1260, by Gerald Kaufman.
+ *Opera News* 53, 5 (November 1988): 67, by Harvey E. Phillips.
  + singing, • Losey's production
• *Opera Quarterly* 8, 3 (Autumn 1991): 135-136, by David McKee.
+ *Opern Welt* 30, 1 (Januar 1989): 60, by Thomas Voigt.
+ *Ovation* 9, 10 (November 1988): 45, by Robert Levine.

33.5. DON GIOVANNI by Wolfgang Amadeus Mozart.
1987. SVS, Inc. (SONY)

Stage production, Salzburg Festival, Austria, 193 min., stereo hi-fi, color, sung in Italian.

CAST:
Don Giovanni .... Samuel Ramey
Donna Anna .... Anna Tomowa-Sintow
Donna Elvira .... Julia Varady
Zerlina .... Kathleen Battle
Don Ottavio .... Gösta Winbergh
Leporello .... Ferruccio Furlanetto
Masetto .... Alexander Malta
Il Commendatore .... Paata Burchuladze

Herbert von Karajan, Vienna Philharmonic Orchestra.

+ *Fanfare* 16, 4 (March/April 1993): 419-420, by James Reel.

33.6. DON GIOVANNI by Wolfgang Amadeus Mozart.
1990. London (PolyGram)

Film version, 190 min., stereo hi-fi, color, sung in Italian with English subtitles.
Director, Peter Sellars; sets, George Tsypin; costumes, Dunya Ramicova; continuo: Myron Lutzke, cello, Suzanne Cleverdon, fortepiano. Action takes place in present-day Spanish Harlem.

CAST:
Don Giovanni .... Eugene Perry
Donna Anna .... Dominique Labelle

Donna Elvira .... Lorraine Hunt
Zerlina .... Ai Lan Zhu
Don Ottavio .... Carroll Freeman
Leporello .... Herbert Perry
Masetto .... Elmore James
The Commendatore .... James Patterson
Small Girl (non-singing) .... Lisi Ortner
Don Giovanni's Four Companions (non-singing) ......
Clark Abraham
Jake Eberle
Anthony Egbowen
Christopher Fischer

Craig Smith, Vienna Symphonic Orchestra and Arnold-Schoenberg-Choir.

+– *Fanfare* 16, 2 (November/December 1992): 482-485, by James Reel. + singing, – Sellars's production
– *New York* 25, 22 (June 1, 1992): 62-63, by Peter G. Davis.
– *Opera News* 56, 1 (July 1991): 42-43, by Patrick J. Smith.
+ *Video Magazine* 16, 5 (August 1992): 41, "Editor's Choice," by Kenneth Kormon.

34. DON PASQUALE by Gaetano Donizetti.
1948. Archival Film, Indiana University; 16mm non-circulating film at California State University, Chico, Chico, CA 95929

Film version, about 25 min., abridged, mono, black and white, sung in Italian with a commentator explaining the plot in English, no subtitles.
Produced by George Richfield; musical arrangement and script, Raffaele Gervasio. Filmed on stage at the Rome Opera House, Italy. Part of the *First Opera Film Festival* series. Giulio Tomei is a singer who also appears as an actor.

CAST:
Singers are listed first; actors and actresses are listed second.

Don Pasquale .... Luciano Neroni/Giulio Tomei
Ernesto .... Cesare Valletti/Mino Rosso
Norina .... Angelica Tuccari/Pina Malagarina
Dr. Malatesta .... Tito Gobbi
A Notary .... Gino Conti

Angelo Questa, Orchestra of the Rome Opera House.

+ *EFLA* (1965), p. 114 [EFLA No. 1951.2256]

35.1. DIE DREIGROSCHENOPER by Kurt Weill.
1931. Nelson Entertainment; Voyager's *Criterion Collection*

Feature film, 110 min., mono, black and white, sung and spoken in German with English subtitles.
Director, G.W. Pabst; settings, Andrei Andreiev; photography, Fritz Arno Wagner; adapted from the play by Bertolt Brecht with screenplay by Leo Lania, Ladislas Vajda, Bela Balazs.

CAST:

Macheath (Mack the Knife) .... Rudolph Forster
Polly Peachum .... Carola Neher
Jenny .... Lotte Lenya
Peachum .... Fritz Rasp
Street Singer .... Ernst Busch
Mrs. Peachum .... Valeska Gert
Tiger Brown .... Reinhold Schünzel
The Vicar .... Hermann Thimig
Smith .... Vladimir Sokolov
Filch .... Herbert Grünbaum
Mack's Gang .... Paul Kemp
Gustav Püttjer
Oscar Höcker
Kraft Raschig

Musical director, Theo Mackeben.

35.2. DIE DREIGROSCHENOPER by Kurt Weill.
1990. Columbia Tristar Home Video

Feature film, 122 min., stereo hi-fi, color, sung and spoken in English.
Producer, Stanley Chase; director, Menahem Golan; production designer, Tivadar Bertalan; photography, Elemer Ragalyi. Adapted from Weill's and Brecht's work by Marc Blitzstein. Released as *Mack the Knife* by Menahem Golan/21st Century.

CAST:

Macheath (Mack the Knife) .... Raul Julia
Polly Peachum .... Rachel Robertson
Jenny .... Julia Migenes-Johnson
Peachum .... Richard Harris
Mrs. Peachum .... Julie Walters
Tiger Brown .... Bill Nighy
Reverend Kimball .... John Woodnut
Street Singer .... Roger Daltrey
Smith .... Steven Law
Filch .... Iain Rogerson
Money Matthew .... Clive Revill
Lucy Brown .... Erin Donovan

Coaxer	Julie T. Wallace
Dolly	Louise Plowright
Molly	Elizabeth Seal
Betty	Chrissie Kendall
Esmerelda	Miranda Garrison
Jimmy Jewels	Mark Northover
Wally the Weeper	Roy Holder
Johnny Ladder	Clive Mantle
Hookfinger Jake	Russel Gold
Reverend Kimball	John Woodnut
Warden	Peter Rutherford
Filch	Iain Rogerson
Sergeant Smith	Steven Law
Sukey Tawdry	Dong Ji Hong
Organ Grinder	Sandor Kaposi

Musical director, Dov Seltzer.

– *Motion Picture Guide, 1991*, p. 108.
• *New York Times Film Reviews, 1989-90*, p. 235, by Janet Maslin.

36. ECHO ET NARCISSE by Christoph Willibald Gluck.
1987. Home Vision, issued with *Le Cinesi* as *L'Innocenza ed il Piacer*

Stage production, Schwetzinger Festival, performed at the Rococo Theater at the Schwetzinger Palace in the small town of Schwetzingen near Heidelberg, 99 min. (total timing, 168 min.), stereo hi-fi, color, sung in French with English subtitles.

CAST:

Amor	Deborah Massell
Echo	Sophie Boulin
Narcisse	Kurt Streit
Cynire	Peter Galliard
Eglé	Gertrud Hoffstedt
Algaé	Christina Högman
Thanais, a Nymph	Hanne Krogen
Sylphie, a Nymph	Eva Maria Tersson

René Jacobs, Concerto Köln.

37.1. ELEKTRA by Richard Strauss.
1980. Bel Canto/Paramount Home Video

Stage production, Metropolitan Opera, New York City, videotaped on Saturday afternoon, February 16, 1980, 112 min., stereo hi-fi, color, sung in German with English subtitles.
Production, Herbert Graf; director, Paul Mills; set and costume designer, Rudolf Heinrich; video director, Brian Large.

CAST:

Elektra	Birgit Nilsson
Chrysothemis	Leonie Rysanek
Klytemnestra	Mignon Dunn
Aegisth	Robert Nagy
Orest	Donald McIntyre
Confidante of Klytemnestra	Constance Webber
Trainbearer of Klytemnestra	Elizabeth Anguish
Young Servant	Charles Anthony
Old Servant	Talmage Harper
Tutor of Orest	John Cheek
Overseer	Elizabeth Cross
Five maidservants	Batyah Godfrey
	Shirley Love
	Ariel Bybee
	Loretta Di Franco
	Alma Jean Smith

James Levine, Orchestra and Chorus of the Metropolitan Opera.

++ *Levine*, p. 30-31.
• *Opera News* 56, 2 (August 1991): 44-45, "The Basics," by Harvey E. Phillips.

37.2. ELEKTRA by Richard Strauss.
1981. London (PolyGram)

Film version, 117 min., stereo hi-fi, color, sung in German with English subtitles.
Staged and directed by Götz Friedrich; designed by Josef Svoboda; photography, Rudolf Blahacek. Filmed on location in the outskirts of Vienna in a constant drizzle.

CAST:

Elektra	Leonie Rysanek
Chrysothemis	Catarina Ligendza
Klytemnestra	Astrid Varnay
Aegisth	Hans Beirer
Orest	Dietrich Fischer-Dieskau
Confidante of Klytemnestra	Carmen Reppel
Trainbearer of Klytemnestra	Olga Warla

Young Servant .... Christopher Doig
Old Servant .... Kurt Böhme
Tutor of Orest .... Josef Greindl
Overseer .... Colette Lorand
Five maidservants .... Kaja Borris
Axelle Gall
Rohangiz Yachmi
Milkana Nikolova
Marjorie Vance
Agamemmon (actor) .... Rolf Boysen

Karl Böhm, Vienna Philharmonic Orchestra, Vienna State Chorus Concert Ensemble.

+– *New York* 21, 38 (September 26, 1988): 127, by Peter G. Davis.
– production, + sound track
+ *Opera Canada* 31, 4 (Winter 1990): 52, by Neil Crory.
++ *Opera News* 53, 13 (March 18, 1989): 44, by C.J. Luten.
+ *Ovation* 9, 11 (December 1988): 58, 60, by David Hurwitz.
+– *Video Review* 10, 5 (August 1989): 60, by Thor Eckert, Jr.
+ music, – color on laser disc

37.3. ELEKTRA by Richard Strauss.
1989. Home Vision

Stage production, Vienna State Opera, Austria, 108 min., stereo hi-fi, color, sung in German with English subtitles.
Production, Harry Kupfer; sets, Hans Schavernoch; costumes, Reinhard Heinrich; video director, Brian Large.

CAST:
Elektra .... Eva Marton
Chrysothemis .... Cheryl Studer
Klytemnestra .... Brigitte Fassbaender
Aegisth .... James King
Orest .... Franz Grundheber
Confidante of Klytemnestra ...... Waltraud Winsauer
Trainbearer of Klytemnestra .... Noriko Sasaki
Young Servant .... Wilfried Gahmlich
Old Servant .... Claudio Otelli
Tutor of Orest .... Goran Simich
Overseer .... Gabriele Lechner
Five maidservants .... Margarita Lilova
Gabriele Sima
Margareta Hintermeier
Brigitte Poschner-Klebel
Joanna Borowska

Claudio Abbado, Orchestra and Chorus of the Vienna State Opera.

++ *Landers Film and Video Reviews* 36, 2 (Winter 1991): 60.
+ *Opera (England)* 43, 7 (July 1992): 871-873, by David Murray.

38.1. L'ELISIR D'AMORE by Gaetano Donizetti.
1946. Applause Video (85 Longview Rd., Port Washington, NY 11050)

Film version, 75 min., mono, black and white, sung in Italian with English subtitles.
Director, Mario Costa. The American version featured commentary by Milton Cross at the beginning of the film. Originally issued as a motion picture. The film was shot without sound and the voices were dubbed later. Also known as *This Wine of Love*. Musical director, Giuseppe Morelli.

CAST:
Adina . . . . Nelly Corradi
Nemorino . . . . Gino Sinimberghi
Belcore . . . . Tito Gobbi
Dulcamara . . . . Italo Tajo
Gianetta . . . . Loretta di Lelio

- *Motion Picture Guide*.

38.2. L'ELISIR D'AMORE by Gaetano Donizetti.
1981. Bel Canto/Paramount Home Video

Stage production, Metropolitan Opera, New York City, videotaped on March 2, 1981, 132 min., stereo hi-fi, color, sung in Italian with English subtitles.
Director, Nathaniel Merrill; video director, Kirk Browning.

CAST:
Adina . . . . Judith Blegen
Nemorino . . . . Luciano Pavarotti
Belcore . . . . Brent Ellis
Dulcamara . . . . Sesto Bruscantini
Gianetta . . . . Louise Wohlafka

Nicola Rescigno, Orchestra and Chorus of the Metropolitan Opera.

• *Opera News* 52, 17 (June 1988): 44, by C.J. Luten.
+ Pavarotti
•– *Opera Quarterly* 5, 4 (Winter 1987/88): 110-111, by Thor Eckert, Jr.
+ Pavarotti

38.3. L'ELISIR D'AMORE by Gaetano Donizetti.
1984. European Video Distributors

Film version, 80 min., hi-fi, color, sung in Italian, no subtitles.
Director, Frank De-Quell.

CAST:

Adina . . . . Melanie Holliday
Nemorino . . . . Miroslav Dvorsky
Belcore . . . . Alfredo Mariotti
Dulcamara . . . . Armando Ariostini
Gianetta . . . . Bozena Plonyova

Piero Bellugi, Bratislava Radio Symphony.

– *Opera News* 53, 9 (January 21, 1989): 41, by Harvey E. Phillips.

38.4. L'ELISIR D'AMORE by Gaetano Donizetti.
1991. Deutsche Grammophon (PolyGram)

Stage production, Metropolitan Opera, New York City, videotaped in November 1991, 129 min., stereo hi-fi, color, sung in Italian with English subtitles.
Production, John Copley; sets, Beni Montresor; video director, Brian Large.

CAST:

Adina . . . . Kathleen Battle
Nemorino . . . . Luciano Pavarotti
Belcore . . . . Juan Pons
Dulcamara . . . . Enzo Dara
Gianetta . . . . Korliss Uecker

James Levine, Orchestra and Chorus of the Metropolitan Opera.

The Elixir of Love
SEE L'Elisir d'Amore, 38.1.—38.4.

39.1. L'ENFANT ET LES SORTILÈGES by Maurice Ravel.
1986. Home Vision

Stage production, Netherlands Dance Theatre on stage, singers on sound track, 50 min., stereo hi-fi, color, sung in French, no subtitles.
Director and producer, Hans Hulscher; choreographer, Jiří Kylián; scenery and costumes, John Macfarlane. The sound track for the video production is taken from a Deutsche Grammophon recording dated 1961. Includes an introduction by Kylián, about 7 min.

CAST:

Singers are listed first; dancers are listed second.

The Child .... Françoise Ogéas/Marly Knoben
His Mother .... Janine Collard/Roslyn Anderson
Tom Cat .... Camille Maurane/Nacho Duato
Grandfather Clock ... Camille Maurane/James Vincent
Armchair .... Heinz Rehfuss/Leigh Matthews
Tree .... Heinz Rehfuss
Bat .... Colette Herzog/James Vincent
Owl .... Colette Herzog
Shepherdess ...... Colette Herzog/Sabine Kupferberg
Teapot .... Michel Sénéchal/Michael Sanders
Mr. Arithmetic ... Michel Sénéchal/Jean-Louis Cabané
Chinese Cup .... Janine Collard/Karin Heinjninck
Dragonfly .... Janine Collard
Fire .... Sylvaine Gilma/Pascale Mosseimans
Princess .... Sylvaine Gilma/Joke Zijlstra
Nightingale .... Sylvaine Gilma
Sofa .... Jeanne Berbié
She-Cat .... Jeanne Berbié/Catherine Allard
Squirrel .... Jeanne Berbié/Sabine Kupferberg
Shepherd .... Jeanne Berbié/Jean-Yves Esquerre
Dancers:
Easy-Chair .... Stephen Sheriff
Prince .... Gerald Tibbs
Ashes .... Aryeh Weiner
Bird .... Teresina Mosco

Lorin Maazel, Orchestre national de Paris, Choeur et la Maîtrise de la RTF.

\+ *AFVA Evaluations 1988*, p. 13 [AFVA No. 1987.12,804]
++ *Opera (England)* 40, 6 (June 1989): 749, by Noël Goodwin.

39.2. L'ENFANT ET LES SORTILÈGES by Maurice Ravel.
1987. Home Vision (laser disc issued with *L'Heure Espagnole*, 67.)

Stage production without an audience, filmed at Glyndebourne, England, 46 min., stereo hi-fi, color, sung in French with English subtitles.
Director, Frank Cosaro; designer, Maurice Sendak; film animator and slide designer, Ronald Chase; choreographer, Jenny Weston; video director, Tom Gutteridge.

CAST:

The Child .... Cynthia Buchan
His Mother/The Cat .... Fiona Kimm
Tom Cat/Grandfather Clock .... Malcolm Walker
Armchair/A Tree .... François Loup
Louis XV Chair/The Bat .... Hyacinth Nicholls
Tea Pot/Frog .... Thierry Dran

Chinese Cup/Dragonfly . . . . Louise Winter
Fire/Nightingale . . . . Nan Christie
Shepherd . . . . Jady Pearl
Princess . . . . Harolyn Blackwell
Shepherdess . . . . Carol Smith
Squirrel . . . . Anna Steiger
Owl . . . . Alison Hagley
Mr. Arithmetic . . . . Thierry Dran
Dancers . . . . Coleen Barsley
Paolo Lopes
Nigel Nicholson

Simon Rattle, London Philharmonic Orchestra, Glyndebourne Festival Chorus, members of Trinity Boys Choir.

\+ *Classical* 2, 7 (July 1990): 37, by Tom Di Nardo.

40.1. DIE ENTFÜHRUNG AUS DEM SERAIL by Wolfgang Amadeus Mozart.
1980. Deutsche Grammophon (PolyGram)

Stage production, Bavarian State Opera, Munich, Germany, 147 min., stereo hi-fi, color, sung in German with English subtitles.
Director, August Everding; sets and costumes, Max Bignens.

CAST:

Konstanze . . . . Edita Gruberova
Belmonte . . . . Francisco Araiza
Blonde . . . . Reri Grist
Pedrillo . . . . Norbert Orth
Osmin . . . . Martti Talvela
Pasha Selim (non-singing) . . . . Thomas Holtzmann

Karl Böhm, Orchestra and Chorus of the Bavarian State Opera.

- *Fanfare* 15, 4 (March/April 1992): 452-453, by James Reel.
- *Opera News* 56, 7 (December 21, 1991): 52, by Harvey E. Phillips.

40.2. DIE ENTFÜHRUNG AUS DEM SERAIL by Wolfgang Amadeus Mozart.
1980. V.I.E.W. Video

Stage production, Dresden State Opera, Germany, 129 min., stereo hi-fi, color, sung in German, no subtitles.
Staged and directed by Harry Kupfer.

CAST:

Konstanze . . . . Caroline Smith-Meyer
Belmonte . . . . Armin Uhde
Blonde . . . . Barbara Sternberger

Pedrillo . . . . Uwe Peper
Osmin . . . . Rolf Tomaszewki
Pasha Selim (non-singing) . . . . Werner Haseleu

Peter Gülke, Orchestra and Chorus of the Dresden State Opera.

40.3. DIE ENTFÜHRUNG AUS DEM SERAIL by Wolfgang Amadeus Mozart.
1980. Video Artists International

Stage production, Glyndebourne Festival, England, 145 min., mono hi-fi, color, sung in German with English subtitles.
Production, Peter Wood; contributions by William Dudley; director, Dave Heather; sets, William Dudley.

CAST:
Konstanze . . . . Valerie Masterson
Belmonte . . . . Ryland Davies
Blonde . . . . Lillian Watson
Pedrillo . . . . James Hoback
Osmin . . . . Willard White
Pasha Selim (non-singing) . . . . Joachim Bissmeier

Gustav Kuhn, London Philharmonic Orchestra, Glyndebourne Festival Chorus.

+– *Levine*, p. 31-32. + performance, – sound track
+– *Ovation* 7, 11 (December 1986): 46, by Robert Levine.
+ performance, – sound track

40.4. DIE ENTFÜHRUNG AUS DEM SERAIL by Wolfgang Amadeus Mozart.
1986. Home Vision

Stage production, Royal Opera House, Covent Garden, London, England, 145 min., stereo hi-fi, color, sung in German with English subtitles.
Producer, Elijah Moshinsky; designers, Timothy O'Brien, Sir Sidney Nolan; video director, Humphrey Burton.

CAST:
Konstanze . . . . Inga Nielsen
Belmonte . . . . Deon van der Walt
Blonde . . . . Lillian Watson
Pedrillo . . . . Lars Magnusson
Osmin . . . . Kurt Moll
Pasha Selim (non-singing) . . . . Oliver Tobias

Sir Georg Solti, Orchestra and Chorus of the Royal Opera House, Covent Garden.

•– *Opera Quarterly* 8, 3 (Autumn 1991): 125-128, by Roger Pines.
\+ *Video Choice* 1, 9 (November 1988): 39-40.

41.1. ERNANI by Giuseppe Verdi.
1982. HBO Video

Stage production, Teatro alla Scala, Milan, Italy, 135 min., stereo hi-fi, color, sung in Italian. This video was initially released without English subtitles; later issues may have subtitles.
Producer, Luca Ronconi; sets, Ezio Frigerio; costumes, Franca Squarciapino; video director, Preben Montell.

CAST:

Ernani	Plácido Domingo
Donna Elvira	Mirella Freni
Don Carlo	Renato Bruson
Don Ruy Gomez di Silva	Nicolai Ghiaurov
Giovanna	Jolanda Michieli
Iago	Alfredo Giacomotti
Don Riccardo	Gianfranco Manganotti

Riccardo Muti, Orchestra and Chorus of Teatro alla Scala.

+– *Levine*, p. 32-33. + singing, – production
+– *Opera Monthly* 1, 3 (July 1988): 57-59, by Robert Levine. + singing, – production
\+ *Opera News* 49, 1 (July 1984): 45, John W. Freeman.
\+ *Opera News* 50, 4 (October 1985): 60, by Richard Hornak.
+– *Opera Quarterly* 5, 2-3 (Summer/Autumn 1987): 148-149, by Robert Levine. + singing, – production

41.2. ERNANI by Giuseppe Verdi.
1983. Bel Canto/Paramount Home Video

Stage production, Metropolitan Opera, New York City, videotaped on December 12 and 17, 1983, 142 min., stereo hi-fi, color, sung in Italian with English subtitles.
Producer, Clemente D'Alessio; sets, Pier Luigi Samaritani; costumes, Peter J. Hall; video director, Kirk Browning. This is a complete recording including all repeats. Pavarotti sings an additional aria composed by Verdi for the Russian tenor, Nicola Ivanoff, in 1844.

CAST:

Ernani	Luciano Pavarotti
Donna Elvira	Leona Mitchell
Don Carlo	Sherrill Milnes
Don Ruy Gomez di Silva	Ruggero Raimondi
Giovanna	Jean Kraft
Iago	Richard Vernon
Don Riccardo	Charles Anthony

James Levine, Orchestra and Chorus of the Metropolitan Opera.

+– *Levine*, p. 34-35. –Mitchell, + others, • production
• *Opera Monthly* 1, 3 (July 1988): 57-59, by Robert Levine.
•– *Opera News* 51, 12 (February 28, 1987): 44, by Thor Eckert, Jr.
• *Opera Quarterly* 5, 2-3 (Summer/Autumn 1987): 148-149, by Robert Levine.

42.1. EUGENE ONEGIN by Peter Ilich Tchaikovsky.
1958. Corinth Video; Kultur; Corinth/Image Entertainment

Film version, Bolshoi Theatre, Russia/Soviet Union, 106 min., mono hi-fi, color, sung in Russian with English subtitles.
Producer, Mosfilm; director, Roman Tikhomirov; screenplay, Alexander Ivanovsky. Actors and actresses lip sync to a prerecorded sound track.

CAST:
Singers are listed first; actors and actresses are listed second.

Tatiana .... Galina Vishnevskaya/Adriadna Shengelaya
Eugene Onegin .... Evgeny Gavrilovich Kibkalo/ Vadim Medvedev
Lensky .... Anton Grigoriev/Igor Ozerov
Prince Gremin .... Ivan Ivanovich Petrov
Olga .... Larissa Avdeeva/Svetlana Nemolyaeva

Boris Ėmmanuilovich Khaikin, Orchestra and Chorus of the Bolshoi Theatre.

+ *Levine*, p. 87-88.
+ *Library Journal* 116, 11 (June 15, 1991): 118, by Adam Paul Hunt.
+ *Opera News* 49, 14 (March 30, 1985): 25, by Richard Hornak.
– *Opera News* 55, 17 (June 1991): 52-53, by Harvey E. Phillips.
+ *Opera Quarterly* 3, 2 (Summer 1985): 139-141, by Christopher J. Thomas.

42.2. EUGENE ONEGIN by Peter Ilich Tchaikovsky.
1984. Kultur

Stage production, Kirov Opera Company, Kirov Opera and Ballet Theatre, Leningrad, 155 min., stereo hi-fi, color, sung in Russian with English subtitles.
Director, Elena Gorbunova; video, Vasily Tarasiok.

CAST:
Tatiana .... Tatyana Novikova
Eugene Onegin .... Sergei Leiferkus
Lensky .... Yuri Marusin
Prince Gremin .... Nikolai Okhotnikov
Olga .... Larissa Dyadkova
Madame Larina .... Evgenia Gorokhovskaya
Filipievna .... Ludmilla Filatova

Yuri Temirkanov, Orchestra and Chorus of the Kirov Opera.

\+ *Opera News* 54, 13 (March 17, 1990): 38, by Harvey E. Phillips.
• *Variety* 336 (August 2-8, 1989): 35, by Tyl.
++ *Video Rating Guide* 1, 2 (Spring 1990): 763, F.W. Lancaster

42.3. EUGENE ONEGIN by Peter Ilich Tchaikovsky.
1985. Home Vision

Stage production, Lyric Opera of Chicago, Illinois, 158 min., stereo hi-fi, color, sung in Russian with English subtitles.
Producer, Peter Weinberg; director, Pier Luigi Samartini; video director, Kirk Browning.

CAST:

Tatiana	Mirella Freni
Eugene Onegin	Wolfgang Brendel
Lensky	Peter Dvorský
Prince Gremin	Nicolai Ghiaurov
Olga	Sandra Walker
Madame Larina	Jean Kraft
Filipievna	Gweneth Bean
Monsieur Triquet	John Fryatt
Captain	Paul Kreider
Zaretsky	Mark Doss
Guillot	Reinert Lindland

Bruno Bartoletti, Orchestra and Chorus of the Lyric Opera of Chicago.

+– *Levine*, p. 35-36. + singing, – technical aspects
\+ *Opera News* 52, 1 (July 1987): 50, by Thor Eckert, Jr.
+– *Ovation* 8, 9 (October 1987): 46, by Robert Levine.
+ singing, – technical aspects

42.4. EUGENE ONEGIN by Peter Ilich Tchaikovsky.
1991. London (PolyGram)

Film version, 116 min., stereo hi-fi, color, sung in Russian with English subtitles.
Filmmaker, Petr Weigl; Royal Opera House, Covent Garden, singers recorded the sound track in Kingsway Hall, London, June and July, 1974. Actors and actresses lip sync to a prerecorded sound track. Shot on location.

CAST:
Singers are listed first; actors and actresses are listed second.

Tatiana	Teresa Kubiak/Magdalena Vásáryová
Eugene Onegin	Bernd Weikl/Michal Docolomansky
Lensky	Stuart Burrows/Emil Horváth
Prince Gremin	Nicolai Ghiaurov/Premysl Koci

Olga . . . . Julia Hamari/Kamila Magálová
Madame Larina . . Anna Reynolds/Antonie Hegerliková
Filipievna . . . . Enid Hartle/Vlasta Fabiánová
Monsieur Triquet . . . . Michel Sénéchal/
Frantisek Filipovsky
Captain . . . . William Mason
Zaretsky . . . . Richard Van Allan/Andrej Hrye

Sir Georg Solti, Orchestra of the Royal Opera House, Covent Garden, the John Alldis Choir.

– *Opera (England)* 42, 12 (December 1991): 1492-1493, by John Allison.
+ *Opera News* 56, 11 (February 15, 1992): 35, by Shirley Fleming.

43.1. FALSTAFF by Giuseppe Verdi.
1976. Video Artists International

Stage production, Glyndebourne Festival, England, 123 min., hi-fi, color, sung in Italian with English subtitles.
Production, Jean-Pierre Ponnelle; television director, Dave Heather.

CAST:
Sir John Falstaff . . . . Donald Gramm
Alice Ford . . . . Kay Griffel
Ford . . . . Benjamin Luxon
Dame Quickly . . . . Nucci Condò
Meg Page . . . . Reni Penkova
Nanetta . . . . Elizabeth Gale
Bardolph . . . . Bernard Dickerson
Pistol . . . . Ugo Trama
Fenton . . . . Max René Cosotti
Dr. Caius . . . . John Fryatt
Innkeeper . . . . Graeme Matheson-Bruce
Mr. Page . . . . Richard Robson
Boy, Falstaff's Page (non-singing) . Paul Jackson Robin

John Pritchard, London Philharmonic Orchestra, Glyndebourne Festival Chorus.

+ *Levine*, p. 38-39.
+ *Opera (England)* 39, 9 (September 1988): 1147, by Noël Goodwin.
+ *Opera News* 50, 4 (October 1985): 60, by Richard Hornak.
+ *Opera Quarterly* 5, 2-3 (Summer/Autumn 1987): 161-163, by Robert Levine.

43.2. FALSTAFF by Giuseppe Verdi.
1979. London (PolyGram)

Film version, 126 min., stereo hi-fi, color, sung in Italian with English subtitles.
Director, Götz Friedrich; sets, Jörg Neumann, Thomas Riccabona; costumes, Bernd Muller; photography, Wolfgang Treu, Theo Rose. A movie made on specially-constructed sets.

CAST:

Sir John Falstaff . . . . Gabriel Bacquier
Alice Ford . . . . Karan Armstrong
Ford . . . . Richard Stilwell
Dame Quickly . . . . Márta Szirmay
Meg Page . . . . Sylvia Lindenstrand
Nanetta . . . . Jutta-Renate Ihloff
Bardolph . . . . Peter Maus
Pistol . . . . Ulrik Cold
Fenton . . . . Max René Cosotti
Dr. Caius . . . . John Lanigan

Sir Georg Solti, Vienna Philharmonic Orchestra.

++ *Classical* 6, 2 (February 1990): 24-25, by Robert Levine.
+ *New York* 22, 15 (April 10, 1989): 110, by Peter G. Davis.

43.3. FALSTAFF by Giuseppe Verdi.
1982. HBO Video

Stage production, Royal Opera House, Covent Garden, London, England, videotaped on July 16, 1982, 139 min., stereo hi-fi, color, sung in Italian. This opera was originally released without English subtitles; later issues may have subtitles.
Producer, Ronald Eyre; scenery, Hayden Griffin; costumes, Michael Stennett; video director, Brian Large.

CAST:

Sir John Falstaff . . . . Renato Bruson
Alice Ford . . . . Katia Ricciarelli
Ford . . . . Leo Nucci
Dame Quickly . . . . Lucia Valentini-Terrani
Meg Page . . . . Brenda Boozer
Nanetta . . . . Barbara Hendricks
Bardolph . . . . Francis Egerton
Pistol . . . . William Wildermann
Fenton . . . . Dalmacio Gonzalez
Dr. Caius . . . . John Dobson
Host of the Garter Inn . . . . George MacPherson

Carlo Maria Giulini, Orchestra and Chorus of the Royal Opera House, Covent Garden.

+ *Levine*, p. 36-37.
+ *Opera News* 49, 1 (July 1984): 45, by John W. Freeman.
+ *Opera News* 50, 4 (October 1985): 60, by Richard Hornak.
+ *Opera Quarterly* 5, 2-3 (Summer/Autumn 1987): 161-163, by Robert Levine.

44.1. LA FANCIULLA DEL WEST by Giacomo Puccini.
1983. HBO Video

Stage production, Royal Opera House, Covent Garden, London, England, 139 min., stereo hi-fi, color, sung in Italian. This video was originally released without English subtitles; later issues may have subtitles.
Producer, Piero Faggioni; sets, Ken Adam; television director, John Vernon.

CAST:

Minnie	Carol Neblett
Dick Johnson (Ramirez)	Plácido Domingo
Jack Rance	Silvano Carroli
Nick	Francis Egerton
Ashby	Robert Lloyd
Jake Wallace	Gwynne Howell
Sonora (Miner)	John Rawnsley
Trim (Miner)	John Dobson
Handsome [Bello] (Miner)	Tom McDonnell
Happy (Miner)	Ian Caddy
Joe (Miner)	Robin Leggate
Larkens (Miner)	Roderick Earle
Harry (Miner)	Paul Crook
Sid (Miner)	Norman Welsby
Billy Jackrabbit	Paul Hudson
Wowkle	Jean Bailey
José Castro	John Gibbs
Pony Express Rider	Handel Owen

Nello Santi, Orchestra and Chorus of the Royal Opera House, Covent Garden.

44.2. LA FANCIULLA DEL WEST by Giacomo Puccini.
1991. Home Vision

Stage production, Teatro alla Scala, Milan, Italy, 145 min., stereo hi-fi, color, sung in Italian with English subtitles.
Director, Jonathon Miller; sets, Stephanos Lazaridis; television director, Peter Wood.

CAST:

Minnie	Mara Zampieri
Dick Johnson (Ramirez)	Plácido Domingo
Jack Rance	Juan Pons

Nick .... Sergio Bertocchi
Ashby .... Luigi Roni
Jake Wallace .... Marco Chingari
Sonora (Miner) .... Antonio Salvadori
Trim (Miner) .... Ernesto Gavazzi
Handsome [Bello] (Miner) .... Orazio Mori
Happy (Miner) .... Ernesto Panariello
Joe (Miner) .... Aldo Bottion
Larkens (Miner) .... Pietro Spagnoli
Harry (Miner) .... Francesco Memeo
Sid (Miner) .... Giovanni Savoiardo
Billy Jackrabbit .... Aldo Bramante
Wowkle .... Nella Verri
José Castro .... Claudio Giombi
Pony Express Rider .... Ivan Del Manto

Loren Maazel, Orchestra and Chorus of Teatro alla Scala.

- *Opera News* 57, 12 (February 27, 1993): 42, by Harvey E. Phillips.

45. **LA FAVORITA** by Gaetano Donizetti.
1952. V.I.E.W. Video; Video Yesteryear

Film version, 80 min., abridged, mono, black and white, sung in Italian with English narration, no subtitles.
Production, Giuseppe Fieno; director, Cesare Barlacchi; costumes, Ditta Ferroni. Actors and actresses lip sync to a prerecorded sound track. Sophia Loren is listed as Sophia Lazarro in the credits. Although Gino Sinimberghi and Franca Tamantini are listed as actors, both are also singers: Sinimberghi, tenor; Tamantini, mezzo-soprano.

CAST:
Singers are listed first; actors and actresses are listed second.

Leonora di Gusman .... Palmira Vitali-Marini/ Sophia Loren
Fernando .... Piero Sardelli/Gino Sinimberghi
Alfonso .... Paolo Silveri
Baldassare .... Alfredo Colella
Don Gasparo .... Nino Russo
Ines .... Miriam Di Giove/Franca Tamantini
An Official of the King .... Giorgio Costantini

Nicola Rucci, Organizzazione Rucci and the Ballet di Teatro dell'Opera di Roma.

– *Opera News* 55, 3 (September 1990): 50-51, by Harvey E. Phillips.

La Favorite
See La Favorita, 45.

46.1. FIDELIO by Ludwig van Beethoven.
1955.

Feature film, Vienna State Opera, Austria, 90 min., mono, black and white, sung in German with English subtitles. Formerly available (1984) as a film rental from Corinth Films.
Director, Walter Felsenstein; music director, Erich Bertel. Based on Beethoven's opera with additional music by Pierre Gaveaux, libretto by Jean Nicolas Bouilly. Originally issued as a motion picture by Akkord/Brandon Films (Austria). Filmed in 1955, released in 1961.

CAST:
Leonore .... Claude Nollier
Florestan .... Richard Holm
Rocco .... Georg Wieter
Marzelline .... Sonja Schoner
Don Pizarro .... Hannes Schiel
Jaquino .... Fritz Berger
Don Fernando .... Erwin Gross
First Prisoner .... Michael Tellering
Second Prisoner .... Harry Payer

Erich Bertel, Orchestra and Chorus of the Vienna State Opera.

- *Motion Picture Guide.*

46.2. FIDELIO by Ludwig van Beethoven.
1968. 16mm rental (magnetic sound track), West Glen Communications, 1430 Broadway, New York, NY 10138 212-921-2800

Television production, Hamburg State Opera, Hamburg, Germany, 126 min., mono, color, sung in German, no subtitles.
Production, Rolf Liebermann; director, Joachim Hess; camera, Hannes Schindler; Productionsleitung, Rudolf Sander. Made for German television and released theatrically in the United States.

CAST:
Leonore .... Anja Silja
Florestan .... Richard Cassilly
Rocco .... Ernst Wiemann
Marzelline .... Lucia Popp
Don Pizarro .... Theo Adam
Jaquino .... Erwin Wohlfahrt
Don Fernando .... Hans Sotin
First Prisoner .... Kurt Marschner
Second Prisoner .... William Workman

Leopold Ludwig, Philharmonische Staatsorchester and the Chorus of the Hamburg State Opera.

- *Motion Picture Guide.*

46.3. FIDELIO by Ludwig van Beethoven.
1979. Video Artists International

Stage production, Glyndebourne Festival, England, 130 min., mono hi-fi, color, sung in German with English subtitles.
Director, Peter Hall; designer, John Bury; television production, Dave Heather.

CAST:

Leonore	Elisabeth Söderström
Florestan	Anton de Ridder
Rocco	Curt Appelgren
Marzelline	Elizabeth Gale
Don Pizarro	Robert Allman
Jaquino	Ian Caley
Don Fernando	Michael Langdon

Bernard Haitink, London Philharmonic Orchestra, Glyndebourne Festival Chorus.

• *Levine*, p. 39-40. – Ridder, Allman, Langdon, ++ Söderström
\+ *Opera News* 50, 2 (August 1985): 36, by Richard Hornak.
•– *Opera Quarterly* 4, 1 (Spring 1986): 137-130, by Christopher J. Thomas. – Ridder, Langdon, + Gale, Söderström, Haitink

46.4. FIDELIO by Ludwig van Beethoven.
1990. Home Vision

Stage production, Royal Opera House, Covent Garden, London, England, 129 min., stereo hi-fi, color, sung in German with English subtitles.
Production, Adolf Dresen; video director, Derek Bailey.

CAST:

Leonore	Gabriela Beňačková-Čápová
Florestan	Josef Protschka
Rocco	Robert Lloyd
Marzelline	Marie McLaughlin
Don Pizarro	Monte Pederson
Jaquino	Neill Archer
Don Fernando	Hans Tschammer
First Prisoner	Lynton Atkinson
Second Prisoner	Mark Beesley

Christoph von Dohnányi, Orchestra and Chorus of the Royal Opera House, Covent Garden.

+– *Opera (England)* 43, 5 (May 1992): 610-611, by Noël Goodwin.
 – sets
• *Opera News* 57, 9 (January 16, 1993): 44, by Harvey E. Phillips.
+• *Opera Now* (December 1991): 56-57, by Richard Fawkes.
 + singing, • stage production

47.1. LA FILLE DU RÉGIMENT by Gaetano Donizetti.
1974. Video Artists International

Stage production, Filene Center Auditorium in Wolf Trap Farm Park for the Performing Arts, Vienna, Virginia, 118 min., mono hi-fi, color, sung in English, English translation by Ruth and Thomas Martin.
Producer, David Prowitt; director, Lotfi Mansouri; sets, Beni Montressor; camera, Kip Durrin; video director, Kirk Browning.

CAST:
Marie .... Beverly Sills
Tonio .... William McDonald
Sergeant Suplice .... Spiro Malas
Marquise de Birkenfeld ..... Muriel Costa-Greenspon
Hortensius .... Stanley Wexler
Corporal .... Reader Anderson
Duchess de Krakenthorp .... Evelyn Freyman
Notary .... David Wylie
Dancing master (non-singing) .... Ben Stevenson

Charles Wendelken-Wilson, Filene Center Orchestra, Wolf Trap Company Chorus.

– *Opera News* 57, 13 (March 13, 1993): 44, by Harvey E. Phillips.

47.2. LA FILLE DU RÉGIMENT by Gaetano Donizetti.
1986. Kultur

Stage production, Australian Opera, Sydney, videotaped on August 9, 1986, 122 min., stereo hi-fi, color, sung in French with English subtitles.
Production, Sandro Sequi; sets, Henry Bardon; costumes, Michael Stennett; television director, Peter Butler. Includes "Pour me rapprocher de Marie."

CAST:
Marie .... Joan Sutherland
Tonio .... Anson Austin
Sergeant Suplice .... Gregory Yurisich
Marquise de Birkenfeld .... Heather Begg
Peasant .... Stephen Bennett
Hortensius .... Gordon Wilcock
Corporal .... David Lemke
Duchess de Krakenthorp .... Marie-Claire

Richard Bonynge, Elizabethan Sydney Orchestra, Australian Opera Chorus.

\+ *Opera (England)* 42, 7 (July 1991): 854-855, by Noël Goodwin.

First Opera Film Festival series

SEE Il Barbiere di Siviglia, 13.2.
Carmen, 22.1.
Don Pasquale, 34.
Fra Diavolo, 52.
Guglielmo Tell, A15.
Lucia di Lammermoor, 82.1.
Le Nozze di Figaro, 101.2.

48.1. DIE FLEDERMAUS by Johann Strauss.
1982. SVS, Inc. (SONY)

Stage production, Australian Opera, Sydney, videotaped on July 10, 1982, 142 min., stereo hi-fi, color, sung in English.
Produced and staged by Anthony Besch; director, Hugh Davidson; designer, John Stoddart; television producer, Brian Adams. Lois Strike and Kelvin Cole dance the *Pas de deux* from *Don Quixote* in the second act.

CAST:

Roselinde . . . . Joan Sutherland
Gabriel von Eisenstein . . . . Robert Gard
Adele . . . . Monique Brynnel
Prince Orlofsky . . . . Heather Begg
Dr. Falke . . . . Michael Lewis
Alfred . . . . Anson Austin
Dr. Blind . . . . Gordon Wilcock
Frank . . . . Gregory Yurisich
Ida . . . . Anne-Marie McDonald
Frosch . . . . Graeme Ewer

Richard Bonynge, Elizabethan Sydney Orchestra, Australian Opera Chorus.

\- *Classical* 2, 5 (May 1990): 35, by Robert Levine
\- *Levine*, p. 40-41.
\+ *Opera Canada* 28, 3 (Fall 1987): 52, by Ruby Mercer.

48.2. DIE FLEDERMAUS by Johann Strauss.
1983. HBO Video

Stage production, Royal Opera House, Covent Garden, London, England, videotaped on December 31, 1983, 180 min., stereo hi-fi, color, sung in German with added dialogue in German and English. This video was originally released without English subtitles; later issues may have subtitles.

Producers, Leopold Lindtberg and Richard Gregson; sets and costumes, Julia Trevelyan Oman; video director, Humphrey Burton. Special appearances in the second act by Dr. Evadne Hinge and Dame Hilda Bracket, Charles Aznavour, Merle Park and Wayne Eagling.

CAST:

Roselinde	Kiri Te Kanawa
Gabriel von Eisenstein	Hermann Prey
Adele	Hildegard Heichele
Prince Orlofsky	Doris Soffel
Dr. Falke	Benjamin Luxon
Alfred	Dennis O'Neill
Dr. Blind	Paul Crook
Frank	Michael Langdon
Ida	Ingrid Baier
Ivan	Richard Hazell
Frosch	Josef Meinrad

Plácido Domingo, Orchestra and Chorus of the Royal Opera House, Covent Garden.

\+ *Opera News* 49, 14 (March 30, 1985): 25, by Richard Hornak.
– *Opera News* 50, 17 (June 1986): 49, by John W. Freeman.

48.3. DIE FLEDERMAUS by Johann Strauss.
1987. Deutsche Grammophon (PolyGram)

Stage production, Bavarian State Opera, National Theater, Munich, Germany, 146 min., stereo hi-fi, color, sung in German with English subtitles.
Staged and directed by Otto Schenk; sets, Günther Schneider-Siemssen; costumes, Silvia Strahammer; television director, Brian Large. Dialogue adapted by Otto Schenk and Peter Weiser.

CAST:

Roselinde	Pamela Coburn
Gabriel von Eisenstein	Eberhard Wächter
Adele	Janet Perry
Prince Orlofsky	Brigitte Fassbaender
Dr. Falke	Wolfgang Brendel
Alfred	Josef Hopferwieser
Dr. Blind	Ferry Gruber
Frank	Benno Kusche
Ida	Irene Steinbeisser
Ivan	Ivan Unger
Frosch	Franz Muxeneder

Carlos Kleiber, Bavarian State Orchestra, Bavarian State Opera Chorus.

\+ *New York* 22, 15 (April 10, 1989): 109, by Peter G. Davis.

48.4. DIE FLEDERMAUS by Johann Strauss.
1990. Home Vision

Stage production, Royal Opera House, Covent Garden, London, England, 197 min., stereo hi-fi, color, sung in English, translation by John Mortimer.
Producer, John Cox; television director, Humphrey Burton. A document of Joan Sutherland's farewell to Covent Garden. Prince Orlofsky is sung by a countertenor. Viviana Durante and Stuart Cassidy dance Ashton's *Voices of Spring* in the second act.

CAST:

Roselinde . . . . Nancy Gustafson
Gabriel von Eisenstein . . . . Louis Otey
Adele . . . . Judith Howarth
Prince Orlofsky . . . . Jochen Kowalski
Dr. Falke . . . . Anthony Michaels-Moore
Alfred . . . . Bonaventura Bottone
Frank . . . . Eric Garrett
Frosch . . . . John Sessions
Orlofsky's guests . . . . Joan Sutherland
Marilyn Horne
Luciano Pavarotti

Richard Bonynge, Orchestra and Chorus of the Royal Opera House, Covent Garden.

- *Opera (England)* 43, 1 (January 1992): 119, by Noël Goodwin.
+ *Opera News* 57, 14 (March 27, 1993): 46, by Harvey E. Phillips.

49.1. DER FLIEGENDE HOLLÄNDER by Richard Wagner.
1984. Philips (PolyGram)

Stage production, Bayreuth Festival, Germany, 136 min., stereo hi-fi, color, sung in German with English subtitles.
Director, Harry Kupfer; television director, Brian Large.

CAST:

Senta . . . . Lisbeth Balslev
The Dutchman . . . . Simon Estes
Mary . . . . Anny Schlemm
Erik . . . . Robert Schunk
Daland's Steersman . . . . Graham Clark
Daland . . . . Matti Salminen

Woldemar Nelsson, Orchestra and Chorus of the Bayreuth Festival.

- *Opera News* 57, 4 (October 1992): 58, by Patrick J. Smith.
+ Estes

49.2. DER FLIEGENDE HOLLÄNDER by Richard Wagner.
1989. Teldec

Stage production, Savonlinna Opera Festival, Finland, 139 min., stereo hi-fi, color, sung in German with English subtitles.
Producer, Ilkka Bäckman; director, Juhani Pirskanen; video director, Aarno Cronvall. Videotaped on location in the courtyard of the fifteenth century Olavinlinna Castle.

CAST:

Senta	Hildegard Behrens
The Dutchman	Franz Grundheber
Mary	Anita Välkki
Erik	Raimo Sirkiä
Daland's Steersman	Jorma Silvasti
Daland	Matti Salminen

Leif Segerstam, Orchestra and Chorus of the Savonlinna Opera Festival.

- *Fanfare* 16, 1 (September/October 1992): 468, by James Reel.
- *Opera (England)* 42, 8 (August 1991): 982-983, by Charles Osborne. + Behrens
- *Opera News* 57, 4 (October 1992): 58, by Patrick J. Smith.
- *Opera Now* (December 1991): 56-57, by Richard Fawkes.

50. THE FLOOD by Igor Stravinsky.
1962. Home Vision (issued with *Oedipus Rex*, 102.2.)

Television/studio production, 90 min. (inclusive timing with *Oedipus Rex* on the same cassette), mono, color, sung in English.
Producers, John McClure, Milka Henriques de Castro; designed and directed by Jaap Drupsteen. *The Flood* was composed in 1962 for CBS Television. This video release incorporates the original sound track with a new video component by Jaap Drupsteen. Actors and actresses lip sync to a prerecorded sound track.

CAST:
Singers and narrators are listed first; actors and actresses are listed second.

Narrator	Laurence Harvey
Noah	Sebastian Cabot/Rudi Van Vlaanderen
Noah's wife	Elsa Lanchester/Kitty Courbois
The Caller	Paul Tripp
God (singers)	John Reardon, Robert Oliver
God (actors)	Rudolf Grasman Emile Linssen Carel Willink
Lucifer	Richard Robinson/Pauline Daniels

Actors and actresses:
Eva . . . . Silvia Millecam
Adam . . . . Julian Beusker
Noah's Son . . . . Fried Keesttulst
Mertens . . . . Glenn Durfort
Wives . . . . Bambi Uden
Liesbeth Coops
Annet Malherbe

Robert Craft, Columbia Symphony Orchestra and Chorus.

The Flying Dutchman
SEE Der Fliegende Holländer, 49.1.—49.2.

Focus on Opera series
SEE Il Barbiere di Siviglia, 13.4.
Les Contes d'Hoffmann, 27.2.
Il Pagliacci, 107.4.
Rigoletto, 117.3.
La Traviata, 136.3.

51. LA FORZA DEL DESTINO by Giuseppe Verdi.
1984. Bel Canto/Paramount Home Video

Stage production, Metropolitan Opera, New York City, videotaped on March 24, 1984, 179 min., stereo hi-fi, color, sung in Italian with English subtitles.
Production, John Dexter; sets, Eugene Berman; costumes, Peter J. Hall.

CAST:
Leonora di Vargas . . . . Leontyne Price
Don Alvaro . . . . Giuseppe Giacomini
Don Carlo di Vargas . . . . Leo Nucci
Preziosilla . . . . Isola Jones
Padre Guardiano . . . . Bonaldo Giaiotti
Fra Melitone . . . . Enrico Fissore
Marquis di Calatrava . . . . Richard Vernon
Curra . . . . Diane Kesling
Mayor of Hornachuelos . . . . James Courtney
Trubucco . . . . Anthony Laciura
A Surgeon . . . . John Darrenkamp

James Levine, Orchestra and Chorus of the Metropolitan Opera.

- *Opera News* 53, 15 (April 15, 1989): 22, by Harvey E. Phillips.
- *Video Review* 9, 9 (December 1988): 85, by Bert Wechsler.

52. FRA DIAVOLO by Daniel François Auber.
About **1948**. 16mm rental, Budget Films

Film version, about 25 min., abridged, mono, black and white, sung in Italian with a commentator explaining the plot in English, no subtitles.
Produced by George Richfield; musical arrangement and script, Raffaele Gervasio; stage director, E. Fulchignoni; film director, E. Cancellieri. Filmed on stage at the Rome Opera House, Italy. Part of the *First Opera Film Festival* series.

CAST:

Fra Diavolo	Nino Adami
Lord Cockburn	Pietro Passarotti
Lady Pamela	Palmira Vitali-Marini
Lorenzo	Giuseppe Biondi/Zwonko Gluk (actor)
Matteo	Gino Conti
Zerlina	Magda Laselo
Giacomo	Luciano Neroni
Beppo	Blando Giusti

Angelo Questa, Orchestra and Chorus of the Rome Opera House.

53. FRANCESCA DA RIMINI by Riccardo Zandonai.
1984. Bel Canto/Paramount Home Video

Stage production, Metropolitan Opera, New York City, videotaped on April 4 and 7, 1984, 148 min., stereo hi-fi, color, sung in Italian with English subtitles.
Production, Piero Faggioni; designed by Ezio Frigerio; costumes, Franca Squarciapino; video director, Brian Large.

CAST:

Francesca da Rimini	Renata Scotto
Paolo Malatesta	Plácido Domingo
Gianciotto	Cornell MacNeil
Malatestino	William Lewis
Simonetto, A Jester	Brian Schexnayder
Smaragdi, Francesca's Slave	Isola Jones
Ostasio, Francesca's Brother	Richard Fredricks
Ser Toldo Berardengo, Lawyer	Anthony Laciura
Samaritana, Francesca's Sister	Nicole Lorange
Berlingerio, Tower Guard	John Darrenkamp
An Archer	John Gilmore
A Prisoner	John Bills
Garsenda	Gail Robinson
Biancofiore	Natalia Rom
Altichiara	Gail Dubinbaum
Adonella	Claudia Catania

James Levine, Orchestra and Chorus of the Metropolitan Opera.

+ *Landers Film and Video Reviews* 34, 3 (Spring 1990): 115.
+– *Levine*, p. 41-42. – Scotto's singing
+ *Opera News* 52, 4 (October 1987): 44, by Thor Eckert, Jr.
+ *Opera Quarterly* 5, 4 (Winter 1987/88): 106-108, by Thor Eckert, Jr.
+ *Ovation* 9, 2 (March 1988): 36, by Dick Adler.
+ *Ovation* 10, 2 (March 1989): 55, 57, by Robert Levine.

54. LO FRATE 'NNAMORATO by Giovanni Battista Pergolesi.
1990. Home Vision

Stage production, Teatro alla Scala, Milan, Italy, 130 min., stereo hi-fi, color, sung in Italian with English subtitles.
Director, Roberto De Simone; scenic designer, Mauro Carosi; costumes, Odette Nicoletti; television director, John Michael Philips. Critical edition by Francesco Degrada.

CAST:

Ascanio . . . . Nuccia Focile
Nena . . . . Amelia Felle
Nina . . . . Bernadette Manca di Nissa
Marcaniello . . . . Alessandro Corbelli
Carlo . . . . Ezio Di Cesare
Luggrezia . . . . Luciana D'Intino
Vannella . . . . Elizabeth Norberg-Schulz
Cardella . . . . Nicolleta Curiel
Don Pietro . . . . Bruno De Simone
Swordsman . . . . Luca Bonini

Riccardo Muti, Orchestra and Chorus of Teatro alla Scala.

55.1. DER FREISCHÜTZ by Carl Maria von Weber.
1970.

Film version, Hamburg State Opera, Germany, 127 min., mono, color, sung in German.
Producer, Rolf Liebermann; director, Joachim Hess; photography, Hannes Schindler. Made for German television and released theatrically in the United States. Originally issued as a motion picture by Polyphon/Polytel Films (Germany).

CAST:

Max, the Huntsman . . . . Ernst Kozub
Agathe . . . . Arlene Saunders
Aennchen . . . . Edith Mathis
Samiel . . . . Bernard Minetti
Prince Ottokar . . . . Tom Krause
Kuno . . . . Toni Blankenheim
Kaspar . . . . Gottlob Frick
Kilian . . . . Franz Grundheber

A Hermit .... Hans Sotin
Bridesmaid .... Regina Marheineke

Music director, Leopold Ludwig, Orchestra and Choir of the Hamburg State Opera.

• *Motion Picture Guide.*

55.2. DER FREISCHÜTZ by Carl Maria von Weber.
1981. Home Vision

Stage production, Württemberg State Opera, Stuttgart, Germany, 150 min., stereo hi-fi, color, sung in German with English subtitles.
Production, Achim Freyer; video director, Hartmut Schottler. Includes the prologue.

CAST:
Max, the Huntsman .... Toni Krämer
Agathe .... Catarina Ligendza
Aennchen .... Raili Viljakainen
Samiel .... Wolfram Raub
Prince Ottokar .... Wolfgang Schöne
Kuno .... Fritz Linke
Kaspar .... Wolfgang Probst
Kilian .... Helmut Holzapfel
A Hermit .... Roland Bracht
Hunters .... Raimund Ade, Kurt Zeiher
Bridesmaids .... Astrid Burden
Nicole Schneider
Alexandera Turni
Christina Wachtler
Margot Wohlers
Heidi Brunig
Petra Kollakowsky

Dennis Russell Davies, Orchestra and Chorus of the Württemberg State Opera.

+ *Levine*, p. 42-43.

56. LA GAZZA LADRA by Gioacchino Rossini.
1984. Home Vision

Stage production, the Cologne Opera, Germany, 176 min., stereo hi-fi, color, sung in Italian with English subtitles.
Sets and costumes, Mauro Pagano; video director, José Montes-Baquer.

CAST:
Ninetta .... Ileana Cotrubas
Fernando .... Brent Ellis
Gianetto .... David Kuebler

Il Podesta .... Alberto Rinaldi
Fabrizio .... Carlos Feller
Lucia .... Nucci Condò
Pippo .... Elena Zilio
Isacco .... Erlingur Vigfusson
Antonio .... Eberhard Katz
Giorgio .... Klaus Bruch
Ernesto .... Ulrich Hielscher
Il Pretore .... Francisco Varga

Bruno Bartoletti, Gürzenich Orchestra of Cologne, Chorus of the Cologne Opera.

57. GIANNI SCHICCHI by Giacomo Puccini.
1983. Home Vision (issued with the other operas of *Il Trittico, Suor Angelica* and *Il Tabarro*)

Stage production, Teatro alla Scala, Milan, Italy, 150 min. (total timing for the three operas in *Il Trittico*), stereo hi-fi, color, sung in Italian with English subtitles.
Producer, Sylvano Bussotti; television director, Brian Large.

CAST:
Gianni Schicchi .... Juan Pons
Lauretta .... Cecilia Gasdia
Zita .... Eleonora Jankovic
Rinuccio .... Yuri Marusin
Gherardo .... Ferreo Poggi
Nella .... Anna Baldasserini
Gherardino .... Alessandra Cesareo
Betto di Signa .... Franco Boscolo
Simone .... Mario Luperi
Marco .... Giorgio Tadeo
La Ciesca .... Nella Verri
Maestro Spinelloccio .... Claudio Giombi
Ser Amantio di Nicol .... Virgilio Carbonari
Pinellino .... Pio Bonfanti
Guccio .... Ruggero Altavilla

Gianandrea Gavazzeni, Orchestra and Chorus of Teatro alla Scala.

+ *Levine*, p. 78-79.
+ *Ovation* 10, 8 (September 1989): 64, by Robert Levine.

58. LA GIOCONDA by Amilcare Ponchielli.
1986. Home Vision

Stage production, Vienna State Opera, Austria, 169 min., stereo hi-fi, color, sung in Italian with English subtitles.
Produced and designed by Filippo Sanjust; *Dance of the Hours* choreographed by Gerlinde Dill; video director, Hugo Käch.

CAST:

La Gioconda	Eva Marton
Enzo Grimaldo	Plácido Domingo
Barnaba	Matteo Manuguerra
Alvise Badoero	Kurt Rydl
Laura	Ludmilla Semtschuk
La Cieca	Margarita Lilova
Zuane	Alfred Sramek
Isèpo	Jorge Pita
A Minstrel	Alfred Burgstaller
A Pilot	Goran Simich
First Gondolier	Benedikt Kobel
Second Gondolier	Peter Köves
A Monk	Francisco Valls

Adam Fischer, Orchestra, Chorus, and Ballet of the Vienna State Opera.

\+ *Landers Film and Video Reviews* 34, 4 (Summer 1990): 170.
\+ *Opera Canada* 32, 1 (Spring 1991): 51, by Ruby Mercer.
+– *Opera Monthly* 4, 1 (May 1991): 45, by David McKee.
– Sanjust's sets, ++ Marton

59. GIOVANNA D'ARCO by Giuseppe Verdi.
1989. Teldec

Stage production, Teatro comunale di Bologna, Italy, videotaped in December, 1989, 127 min., stereo hi-fi, color, sung in Italian with English subtitles.
Producer, Fiona Morris; directors, Werner Herzog and Henning von Gierke; television directors, Keith Cheetham, Werner Herzog.

CAST:

Giovanna d'Arco	Susan Dunn
Carlo (Charles VII)	Vincenzo La Scola
Delil	Pierre Lefebvre
Giacomo	Renato Bruson
Talbot	Pietro Spagnoli

Riccardo Chailly, Orchestra and Chorus of the Teatro comunale di Bologna, coro di Parma.

– *Fanfare* 16, 1 (September/October 1992): 469, by James Reel.
+ *Opera (England)* 42, 8 (August 1991): 982-983, by Charles Osborne.
+ *Opera News* 57, 3 (September 1992): 54, by Shirley Fleming.
•– *Opera Now* (December 1991): 56-57, by Richard Fawkes.

The Girl of the Golden West
SEE La Fanciulla del West, 44.1.—44.2.

60.1. GIULIO CESARE by George Frideric Handel.
1977. V.I.E.W. Video

Stage production, Berlin State Opera, Germany, 124 min., stereo hi-fi, color, sung in German, no subtitles.
Director, Georg F. Mielke; staging, Erhard Fischer; sets, Gustav Hoffmann; costumes, Christine Stromberg; choreography, Ingeborg-Gerda Funke.

CAST:

Giulio Cesare	Theo Adam
Cleopatra	Celestina Casapietra
Cornelia	Annelies Burmeister
Sextus	Eberhard Büchner
Achillas	Günther Leib
Ptolemy	Siegfried Vogel
Curio, Roman Officer	Horst Lunow
Nirenus	Günther Fröhlich

Peter Schreier, Orchestra, Chorus, and Ballet of the Berlin State Opera.

60.2. GIULIO CESARE by George Frideric Handel.
1984. HBO Video

Film version/Studio production, English National Opera, England, 180 min., stereo hi-fi, color, sung in English, English translation by Brian Trowell.
Producer, John Copley; sets, John Pascoe; costumes, Michael Stennett; video director, John Michael Phillips. Recorded at Limehouse Studios in London's Docklands.

CAST:

Giulio Cesare	Janet Baker
Cleopatra	Valerie Masterson
Cornelia	Sarah Walker
Sextus	Della Jones
Achillas	John Tomlinson
Ptolemy	James Bowman
Curio, Roman Officer	John Kitchiner
Nirenus	Tom Emlyn Williams
Pothinus	Brian Casey

Sir Charles Mackerras, Orchestra and Chorus of the English National Opera.

++ *Levine*, p. 88-90.
+ *Opera Quarterly* 4, 4 (Winter 1986/87): 116-118, by London Green.
+ *Ovation* 9, 5 (June 1988): 44, by Robert Levine.

60.3. GIULIO CESARE by George Frideric Handel.
1990. London (PolyGram)

Film version, produced in the studios of Defa-Film, Babelsberg, 222 min., stereo hi-fi, color, sung in Italian with English subtitles.
Director, Peter Sellars. The score is performed complete with some substitutions of arias. There are two countertenors in the cast. In Sellars's version, Caesar becomes an American president staying at the Nile Hilton.

CAST:

Giulio Cesare	Jeffrey Gall
Cleopatra	Susan Larson
Cornelia	Mary Westbrook-Geha
Sextus	Lorraine Hunt
Achillas	James Maddalena
Ptolemy	Drew Minter
Curio, Roman Officer	Herman Hildebrand
Nirenus	Cheryl Cobb

Craig Smith, Sächsische Staatskapelle Dresden.

+ *Fanfare* 16, 5 (May/June 1993): 435-436, by James Reel.
+– *Opera News* 57, 11 (February 13, 1993): 45, by Patrick J. Smith.

61. GLORIANA by Benjamin Britten.
1984. HBO Video

Stage production, English National Opera at the London Coliseum, England, 146 min., stereo hi-fi, sung in the original English.
Producer, Colin Graham; video director, Derek Bailey.

CAST:

Queen Elizabeth I	Sarah Walker
Robert Devereux, Lord Essex	Anthony Rolfe Johnson
Frances, Countess of Essex	Jean Rigby
Sir Walter Raleigh	Richard Van Allan
Penelope, Lady Rich	Elizabeth Vaughan
Sir Robert Cecil	Alan Opie
Charles Blount, Lord Mountjoy	Neil Howlett
Henry Cuffe	Malcolm Donnelly
Blind Ballad Singer	Norman Bailey
Recorder of Norwich	Dennis Wicks
Lady-in-waiting to the Queen	Lynda Russell
Master of Ceremonies	Alan Woodrow
Morris Dancer	Robert Huguenin

A Housewife	Shelagh Squires
City Crier	Leigh Maurice
Characters of the Masque:	
Spirit of Masque (tenor)	Adrian Martin
Time	Ian Stewart
Concord	Amanda Maxwell
Country Girls	Jocelyn Bowland
	Loraine Gill
	Cornelia Hayes
Rustic Boys	Peter Allan
	David Turner
	Kent Bradford
Actors and dancers	Mary Anne Kraus
	Roy Morto
	Graham T. Phillips

Mark Elder, Orchestra and Chorus of the English National Opera.

+ *Levine*, p. 43-44.
++ *Opera (England)* 39, 10 (October 1988): 1258-1259, by Alan Blyth.
+ *Opera News* 52, 6 (December 5, 1987): 56, by Thor Eckert, Jr.
+ *Ovation* 10, 1 (February 1989): 51-52, by Robert Levine.

62.1. THE GONDOLIERS by W.S. Gilbert & Sir Arthur Sullivan.
1974. 16mm film rental available prior to June 1993 from the University of Illinois Film Center

Film version, 50 min., abridged, mono, color, sung in the original English.
Producer, John Seabourne; director, Trevor Evans; script, David Maverovitch; photography, Adrian Jenkins; narrators, Johnny Wayne, Frank Shuster. Part of the *World of Gilbert and Sullivan* series.

CAST:

Duchess of Plaza-Toro	Helen Landis
Duke of Plaza-Toro	John Cartier
Grand Inquisitor	Donald Adams
Marco Palmieri	Thomas Round
Giuseppe Palmieri	Michael Wakeham
Gianetta	Gillian Humphreys
Tessa	Ann Hood
Casilda	Joy Roberts
Luiz	Glyn Adams
Antonio	Philip Fraser
Inez	Alice Hynd

Gilbert and Sullivan Festival Orchestra and Chorus of England.

62.2. THE GONDOLIERS by W.S. Gilbert & Sir Arthur Sullivan.
1982. CBS/Fox Video

Film version, 117 min., stereo hi-fi, color, sung in the original English.
Producer, Judith de Paul; stage producer, Peter Wood; director, Dave Heather; costume coordinator, Jenny Beavan; executive producer, George Walker. Videotaped at Twickenham Film Studios

CAST:

Duchess of Plaza-Toro . . . . Anne Collins
Duke of Plaza-Toro . . . . Eric Shilling
Grand Inquisitor . . . . Keith Michell
Marco Palmieri . . . . Francis Egerton
Giuseppe Palmieri . . . . Tom McDonnell
Gianetta . . . . Nan Christie
Tessa . . . . Fiona Kimm
Luiz . . . . Christopher Booth-Jones
Antonio . . . . Peter Savidge
Giorgio . . . . Alan Watt

Alexander Faris, London Symphony Orchestra, Ambrosian Opera Chorus.

\+ *Opera News* 50, 2 (August 1985): 37, by Richard Hornak.

62.3. THE GONDOLIERS by W.S. Gilbert & Sir Arthur Sullivan.
1983. Home Vision

Stage production, Stratford Festival of Canada, Avon Theatre, 154 min., stereo hi-fi, color, sung in the original English.
Producer and director, Norman Campbell; sets and costumes, Susan Benson and Douglas McLean. Additional lyrics by John Banks. Musical director and additional music arranged by Berthold Carrière. Original Stratford production directed and choreographed by Brian Macdonald.

CAST:

Duchess of Plaza-Toro . . . . Douglas Chamberlain
Duke of Plaza-Toro . . . . Eric Donkin
Grand Inquisitor . . . . Richard McMillan
Marco Palmieri . . . . John Keane
Giuseppe Palmieri . . . . Paul Massel
Gianetta . . . . Marie Baron
Tessa . . . . Karen Skidmore
Casilda . . . . Deborah Milsom
Annibale . . . . Jim White
Luiz . . . . Kimble Hall
Antonio . . . . Stephen Beamish
Giulia . . . . Aggie Cekuta
Francesco . . . . Richard March
Giorgio . . . . Dale Mieske
Inez . . . . Jean Stilwell

Fiametta .... Marcia Tratt
Vittoria .... Karen Wood
Zanies (non-singing) .... Allison Grant
Larry Herbert
Debora Joy
Kelly Robinson
David Smith
Timothy Cruichshank
Cynthia Dale
Glori Cage
James Leatch
Eileen Smith
Martin Spencer
Gwynyth Walsh

Berthold Carrière, Orchestra and Chorus of the Stratford Festival (Canada).

+– *Levine*, p. 63-65. + singing, sets, and costumes, – additional lyrics
+ *Opera Canada* 30, 1 (Spring 1989): 52, by Ruby Mercer.

63.1. DIE GÖTTERDÄMMERUNG by Richard Wagner.
1980. Philips (PolyGram)

Stage production, Bayreuth Festival, Germany, 266 min., stereo hi-fi, color, sung in German with English subtitles.
Modern version by Pierre Boulez and director Patrice Chéreau; design, Richard Peduzzi; costumes, Jacques Schmidt; video director, Brian Large.

CAST:
Brünnhilde .... Gwyneth Jones
Siegfried .... Manfred Jung
Gutrune .... Jeannine Altmeyer
Gunther .... Franz Mazura
Hagen .... Fritz Hübner
Waltraute .... Gwendolyn Killebrew
Alberich .... Hermann Becht
First Norn .... Ortrun Wenkel
Second Norn .... Gabriele Schnaut
Third Norn .... Katie Clarke
Woglinde .... Norma Sharp
Wellgunde .... Ilse Gramatzki
Flosshilde .... Marga Schiml

Pierre Boulez, Orchestra and Chorus of the Bayreuth Festival.

+ *Classical* 14, 5 (November 1991): 43-44, by Neil Crory.
++ *New York* 25, 20 (May 18, 1992): 65-66, by Peter G. Davis.

63.2. DIE GÖTTERDÄMMERUNG by Richard Wagner.
1990. Deutsche Grammophon (PolyGram)

Stage production, Metropolitan Opera, New York City, 280 min., stereo hi-fi, color, sung in German with English subtitles.
Production by Otto Schenk; sets and projection designer, Günther Schneider-Siemssen; costumes, Rolf Langenfass; video director, Brian Large.

CAST:
Brünnhilde .... Hildegard Behrens
Siegfried .... Siegfried Jerusalem
Hagen .... Matti Salminen
Waltraute .... Christa Ludwig
Gunther .... Anthony Raffell
Gutrune .... Hanna Lisowska
Alberich .... Ekkehard Wlaschiha
First Norn .... Gweneth Bean
Second Norn .... Joyce Castle
Third Norn .... Andrea Gruber
Woglinde .... Kaaren Erickson
Wellgunde .... Diane Kesling
Flosshilde .... Meredith Parsons

James Levine, Orchestra and Chorus of the Metropolitan Opera.

– *New York* 25, 20 (May 18, 1992): 65-66, by Peter G. Davis.

Gustavo III
SEE Un Ballo in Maschera, 12.1.—12.2.

64.1. H.M.S. PINAFORE by W.S. Gilbert & Sir Arthur Sullivan.
1973. Magnetic Video, a Twentieth Century-Fox Company

Television production, D'Oyly Carte Opera Company, 66 min., hi-fi, color, sung in the original English.
Production director, Michael Heyland; producer and director for television, John Sichel. Musical director, Royston Nash.

CAST:
Sir Joseph Porter .... John Reed
Captain Corcoran .... Michael Rayner
Ralph Rackstraw .... Malcolm Williams
Josephine .... Pamela Field
Little Buttercup .... Lyndsie Holland
Dick Deadeye .... John Ayldon
Hebe .... Pauline Williams
Boatswain's Mate .... Jon Ellison
Carpenter's Mate .... John Broad

64.2. H.M.S. PINAFORE by W.S. Gilbert & Sir Arthur Sullivan.
1974. 16mm film rental available prior to June 1993 from the University of Illinois Film Center

Film version, 50 min., abridged, mono, color, sung in the original English.
Producer, John Seabourne; director, Trevor Evans; script, David Maverovitch; photography, Adrian Jenkins; narrators, Johnny Wayne, Frank Shuster. Part of the *World of Gilbert and Sullivan* series.

CAST:

Sir Joseph Porter	John Cartier
Captain Corcoran	Michael Wakeham
Ralph Rackstraw	Thomas Round
Josephine	Valerie Masterson
Little Buttercup	Helen Landis
Dick Deadeye	Donald Adams
Hebe	Vera Ryan
Boatswain's Mate	Lawrence Richard

The Gilbert and Sullivan Festival Orchestra and Chorus of England.

64.3. H.M.S. PINAFORE by W.S. Gilbert & Sir Arthur Sullivan.
1982. CBS/Fox Video

Television production, 90 min., stereo hi-fi, color, sung in the original English.
Producer, Judith De Paul; stage production, Michael Geliot; director, Rodney Greenway; production designer, Allan Cameron; costume coordinator, Jenny Beavan; executive producer, George Walker.

CAST:

Sir Joseph Porter	Frankie Howerd
Captain Corcoran	Peter Marshall
Ralph Rackstraw	Michael Bulman
Josephine	Meryl Drower
Little Buttercup	Della Jones
Dick Deadeye	Alan Watt

Alexander Faris, London Symphony Orchestra, Ambrosian Opera Chorus.

\+ *Opera Now* (January 1992): 56, by Richard Fawkes.

65.1. HÄNSEL UND GRETEL by Engelbert Humperdinck.
1954. 16mm rental, Budget Films; VHS purchase, Vestron Video c/o Live Entertainment, 15400 Sherman Way, Box 10124, Van Nuys, CA 91410-0124 818-988-5060

Feature film, 75 min., mono, color, sung in English.
Producer, Michael Meyerberg; director, John Paul; sets, Evalds Dajevskis; costumes, Ida Vendicktow. Originally issued as a motion picture by RKO. The opera is staged by electronically controlled Kinemins designed by sculptor-painter James Summers. The voices on the sound track are listed below.

CAST:

Gretel	Constance Brigham
Hänsel	Constance Brigham
Gertrude (Mother)	Mildred Dunnock
Peter (Father)	Frank Rogier
The Witch (Rosina Rubylips)	Anna Russell
The Sandman	Delbert Anderson
The Dewfairy	Helen Boatwright

Franz Allers, with the Apollo Boy's Choir (Angels and children).

- *Motion Picture Guide*.

+– *Video Librarian* 5, 2 (April 1990): 3.

65.2. HÄNSEL UND GRETEL by Engelbert Humperdinck.
1981. London (PolyGram)

Television production, Vienna, 107 min., stereo hi-fi, color, sung in German with English subtitles.
Director, August Everding; design, Gerhard Janda; paintings, designs, and costumes, Friedrich Hechelmann; photography, Wolfgang Tren; animation, Theo Nischwitz, Hal Clay.

CAST:

Gretel	Edita Gruberova
Hänsel	Brigitte Fassbaender
Gertrude (Mother)	Helga Dernesch
Peter (Father)	Hermann Prey
The Witch	Sena Jurinac
The Sandman	Norma Burrowes
The Dewfairy	Elfriede Höbarth

Sir Georg Solti, Vienna Philharmonic Orchestra, Wiener Sängerknaben.

65.3. HÄNSEL UND GRETEL by Engelbert Humperdinck.
1982. Bel Canto/Paramount Home Video

Stage production, Metropolitan Opera, New York City, videotaped on December 25, 1982, 104 min., stereo hi-fi, color, sung in English, English text by Norman Kelley.
Production, Nathaniel Merrill; stage direction, Bruce Donnell; sets and costumes, Robert O'Hearn; video director, Kirk Browning.

CAST:

Gretel . . . . Judith Blegen
Hänsel . . . . Frederica Von Stade
Gertrude (Mother) . . . . Jean Kraft
Peter (Father) . . . . Michael Devlin
The Witch . . . . Rosalind Elias
The Sandman . . . . Diane Kesling
The Dewfairy . . . . Betsy Norden

Thomas Fulton, Orchestra and Chorus of the Metropolitan Opera.

++ *Levine*, p. 44-45.
•– *Opera News* 50, 17 (June 1986): 49, by John W. Freeman.
\+ *Opera Quarterly* 4, 2 (Summer 1986): 162-165, by M. Owen Lee.
\+ *Ovation* 10, 3 (April 1989): 73, by Robert Levine.

66. THE HAUNTED MANOR by Stanisław Moniuszko.
1988. Contal International Ltd., 250 West 54 St., Suite 711, New York, NY 10019 212-265-5770

Grand Theater of Warsaw, Poland, 134 min., hi-fi, color, sung in Polish, no subtitles.
Director, Marek Grzesinski; costumes, Irena Bieganska.

CAST:

Miecznik . . . . Andrzej Hiolski
Hanna . . . . Izabella Kłosińska
Jadwiga . . . . Elzbieta Panko
Pan (Mr.) Damazy . . . . Krzysztof Szmyt
Stefan . . . . Stanisław Kowalski
Zbigniew . . . . Leonard Mroz
Czesnikowa (Butler's Wife) . . . .
Krystyna Szostek-Radkowa
Maciej . . . . Wieslaw Bednarek
Skoluba . . . . Jerzy Ostapiuk
Marta . . . . Krystyna Jazwinska
Grzes . . . . Piotr Czajkowski
Stara niewiasta (Elderly Woman) . Elzbieta Kolasinska

Robert Satanowski, Orchestra and Chorus of the Grand Theater of Warsaw, Poland.

67. L'HEURE ESPAGNOLE by Maurice Ravel.
1987. Home Vision (laser disc issued with *L'Enfant et les Sortilèges*, 39.2)

Stage production, Glyndebourne Festival, England, 53 min., stereo hi-fi, color, sung in French with English subtitles.
Producer, Frank Corsaro; film animator and slide designer, Roland Chase; sets and costumes, Maurice Sendak; video director, Dave Heather.

CAST:

Concepcion	Anna Steiger
Ramiro	François Le Roux
Torquemada	Rémy Corazza
Golzalve	Thierry Dran
Don Inigo Gomez	François Loup

Sian Edwards, London Philharmonic Orchestra, Glyndebourne Festival Chorus.

\+ *Classical* 2, 7 (July 1990): 37, by Tom Di Nardo.

68. HIGGLETY PIGGLETY POP! or There Must be More to Life by Oliver Knussen.
1985. Home Vision (laser disc issued with *Where the Wild Things Are*, 151.)

Stage production without audience, filmed at Glyndebourne, England, 60 min., stereo hi-fi, color, sung in the original English.
Director and choreographer, Frank Corsaro; designer, Maurice Sendak; video director, Christopher Swann; movement, Clive Duncan, George Reid.

CAST:

Jennie, a Sealyham Terrier	Cynthia Buchan
Potted Plant/Baby/Mother Goose	Deborah Rees
Pig-in-Sandwich Board	Andrew Gallacher
Low Voice of Ash Tree	Andrew Gallacher
Cat-Milkman	Neil Jenkins
High Voice of Ash Tree	Neil Jenkins
Rhoda, a Parlourmaid	Rosemary Hardy
Voice of Baby's Mother	Rosemary Hardy
Lion	Stephen Richardson

Oliver Knussen, the London Sinfonietta.

++ *Levine*, p. 82-83.
\+ *Ovation* 10, 3 (April 1989): 73, 75, by Robert Levine.
\+ *Video Review* 8, 4 (July 1987): 85, by Allan Kozinn.

Hsiang lo pa
SEE The Perfumed Handkerchief, 109.

69. LES HUGUENOTS by Giacomo Meyerbeer.
1990. Home Vision

Stage production, Australian Opera, Sydney, videotaped on October 2, 1990, 200 min., stereo hi-fi, color, sung in French with English subtitles.
Producer and director, Virginia Lumsden; director, Lotfi Mansouri. Sutherland's farewell in Sydney; she sings *Home Sweet Home* at the end.

CAST:

Marguerite de Valois . . . . Joan Sutherland
Valentine . . . . Amanda Thane
Raoul de Nangis . . . . Anson Austin
Count de Nevers . . . . John Pringle
Count de St. Gris . . . . John Wegner
Marcel . . . . Clifford Grant
Urbain . . . . Suzanne Johnston
Cossé . . . . Lindsay Gaffney
Tavannes . . . . David Collins-White
Bois-Rosé . . . . Sergei Baigildin
Méru . . . . David Lemke
Thore . . . . Kerry Henderson
de Retz . . . . Neil Kirkby

Richard Bonynge, Elizabethan Sydney Orchestra, Australian Opera Chorus.

\+ *Landers Film and Video Reviews* 36, 3 (Spring 1992): 127-128.
\+ *Opera (England)* 42, 12 (December 1991): 1493, by Charles Osborne.
•– *Opera News* 56, 9 (January 18, 1992): 35, by Harvey E. Phillips.

70.1. IDOMENEO by Wolfgang Amadeus Mozart.
1974. Video Artists International

Stage production, Glyndebourne Festival, England, 127 min., hi-fi, color, sung in Italian with English subtitles.
Producer, John Cox; sets, Roger Butlin; television director, Dave Heather. This performance follows the Vienna version with some alterations and with many cuts. Approximately half of first act has been cut as well as "Non ho colpa" and "Tutte nel cor vi sento." "D'Oreste, d'Ajace" has been restored.

CAST:

Idomeneo . . . . Richard Lewis
Ilia . . . . Bozena Betley
Idamante . . . . Leo Goeke
Elettra . . . . Josephine Barstow
Arbace . . . . Alexander Oliver
High Priest of Neptune . . . . John Fryatt
Voice of Neptune . . . . Dennis Wicks

John Pritchard, London Philharmonic Orchestra, Glyndebourne Festival Chorus.

- • *Opera News* 51, 4 (October 1986): 50, by Richard Hornak.
  + Barstow
- •– *Opera Quarterly* 4, 4 (Winter 1986/87): 114-116, by Andrew L. Schreiber.
  – sets, Lewis, + Barstow, • others

70.2. IDOMENEO by Wolfgang Amadeus Mozart.
1982. Bel Canto/Paramount Home Video

Stage production, Metropolitan Opera, New York City, videotaped on November 6, 1982, 185 min., stereo hi-fi, color, sung in Italian with English subtitles.

Producer, sets, costumes, and director Jean-Pierre Ponnelle; video director, Brian Large. Cuts include: Ballet music, K. 367, and "Spiegarti non Poss'io," K. 489. Retained are: "Torna la Pace" and "Fuor del Mar." Critical edition by Daniel Heartz.

CAST:

Idomeneo	Luciano Pavarotti
Ilia	Ileana Cotrubas
Idamante	Frederica Von Stade
Elettra	Hildegard Behrens
Arbace	John Alexander
Women of Crete	Loretta Di Franco, Batyah Godfrey
High Priest of Neptune	Timothy Jenkins
Voice of Neptune	Richard J. Clark
Trojan Soldiers	Charles Anthony, James Courtney

James Levine, Orchestra and Chorus of the Metropolitan Opera.

- + *Opera News* 50, 11 (February 15, 1986): 45, by John W. Freeman.
- + *Opera News* 51, 4 (October 1986): 50, by Richard Hornak.
- + *Opera Quarterly* 4, 2 (Summer 1986): 162-165, by M. Owen Lee.
- + *Opera Quarterly* 8, 3 (Autumn 1991): 123-125, by M. Owen Lee.

70.3. IDOMENEO by Wolfgang Amadeus Mozart.
1983. HBO Video

Stage production, Glyndebourne Festival, England, 180 min., stereo hi-fi, color, sung in Italian with English subtitles.

Producer, Trevor Nunn; designer, John Napier; television director, Christopher Swann. Cuts "Torna la Pace" and almost all of Arbace's music.

CAST:

Idomeneo	Philip Langridge
Ilia	Yvonne Kenny
Idamante	Jerry Hadley
Elettra	Carol Vaness
Arbace	Thomas Hemsley
High Priest of Neptune	Anthony Roden
Voice of Neptune	Roderick Kennedy

Bernard Haitink, London Philharmonic Orchestra, Glyndebourne Festival Chorus.

+– *Opera Monthly* 4, 2 (June 1991): 44, by David McKee.

71.1. L'INCORONAZIONE DI POPPEA by Claudio Monteverdi.
1979. London (PolyGram)

Film version (Harnoncourt edition), Monteverdi Ensemble, Zurich Opera, Switzerland, 162 min., stereo hi-fi, color, sung in Italian with English subtitles.

Designer and director, Jean-Pierre Ponnelle. Based on a production for the Zurich Opera House. The castrato roles are taken by countertenors and Arnalta is sung by countertenor Alexander Oliver. Amore (the goddess of love) is sung by a boy soprano.

CAST:

Poppea	Rachel Yakar
Nerone	Eric Tappy
Ottavia	Trudeliese Schmidt
Seneca	Matti Salminen
Drusilla	Janet Perry
Ottone	Paul Esswood
Arnalta	Alexander Oliver
Fortuna	Renate Lenhart
Virtù	Helrun Gardow
Amore	Klaus Brettschneider
Damigella	Suzanne Calabro
Valletto	Peter Keller
Liberto Capitano	Rudolf A. Hartmann
First Soldier	Peter Straka
Lucano	Philippe Huttenlocher
Second Soldier	Fritz Peter
Nutrice	Maria Minetto
Famigliari di Seneca	Francisco Araiza
	Werner Gröschel
	Peter Keller

Nikolaus Harnoncourt, Monteverdi Ensemble and Choir of the Zurich Opera House.

\+ *Fanfare* 16, 1 (September/October 1992): 467-468, by James Reel.
\+ *Opera News* 57, 3 (September 1992): 54-55, by Shirley Fleming.

71.2. L'INCORONAZIONE DI POPPEA by Claudio Monteverdi.
1984. HBO Video

Stage production (Leppard edition, 1962), Glyndebourne Festival, England, 148 min., stereo hi-fi, color, sung in Italian. This video was initially released without English subtitles; later issues may include subtitles.
Producer, stage, and television director, Peter Hall; designer, John Bury; television producer, Robin Lough.

CAST:

Poppea	Maria Ewing
Nerone	Dennis Bailey
Ottavia	Cynthia Clarey
Seneca	Robert Lloyd
Drusilla	Elizabeth Gale
Ottone	Dale Duesing
Arnalta	Anne-Marie Owens
Fortuna	Patricia Kern
Virtù	Helen Walker
Amore	Linda Kitchen
Damigella	Leslie Garrett
Valletto	Petros Evangelides
Liberto Capitano	Roderick Kennedy
First Soldier	Keith Lewis
Lucano	Keith Lewis
Second Soldier	Donald Stephenson
Pallade	Jenny Miller
Littore	Roger Bryson

Raymond Leppard, London Philharmonic Orchestra, Glyndebourne Festival Chorus.

\+ *Opera (England)* 40, 10 (October 1989): 1265, by Noël Goodwin.

L'Innocenza ed il Piacer
SEE Le Cinesi, 25.
Echo et Narcisse, 36.

72. INTERMEZZO by Richard Strauss.
1983. Home Vision

Stage production, Glyndebourne Festival, England, 155 min., stereo hi-fi, color, sung in English, English translation by Andrew Porter.
Director, John Cox; designer, Martin Battersby; television director, David Buckton.

CAST:

Christine	Felicity Lott
Robert Storch	John Pringle

Baron Lummer	Ian Caley
Anna	Elizabeth Gale
Franzl	Rupert Ashford
Therese	Maria Jagusz
Fanny	Yvonne Howard
Marie	Delith Brook
Lawyer's Wife	Rae Woodland
Resi	Cathrine Pierard
Commercial Counselor	Ian Caddy
Opera Singer	Andrew Gallacher
Stroh	Glenn Winslade
Legal Counselor	Brian Donlan
Lawyer	Roger Bryson

Gustav Kuhn, London Philharmonic Orchestra, Glyndebourne Festival Chorus.

\+ *Levine*, p. 45-46.
\+ *Ovation* 10, 7 (August 1989): 60, by Robert Levine.

73. IOLANTHE by W.S. Gilbert & Sir Arthur Sullivan.
1985. Home Vision

Stage production, Stratford Festival of Canada, Avon Theatre, 138 min., stereo-hi-fi, color, sung in the original English, book and lyrics adapted by Jim Betts.

Producer for the Canadian Broadcasting Corporation, James Guthro; sets and costumes, Susan Benson. Additional lyrics by John Banks. Musical director and additional music arranged by Berthold Carrière. Original Stratford production directed and choreographed by Brian Macdonald.

CAST:

Queen of the Fairies	Maureen Forrester
Lord Chancellor	Eric Donkin
Phyllis	Marie Baron
Stephon	Paul Massel
Iolanthe	Katharina Megli
Earl Tolloller	Stephen Beamish
Private Willis	Avo Kittask
Celia	Allison Grant
Leila	Karen Skidmore
Babs	Karen Wood

Berthold Carrière, Orchestra and Chorus of the Stratford Festival (Canada).

+– *Levine*, p. 63-65. + singing, sets and costumes, – additional lyrics

74. JENŮFA by Leoš Janáček.
1989. Home Vision

Stage production, Glyndebourne Festival, England, 119 min., stereo hi-fi, color, sung in Czech with English subtitles.
Producer, John Miller; original stage production by Nikolaus Lehnhoff; designer, Tobias Hoheisel; video director, Derek Bailey.

CAST:

Jenůfa	Roberta Alexander
Kostelnička Buryjovka	Anja Silja
Laca Klemen	Philip Langridge
Števa Buryja	Mark Baker
Karolka	Alison Hagley
Barena	Sarah Pring
Jano	Lynne Davis
Mayor's wife	Linda Ormiston
Grandmother Buryja	Menai Davies
Foreman at the Mill	Robert Poulton
Mayor of the Village	Gordon Sandison

Andrew Davis, London Philharmonic Orchestra, Glyndebourne Festival Chorus.

++ *Landers Film and Video Reviews* 36, 2 (Winter 1991): 73.
+ *Opera (England)* 43, 1 (January 1992): 118-119, by John Allison.
• *Opera News* 56, 5 (November 1991): 36-37, by Harvey E. Phillips.

Julius Caesar
SEE Giulio Cesare, 60.1.—60.3.

75. KATYA KABANOVA by Leoš Janáček.
1988. Home Vision

Stage production, Glyndebourne Festival, England, 100 min., stereo hi-fi, color, sung in Czech with English subtitles.
Original stage production by Nikolaus Lehnhoff; designer, Tobias Hoheisel; video director, Derek Bailey.

CAST:

Katya Kabanova	Nancy Gustafson
Kabanicha	Felicity Palmer
Varvara (Barbara)	Louise Winter
Gláša	Christine Bunning
Fekluša	Linda Ormiston
Tichon Kabanov	Ryland Davies
Boris Grigorievitch	Barry McCauley
Vanya Kudrjaš	John Graham-Hall
Kuligin	Robert Poulton
Dikoy	Donald Adams

Woman . . . . Rachael Hallawell
Bystander . . . . Christopher Ventris

Andrew Davis, London Philharmonic Orchestra, Glyndebourne Festival Chorus.

+ *Library Journal* 116, 19 (November 15, 1991): 124, by Adam Paul Hunt.
+ *Opera (England)* 43, 1 (January 1992): 118-119, by John Allison.
• *Opera News* 56, 5 (November 1991): 36-37, by Harvey E. Phillips.
+ *Opera Quarterly* 9, 2 (Winter 1992): 133-136, by Roger Pines.
– *Video Librarian* 6, 4 (June 1991): 15.

Kékszakállú Herceg Vára
SEE Bluebeard's Castle, 17.

Kennst du das Land
SEE Mignon, 96.

76.1. KHOVANSHCHINA by Modest Petrovich Mussorgsky.
1959. Corinth Video; Corinth/Image Entertainment [released in the original wide-screen ratio, e.g., letterboxed]

Feature film (Shostakovich edition), Bolshoi Theatre, Russia/Soviet Union, 131 min., mono hi-fi, color, sung in Russian with English subtitles.
Director, Vera Stroyeva; sets, A. Borisov. Musical editing and orchestration by Dmitri Dmitrievich Shostakovich; script, A. Abramova, Dmitri Dmitrievich Shostakovich, Vera Stroyeva.

CAST:
Prince Ivan Khovansky . . . . Aleksei Krivchenya
Dosifei . . . . Mark Osipovich Reizen
Marfa . . . . Kira Leonova
Price Vassily Golitsin . . . . Vladimir Petrov
Boyar Shaklovity . . . . Evgeny Gavrilovich Kibkalo
A Popular Leader . . . . Viktor Nechipailo
Prince Andrei Khovansky . . . . Anton Grigoriev
Kouzka . . . . Aleksei Maslennikov
Persian Captive . . . . Maya Plissetskaya
Emma . . . . V. Gromova
Susanna . . . . L. Gritsyenko
Lutheran Pastor . . . . G. Pankov
Varsonofiev . . . . F. Fokin
Streshniev . . . . E. Demyentev

Evgeny Fedorovich Svetlanov, Orchestra, Chorus, and Ballet of the Bolshoi Theatre.

+ *Opera News* 50, 2 (August 1985): 36, by Richard Hornak.
+ *Opera Quarterly* 3, 4 (Winter 1985/86): 125-128, by Christopher J. Thomas.

76.2. KHOVANSHCHINA by Modest Petrovich Mussorgsky.
1979. Kultur

Stage production (Rimsky-Korsakov edition), Bolshoi Theatre, Russia/Soviet Union, 172 min., mono hi-fi, color, sung in Russian with English subtitles.
Orchestration by Nikolay Rimsky-Korsakov.

CAST:
Prince Ivan Khovansky .... Aleksandr Vedernikov
Dosifei .... Evgeny Nesterenko
Marfa .... Irina Konstantinovna Arkhipova
Price Vassily Golitsin .... Evgeny Raikov
Boyar Shaklovity .... Vladimir Romanovsky
Prince Andrei Khovansky ... Georgy Andryushchenko
Scrivener .... Vitaly Vlasov

Yuri Simonov, Orchestra and Chorus of the Bolshoi Theatre.

+– *Classical* 14, 4 (September 1991): 34, by Neil Crory.
– sound, production, + Nesterenko, Arkhipova
+ *Opera News* 53, 1 (July 1988): 45, by Harvey E. Phillips.
+ *Opera News* 56, 13 (March 14, 1992): 37, by Harvey E. Phillips.
+ *Opera Quarterly* 6, 2 (Winter 1988/89): 109-110, by London Green.

76.3. KHOVANSHCHINA by Modest Petrovich Mussorgsky.
1989. Home Vision

Stage production (Shostakovich edition), Vienna State Opera, Austria, 173 min., stereo hi-fi, color, sung in Russian with English subtitles.
Director, Alfred Kirchner; sets, Erich Wonder; costumes, Joachim Herzog; television director, Brian Large. Orchestration by Dmitri Dmitrievich Shostakovich; final scene by Igor Stravinsky.

CAST:
Prince Ivan Khovansky .... Nicolai Ghiaurov
Dosifei .... Paata Burchuladze
Marfa .... Ludmilla Semtschuk
Price Vassily Golitsin .... Yuri Marusin
Boyar Shaklovity .... Anatoly Kotscherga
Prince Andrei Khovansky .... Vladimir Atlantov
Scrivener .... Heinz Zednik
Emma .... Joanna Borowska
Susanna .... Brigitte Poschner-Klebel
Streshniev .... Timothy Breese
Second Strelets .... Goran Simich
Klevret .... Boyidar Nikolov
Kouzka .... Wilfried Gahmlich
Varsonfiev/First Strelets .... Peter Köves

Persian Captives (Dancers) .... Marialuise Jaska
Roswitha Over
Jolantha Seyfried

Claudio Abbado, Orchestra and Chorus of the Vienna State Opera.

+ *Opera News* 56, 13 (March 14, 1992): 37, by Harvey E. Phillips.
+ *Opera Quarterly* 8, 4 (Winter 1991/92): 108-111, by David McKee.

77. KING PRIAM by Michael Tippett.
1985. Home Vision

Film version/Studio recording, Kent Opera, England, 130 min., stereo hi-fi, color, sung in the original English.
Director and producer, Nicholas Hytner; design, David Fielding; television director, Robin Lough. Recorded in Limehouse Studios in London's Docklands.

CAST:
King Priam .... Rodney Macann
Andromache .... Sarah Walker
Helen of Troy .... Anne Mason
Paris .... Howard Haskin
Hecuba .... Janet Price
Hector .... Omar Ebrahim
Achilles .... Neil Jenkins
Patroclus .... John Hancorn
Hermes .... Christopher Gillett
Nurse .... Enid Hartle
Old Man .... Richard Suart
Young Guard .... Mark Curtis
First Huntsman .... Kevin John
Second Huntsman .... Philip Creasy
Third Huntsman .... Ian Platt
Serving Woman .... Margaret Medlyn
Paris as a Boy .... Nana Antwi-Nyanin

Roger Norrington, Orchestra and Chorus of the Kent Opera.

+ *Levine*, p. 90-91.
+ *Opera News* 53, 15 (April 15, 1989): 40, by Harvey E. Phillips.
+ *Opera Quarterly* 9, 2 (Winter 1992): 131-133, by David McKee.
+ *Ovation* 10, 5 (June 1989): 70, by Robert Levine.

Kniaz Igor
SEE Prince Igor, 112.

78. THE LEGEND OF TSAR SALTAN by Nikolay Rimsky-Korsakov.
1978. V.I.E.W. Video

Stage production, Dresden State Opera, Germany, 98 min., hi-fi, color, sung in German, no subtitles.
Staged by Harry Kupfer; sets and costumes, Peter Sykora.

CAST:

Tsar Saltan	Rolf Wollard
Militrissa	Lidija Rushizkaja
Prince Guidon	Stephan Spiewok
Militrissa's Elder Sisters	Elenore Elstermann
	Barbara Gubisch
Barbaricha	Barbara Hoene
Swan Princess	Ilse Ludwig
Additional singers	Ingrid Schuh
	Friederike Riedel
	Karl-Heinz Koch
	Karl-Heinz Hölzke
	Jürgen Muck
	Jürgen Freier
	Hajo Müller
	Roland Giertz
	Ullrich Schaller

Siegfried Kurz, Orchestra and Chorus of the Dresden State Opera.

Liubov k trem Apelsinam
SEE The Love for Three Oranges, 81.

79.1. LOHENGRIN by Richard Wagner.
1982. Philips (PolyGram)

Stage production, Bayreuth Festival, Germany, 200 min., stereo hi-fi, color, sung in German with English subtitles.
Staged and directed by Götz Friedrich; sets, Günther Uecker; costumes, Frieda Parmeggiani, television director, Brian Large. Artistic supervision, Wolfgang Wagner.

CAST:

Lohengrin	Peter Hofmann
Elsa of Brabant	Karan Armstrong
Ortrud	Elizabeth Connell
Henry the Fowler	Siegfried Vogel
Frederick of Telramund	Leif Roar
King's Herald	Bernd Weikl
Nobles	Toni Krämer
	Helmut Pampuch
	Martin Egel
	Heinz-Klaus Ecker

Pages .... Natuse von Stegmann
Irene Hammann
Patricia Lampert-Bucher
Elke Burkert

Woldemar Nelsson, Orchestra and Chorus of the Bayreuth Festival.

• *Fanfare* 16, 2 (November/December 1992): 486, by James Reel.
•– *Opera News* 56, 6 (December 7, 1991): 58-59, by Harvey E. Phillips.

79.2. LOHENGRIN by Richard Wagner.
1986. Bel Canto/Paramount Home Video

Stage production, Metropolitan Opera, New York City, videotaped on Friday, January 10, 1986, 220 min., stereo hi-fi, color, sung in German with English subtitles.
Production, August Everding; sets, Ming Cho Lee; costumes, Peter J. Hall; video director Brian Large.

CAST:
Lohengrin .... Peter Hofmann
Elsa of Brabant .... Eva Marton
Ortrud .... Leonie Rysanek
Henry the Fowler .... John Macurdy
Frederick of Telramund .... Leif Roar
King's Herald .... Anthony Raffell
Duke Godfrey, Elsa's Brother (non-singing) ....
Christian Collins
Nobles .... Charles Anthony
John Gilmore
John Darrenkamp
Richard Vernon
Pages .... George Caputo
Matthew Dobkin
Melissa Fogarty
Gary Lorentzson
Timothy Murtha
Elizabeth Rogers
Zachery Taylor
Dana Watkins

James Levine, Orchestra and Chorus of the Metropolitan Opera.

++ *Levine*, p. 46-47.
– *Opera News* 53, 15 (April 15, 1989): 23, 40, by Harvey E. Phillips.
– overall, + Rysanek
+ *Ovation* 10, 7 (August 1989): 60, by Robert Levine.

79.3. LOHENGRIN by Richard Wagner.
1990. Home Vision

Stage production, Vienna State Opera, Austria, 217 min., stereo hi-fi, color, sung in German with English subtitles.
Staging, Wolfgang Weber; sets, Rudolf and Reinhard Heinrich; television director, Brian Large. Blue Ribbon winner, American Film and Video Association, 1992.

CAST:

Lohengrin . . . . Plácido Domingo
Elsa of Brabant . . . . Cheryl Studer
Ortrud . . . . Dunja Vejzović
Henry the Fowler . . . . Robert Lloyd
Frederick of Telramund . . . . Hartmut Welker
King's Herald . . . . Georg Tichy
Duke Godfrey, Elsa's Brother (non-singing) . . . .
Karl Scheiner
Nobles . . . . Boyidar Nikolov
Franz Kasemann
Claudio Otelli
Peter Köves
Pages . . . . Silvia Panzenböck
Ingrid Sieghart
Ulrike Erfurt
Johanna Graupe
Ladies . . . . Renate Polacek
Gretchen Eder
Elizabeth Kudrna
Eva-Maria Thor

Claudio Abbado, Orchestra and Chorus of the Vienna State Opera.

\+ *AFVA Evaluations 1992*, p. 135.
• *Opera Canada* 34, 1 (Spring 1993): 34, by Neil Crory.
  \+ Welker, Abbado
• *Opera News* 56, 6 (December 7, 1991): Harvey E. Phillips.

80. I LOMBARDI ALLA PRIMA CROCIATA by Giuseppe Verdi.
1984. HBO Video

Stage production, Teatro alla Scala, Milan, Italy, 126 min., stereo hi-fi, color, sung in Italian. This video was initially released without English subtitles; later issues may have subtitles.
Producer, Gabriele Lavia; sets, Giovanni Agostinucci; costumes, Andrea Viotti; television director, Brian Large. Solo violin, Franco Fantini.

CAST:

Oronte . . . . José Carreras
Giselda . . . . Gena Macheva Dimitrova

Pagano . . . . Silvano Carroli
Arvino . . . . Carlo Bini
Viclinda . . . . Luisa Vannini
Pirro . . . . Luigi Roni
Prior of the City of Milan . . . . . Gianfranco Manganotti
Acciano . . . . Giovanni Foiani
Sofia . . . . Laura Bocca

Gianandrea Gavazzeni, Orchestra and Chorus of Teatro alla Scala.

•– *Levine*, p. 47-49.
– *Opera News* 51, 2 (August 1986): 30, by Richard Hornak.
• *Opera News* 51, 8 (January 3, 1987): 42, by John W. Freeman.
•– *Opera Quarterly* 5, 2-3 (Summer/Autumn 1987): 148, by Robert Levine.
+ *Ovation* 7, 8 (September 1986): 46, by Nancy Malitz.
+– *Video Review* 7, 10 (January 1987): 96, by Allan Kozinn.

81. THE LOVE FOR THREE ORANGES by Sergey Prokofiev.
1982. Home Vision

Stage production, Glyndebourne Festival, England, 120 min., stereo hi-fi, color, sung in French with English subtitles.
Director and producer, Frank Corsaro; designer, Maurice Sendak; television director, Rodney Greenberg. Includes animation and large puppets. This opera is also known as *The Love of Three Oranges*.

CAST:
The Prince . . . . Ryland Davies
Princess Ninetta . . . . Colette Alliot-Lugaz
Truffaldino . . . . Ugo Benelli
King of Clubs . . . . Willard White
Tchelio, The Magician . . . . Richard Van Allan
Fata Morgana . . . . Nelly Morpurgo
Princess Clarissa . . . . Nucci Condò
Leandro . . . . John Pringle
Pantaloon . . . . Peter-Christoph Runge
Smeraldina . . . . Fiona Kimm
Princess Nicoletta . . . . Susan Moore
Princess Linetta . . . . Yvonne Lea
Farfarello . . . . Derek Hammond-Stroud
Herald/Cook . . . . Roger Bryson
Master of Ceremonies . . . . Hugh Hetherington

Bernard Haitink, London Philharmonic Orchestra, Glyndebourne Festival Chorus.

+ *Levine*, p. 49.
+ *Opera News* 52, 13 (March 12, 1988): 44, by Harvey E. Phillips.

Love of a Clown
SEE Il Pagliacci, 107.2.

82.1. LUCIA DI LAMMERMOOR by Gaetano Donizetti.
1948. 16mm film rental, Budget Films; 16mm archival film, Indiana University

Film version, about 23 min., abridged, mono, black and white, sung in Italian with a commentator explaining the plot in English, no subtitles.
Produced by George Richfield; musical arrangement and script, Raffaele Gervasio; stage director, E. Fulchignoni; film director, E. Cancellieri. Filmed on stage at the Rome Opera House, Italy. Part of the *First Opera Film Festival* series. Giulio Tomei and Gino Conti are singers who also appear as actors.

CAST:
Singers are listed first; actors and actresses are listed second.

Lucia . . . . Liliana Rossi/Anne Lollohrigida
Edgardo . . . . Giancinto Prandelli/Zwonko Gluk
Lord Enrico Ashton . . . . Tito Gobbi
Raimondo . . . . Luciano Neroni/Giulio Tomei
Alisa . . . . Anna Marcangeli
Lord Arturo Bucklaw . . . . . . Cesare Valletti/Gino Conti

Angelo Questa, Orchestra and Chorus of the Rome Opera House.

\+ *EFLA* (1965), p. 256. [No. 1950.713]

82.2. LUCIA DI LAMMERMOOR by Gaetano Donizetti.
1971. Video Artists International

Film version, 108 min., hi-fi, color, sung in Italian with English subtitles.
Director, Mario Lanfranchi. Filmed on location in Italy.

CAST:
Lucia . . . . Anna Moffo
Edgardo . . . . Lajos Kosma
Lord Enrico Ashton . . . . Giulio Fioravanti
Raimondo . . . . Paolo Washington
Normanno . . . . Glauco Scarlini
Alisa . . . . Anna Maria Segatori
Lord Arturo Bucklaw . . . . Pietro di Vietri

Carlo Felice Cillaro, Rome Symphony Orchestra and the Radiotelevisione Italiana Chorus.

+– *Levine*, p. 50-51. + Moffo, – production
\+ *Opera News* 49, 14 (March 30, 1985): 26, by Richard Hornak.

+– *Opera Quarterly* 3, 2 (Summer 1985): 137-139, by Andrew L. Schreiber. + Moffo, other singers, – director and production

82.3. LUCIA DI LAMMERMOOR by Gaetano Donizetti.
1982. Bel Canto/Paramount Home Video

Stage production, Metropolitan Opera, New York City, videotaped on November 13, 1982, 128 min., stereo hi-fi, color, sung in Italian with English subtitles.
Staging, Bruce Donnell; sets and costumes, Attilio Colonnello; video director, Kirk Browning.

CAST:

Lucia	Joan Sutherland
Edgardo	Alfredo Kraus
Lord Enrico Ashton	Pablo Elvíra
Raimondo	Paul Plishka
Normanno	John Gilmore
Alisa	Ariel Bybee
Lord Arturo Bucklaw	Jeffrey Stamm

Richard Bonynge, Orchestra and Chorus of the Metropolitan Opera.

+ *Levine*, p. 50.
+ *Opera News* 49, 4 (October 1984): 59, by John W. Freeman.
+ *Opera News* 52, 5 (November 1987): 74, by Thor Eckert, Jr.

82.4. LUCIA DI LAMMERMOOR by Gaetano Donizetti.
1986. Kultur

Stage production, Australian Opera, Sydney, 145 min., stereo hi-fi, color, sung in Italian with English subtitles.
Director, John Copley. A complete recording of the opera including the Lucia and Raimondo duet and the Wolf's Craig scene.

CAST:

Lucia	Joan Sutherland
Edgardo	Richard Greager
Lord Enrico Ashton	Malcolm Donnelly
Raimondo	Clifford Grant
Normanno	Robin Donald
Alisa	Patricia Price
Lord Arturo Bucklaw	Sergei Baigildin

Richard Bonynge, Elizabethan Sydney Orchestra, Australian Opera Chorus.

– *Opera News* 54, 13 (March 17, 1990): 38, by Harvey E. Phillips.
+ *Ovation* 10, 6 (July 1989): 61, 64, by Robert Levine.

83.1. DIE LUSTIGE WITWE by Franz Lehár.
1934. MGM/UA Home Video

Feature film, 99 min., mono hi-fi, black and white, sung and spoken in English.
Producer, Irving Thalbert; director, Ernst Lubitsch; writers, Samson Raphaelson, Ernest Vagda (based on Lehár's operetta); set designers, Edwin B. Willis, Gabriel Scognamillo. Also known as: *The Lady Dances*. Music director, Herbert Stothart. Originally issued as a motion picture.

CAST:
Only singers MacDonald and Chevalier are included in the *Index of Singers and Conductors*.

Sonia .... Jeanette MacDonald
Queen Dolores .... Una Merkel
Danilo .... Maurice Chevalier
Ambassador Popoff .... Edward Everett Horton
King Achmed .... George Barbier
Marcelle .... Minna Gombell
Lulu .... Ruth Channing
Mischka .... Sterling Holloway
Turk .... Henry Armetta
Maid .... Barbara Leonard
Valet .... Donald Meek
Maxim's Manager .... Akim Tamiroff
Zizipoff .... Herman Bing
Adamovitch .... Lucien Prival

++ *Motion Picture Guide*.
+ *Video Review* 10, 4 (July 1989): 72, by Roy Hemming.

83.2. DIE LUSTIGE WITWE by Franz Lehár.
1988. Home Vision

Stage production, Australian Opera, Sydney, videotaped on February 23, 1988, 155 min., stereo hi-fi, color, sung in English, English text by Christopher Hassall.
Production, Lotfi Mansouri; costumes, Jose Varona; television director, Virginia Lumsden.

CAST:

Hanna .... Joan Sutherland
Valencienne .... Ann-Marie MacDonald
Danilo .... Ronald Stevens
Camille .... Anson Austin
Olga .... Irene Cassimatis
Sylviane .... Caroline Clack
Praskovia .... Rosina Raisbeck
Zozo .... Jennifer Bermingham

Njegus . . . . Graeme Ewer
St. Broiche . . . . Christopher Dawes
Cascada . . . . Neil Kirkby
Baron Zeta . . . . Gordon Wilcock

Richard Bonynge, Elizabethan Philharmonic Orchestra, Australian Opera Chorus and Ballet.

• *Opera (England)* 42, 7 (July 1991): 855, by Noël Goodwin.
+ *Opera News* 56, 11 (February 11, 1992): 35, by Shirley Fleming.

84.1. DIE LUSTIGEN WEIBER VON WINDSOR by Otto Nicolai. **1952**.

Feature film, about 97 min., mono, black and white, sung in German with English subtitles.
Producer, Walter Lehmann; director, Georg Wildhagen; writers, Wolff von Gordon and Georg Wildhagen (based on Nicolai's opera). Actors and actresses lip sync to a prerecorded sound track. Originally issued as a motion picture by Deutsche Film/Central Cinema.

CAST:
With the voices of . . . . Rita Streich
Martha Mödl
Hans Kramer
Helmut Kregs

Actors and actresses:
Frau Fluth . . . . Sonja Ziemann
Frau Reich . . . . Camilla Spira
Sir John Falstaff . . . . Paul Esser
Herr Fluth . . . . Calus Holm
Herr Reich . . . . Alexander Engel
Fenton . . . . Eckart Dux
Anna Reich . . . . Ina Halley
Junker Sparlich . . . . Joachim Teege
Dr. Caius . . . . Gerhard Frickhoffer

+ *EFLA* (1965), p. 275. [No. 1953. 1753]
• *Motion Picture Guide.*

84.2. DIE LUSTIGEN WEIBER VON WINDSOR by Otto Nicolai. **1966**.

Feature film, 97 min., mono, color, sung in German. Formerly available (1984) as a film rental from Corinth Films.
Producer, Norman Foster; director, George Tressler; writer, Norman Foster (based on Nicolai's opera); sets, Gerd Krauss; costumes, Helga Pinnow. Originally issued as a motion picture by Wien/Sigma III (Austria).

CAST:

Sir John Falstaff	Norman Foster
Frau Fluth	Colette Boky
Herr Fluth	Igor Gorin
Frau Reich	Mildred Miller
Herr Reich	Edmond Hurshell
Anna Reich	Lucia Popp
Fenton	Ernst Schutz
Dr. Caius	John Gittings
Junker Sparlich	Marshall Raynor
Ballerina	Rosella Hightower

Musical director, Milan Howath with the Zagreb Symphony Orchestra.

- *Motion Picture Guide.*

Lyubov k trem Apelsinam
SEE The Love for Three Oranges, 81.

85.1. MACBETH by Giuseppe Verdi.
1972. Video Artists International

Stage production (1865 revision), Glyndebourne Festival, England, 148 min., mono hi-fi, color, sung in Italian with English subtitles.
Production, Michael Hadjimischer; designer, Emanuele Luzzati; television producer, Humphrey Burton; television director, Dave Heather.

CAST:

Macbeth	Kostas Paskalis
Lady Macbeth	Josephine Barstow
Banquo	James Morris
Macduff	Keith Erwen
Malcolm	Ian Caley
Lady-in-Waiting to Lady Macbeth	Rae Woodland
Doctor	Brian Donlan
Murderer	John Tomlinson
First Apparition (A Warrior)	John Tomlinson
Second Apparition (A Bloody Child)	Angela Whittingham
Third Apparition (A Crowned Child)	Linda Esther Gray
King Duncan (non-singing)	Geoffrey Gilbertson
Fleance (non-singing)	Tom Redman
Servant	Ian Caddy

John Pritchard, London Philharmonic Orchestra, Glyndebourne Festival Chorus and Ballet.

++ *Levine*, p. 52-54.
+– *Opera (England)* 39, 8 (August 1988): 1017-1019, by Arthur Jacobs.
+ Barstow, Morris, Paskalis, – sound
+ *Opera News* 51, 4 (October 1986): 82, by Richard Hornak.
++ *Opera Quarterly* 5, 2-3 (Summer/Autumn 1987): 150, by Robert Levine.
+ *Opera Quarterly* 4, 1 (Spring 1986): 136-137, by London Green.
++ Barstow

85.2. MACBETH by Giuseppe Verdi.
1987. Home Vision

Stage production (1865 revision), Deutsche Oper Berlin, Germany, 150 min., stereo hi-fi, color, sung in Italian with English subtitles.
Producer, Luca Ronconi; sets and costumes, Luciano Damiani; television director, Brian Large.

CAST:

Macbeth .... Renato Bruson
Lady Macbeth .... Mara Zampieri
Banquo .... James Morris
Macduff .... Dennis O'Neill
Malcolm .... David Griffith
Lady-in-Waiting to Lady Macbeth ..... Sharon Sweet
Doctor .... Josef Becker
Murderer .... Leopold Clam
Apparitions .... Edelgard Neubert-Imm, Mark Gruett
King Duncan (non-singing) .... Goetz Rose
Fleance (non-singing) .... Claus Endisch
Servant .... Klaus Lang

Giuseppe Sinopoli, Orchestra and Chorus of the Deutsche Oper Berlin.

•– *Levine*, p. 51-52.
•– *Ovation* 10, 5 (June 1989): 70-71, by Robert Levine.

85.3. MACBETH by Giuseppe Verdi.
1987. London (PolyGram)

Film version, 134 min., stereo hi-fi, color, sung in Italian with English subtitles.
Adapted and directed by Claude d'Anna. Filmed on location at the Castle of Godefroy de Bouillon in the Ardennes, Belgium.

CAST:
Singers are listed first; actors and actresses are listed second.

Macbeth .... Leo Nucci
Lady Macbeth .... Shirley Verrett
Banquo .... Samuel Ramey/John Leysen
Macduff .... Veriano Luchetti/Philippe Volter

Malcolm . . . . Antonio Barasorda
Lady-in-Waiting to Lady Macbeth . . . .
Anna Caterina Antonacci
Doctor . . . . Sergio Fontana
Fleance (non-singing) . . . . Nicolas Sansier

Riccardo Chailly, Orchestra and Chorus of the Teatro comunale di Bologna.

\+ *Fanfare* 16, 4 (March/April 1993): 419-420, by James Reel.
– *Opera News* 57, 12 (February 27, 1993): 42-43, by Harvey E. Phillips.
\+ Verrett

Mack the Knife
SEE Die Dreigroschenoper, 35.2.

86.1. MADAMA BUTTERFLY by Giacomo Puccini.
1955.

Feature film, Rome Opera, 114 min., mono, color, sung in Italian, no subtitles.
Producer, Ivao Mori; director, Carmine Gallone; photography, Claude Renoir. Japanese actors and actresses lip sync to a prerecorded sound track sung by Italian singers. Originally issued as a motion picture by Toho-Rizzoli-Gallone (Italian-Japanese production).

CAST:
Singers are listed first; actors and actresses are listed second.

Madama Butterfly . . Orietta Moscucci/Karuo Yachigusa
B.F. Pinkerton . . . Giuseppe Campora/Nicola Filacuridi
Sharpless . . . . Fernando Lidonni
Suzuki . . . . Anna Maria Canali/Michiko Tanaka
Goro . . . . Paolo Caroli/Kiyoshi Takagi
The Bonze . . . . Plinio Clabassi/Yoshio Kosugi
Prince Yamadori . . Adelio Zagonara/Satoshi Nakamura
Kate Pinkerton . . . . Josephine Corry

Music director, Oliviero De Fabritiis, Teatro Reale dell'Opera di Roma; Takarazuka Kabuki Ballet of Tokyo (the Geishas).

\+ *Motion Picture Guide.*

86.2. MADAMA BUTTERFLY by Giacomo Puccini.
1974. London (PolyGram)

Stage production, Vienna State Opera, Austria, 134 min., stereo hi-fi, color, sung in Italian with English subtitles.
Production, Jean-Pierre Ponnelle. Filmed in Berlin in November and December, 1974.

CAST:

Madama Butterfly	Mirella Freni
B.F. Pinkerton	Plácido Domingo
Sharpless	Robert Kerns
Suzuki	Christa Ludwig
Goro	Michel Sénéchal
The Bonze	Marius Rintzler
Prince Yamadori	Giorgio Stendoro
Kate Pinkerton	Elke Schary

Herbert von Karajan, Vienna Philharmonic Orchestra.

- – *Opera (England)* 43, 5 (May 1992): 611-612, by Noël Goodwin.
- + *Opera News* 56, 2 (August 1991): 44-45, "The Basics," by Harvey E. Phillips.
- • *Video Review* 10, 6 (September 1989): 80, by Christie Barter.

86.3. MADAMA BUTTERFLY by Giacomo Puccini.
1983. HBO Video

Stage production, Arena di Verona, Italy, 150 min., stereo hi-fi, color, sung in Italian. This video was initially released without English subtitles; later issues may have subtitles.
Producer, Giulio Chazalettes; sets and costumes, Ulisse Santicchi; video director, Brian Large.

CAST:

Madama Butterfly	Raina Kabaivanska
B.F. Pinkerton	Nazzareno Antinori
Sharpless	Lorenzo Saccomani
Suzuki	Eleonora Jankovic
Goro	Mario Ferrara
The Bonze	Gianni Brunelli
Prince Yamadori	Giuseppe Zecchillo
Kate Pinkerton	Marisa Zotti
Yakuside	Bruno Grella
Imperial Commissioner	Carlo Meliciani
Official Registrar	Bruno Tessari
Cio-Cio-San's Mother (non-singing)	Lina Rossi
Her Aunt (non-singing)	Anna Lia Bazzani
Her Cousin (non-singing)	Sandra Zamuner

Maurizio Arena, Orchestra and Chorus of the Arena di Verona.

– *Levine*, p. 54-55.
+ *Opera News* 49, 14 (March 30, 1985): 26, by Richard Hornak.

86.4. MADAMA BUTTERFLY by Giacomo Puccini.
1986. Home Vision

Stage production, Teatro alla Scala, Milan, Italy, 143 min., stereo hi-fi, color, sung in Italian with English subtitles.
Producer, Keita Asari; sets, Ichiro Takada; costumes, Hanae Mori; video director, Derek Bailey.

CAST:

Madama Butterfly	Yasuko Hayashi
B.F. Pinkerton	Peter Dvorský
Sharpless	Giorgio Zancanaro
Suzuki	Hak-Nam Kim
Goro	Ernesto Gavazzi
The Bonze	Sergio Fontana
Prince Yamadori	Arturo Testa
Kate Pinkerton	Anna Caterina Antonacci
Yakuside	Claudio Giombi
Imperial Commissioner	Claudio Giombi

Lorin Maazel, Orchestra and Chorus of Teatro alla Scala.

+ *Landers Film Reviews* 32, 3 (Spring 1988): 123.
+ *Levine*, p. 54-55.
• *Opera (England)* 39, 10 (October 1988): 1259, by Noël Goodwin.
+– *Opera News* 53, 3 (September 1988): 58, by Harvey E. Phillips.
  + staging, – singing
+ *Ovation* 9, 6 (July 1988): 40, by Dick Adler.
++ *Video Review* 9, 4 (July 1988): 79, by Christie Barter.

The Magic Flute
SEE Die Zauberflöte, 156.1.—156.7.

87. THE MAKROPULOS CASE by Leoš Janáček.
1989. Video Artists International

Stage production, Canadian Opera Company, Canada, 123 min., stereo hi-fi, color, sung in Czech with English subtitles.
Director, Lotfi Mansouri; camera, Norman Campbell.

CAST:

Emilia Marty	Stephanie Sundine
Janek	Benoit Butel
Kristina	Kathleen Brett
Albert Gregor	Graham Clark

A Stagehand . . . . Steven Horst
Vitek . . . . Richard Margison
Jaroslav Prus . . . . Cordells Opthof
Dr. Kolenaty . . . . Robert Orth
A Chambermaid . . . . Gabriella Prata
Count Hauk-Sendorf . . . . Gary Rideout
A Charwoman . . . . Marcia Swanston

Berislav Klobucar, Orchestra of the Canadian Opera Company.

- *Library Journal* 116, 17 (October 15, 1991): 134, by Nick S. Thorndike.
  – sound and lighting
+ *Opera Canada* 33, 1 (Spring 1992): 59, by Ruby Mercer.
+ *Opera News* 55, 15 (April 13, 1991): 49, by P. J. S. [Patrick J. Smith]

88. **MANON** by Jules Massenet.
1977. Bel Canto/Paramount Home Video

Stage production, New York City Opera, New York State Theater, Lincoln Center, New York City, videotaped on October 18, 1977, 152 min., stereo hi-fi, color, sung in French with English subtitles.
Production devised and directed by Tito Capobianco; stage director, Gigi Denda; sets, Marsha Louis Eck; costumes, Jose Varona; video director, Kirk Browning.

CAST:

Manon Lescaut . . . . Beverly Sills
Chevalier des Grieux . . . . Henry Price
Lescaut . . . . Richard Fredricks
Count des Grieux . . . . Samuel Ramey
Guillot de Morfontaine . . . . Nico Castel
De Bretigny . . . . Robert Hale
Pousette . . . . Elizabeth Hynes
Javotte . . . . Gwenlynn Little
Rosette . . . . Sandra Walker
Innkeeper . . . . Harlan Foss
Guards . . . . Don Yule, James Sergi
Maid . . . . Harriet Greene
Tobacco Vendor . . . . Louis Perry
Seminary Porter . . . . Don Carlo
Gambler . . . . Dan Kingman
Sergeant . . . . Don Yule
Cupid . . . . Sandra Balestracci
Ballet Master . . . . Michael Rubino
Prima Ballerina of the Paris Opera . . . .
Toni Ann Gardella
Primier Danseur of the Paris Opera . . . .
Mikhail Korogodsky

Julius Rudel, Orchestra and Chorus of the New York City Opera.

89.1. MANON LESCAUT by Giacomo Puccini.
1980. Bel Canto/Paramount Home Video

Stage production, Metropolitan Opera, New York City, videotaped on Saturday, March 29, 1980, 135 min., stereo hi-fi, color, sung in Italian with English subtitles.
Production, Gian Carlo Menotti; sets and costumes, Desmond Heeley; video director, Kirk Browning.

CAST:

Manon Lescaut .... Renata Scotto
Chevalier des Grieux .... Plácido Domingo
Lescaut .... Pablo Elvíra
Edmondo .... Philip Creech
Innkeeper .... Mario Bertolino
Geronte di Ravoir .... Renato Capecchi
Dancing Master .... Andrea Velis
A Sergeant .... Julien Robbins
A Lamplighter .... John Carpenter
Naval Captain .... Christopher Russell
A Musician .... Isola Jones
Madrigal Singers .... Suzanne Der Derian
Susan Ball
Joyce Olson
Janet Wagner

James Levine, Orchestra and Chorus of the Metropolitan Opera.

\+ *Levine*, p. 56-58.
\+ *Opera News* 53, 13 (March 18, 1989): 45, by C.J. Luten.
\+ *Opera Quarterly* 6, 3 (Spring 1989): 118-120, by Thor Eckert, Jr.
\+ *Ovation* 10, 1 (February 1989): 53, by Dick Adler.

89.2. MANON LESCAUT by Giacomo Puccini.
1983. HBO Video

Stage production, Royal Opera House, Covent Garden, London, England, videotaped on May 17, 1983, 142 min. (timing includes introductory materials), stereo hi-fi, color, sung in Italian. This video was initially released without English subtitles; later issues may have subtitles.
Producer, Götz Friedrich; designer, Günther Schneider-Siemssen; costumes, Aliute Meczies; video director, Humphrey Burton. Includes an interview with Thomas Allen before the opera begins.

CAST:

Manon Lescaut .... Kiri Te Kanawa
Chevalier des Grieux .... Plácido Domingo
Lescaut .... Thomas Allen
Edmondo .... Robin Leggate
Innkeeper .... George MacPherson

Geronte di Ravoir	Forbes Robinson
Dancing Master	John Fryatt
A Sergeant	Handel Thomas
A Lamplighter	Mark Curtis
Naval Captain	Roderick Earle
Madrigal Singer	Anna Cooper
Sergeant of Soldiers	Paschal Allen

Giuseppe Sinopoli, Orchestra and Chorus of the Royal Opera House, Covent Garden.

- *Levine*, p. 56-58. + Domingo
- *Opera News* 49, 7 (December 22, 1984): 44, by John W. Freeman. + Allen

Maria Stuarda
SEE Mary Stuart, 90.

The Marriage of Figaro
SEE Le Nozze di Figaro, 101.1.—101.6.

90. MARY STUART by Gaetano Donizetti.
1982. HBO Video

Stage production, English National Opera at the London Coliseum, England, 138 min., stereo hi-fi, color, sung in English, English translation by Tom Hammond.
Producer, John Copley; director, Peter Butler; designer, Desmond Heeley; video director, Peter Butler.

CAST:

Mary Stuart	Janet Baker
Queen Elizabeth I	Rosalind Plowright
Earl of Leicester	David Rendall
Talbot	John Tomlinson
Sir William Cecil	Alan Opie
Hannah Kennedy	Angela Bostock
Garter King at Arms	Leigh Maurice

Sir Charles Mackerras, Orchestra and Chorus of the English National Opera.

+ *Levine*, p. 59-60.
++ *Opera (England)* 40, 11 (November 1989): 1379, by Noël Goodwin.
+ *Ovation* 7, 9 (October 1986): 47, by Robert Levine.

The Masked Ball
SEE Un Ballo in Maschera, 12.1.—12.2.

91. IL MATRIMONIO SEGRETO by Domenico Cimarosa.
1986. Home Vision

Stage production, Schwetzinger Festival, the Cologne Opera, 140 min., stereo hi-fi, color, sung in Italian with English subtitles.
Director, Michael Hampe; sets, Jan Schlubach; television director, Claus Viller. Performed at the Drottningholm Theatre, Stockholm, Sweden. The orchestra uses period instruments.

CAST:

Elisetta . . . . Barbara Daniels
Geronimo . . . . Carlos Feller
Count Robinson . . . . Claudio Nicolai
Paolino . . . . David Kuebler
Fidalma . . . . Márta Szirmay
Carolina . . . . Georgine Resick
Geronimo's Valet . . . . Werner Sindemann

Hilary Griffiths, Orchestra of the Drottningholm Theatre.

+ *Levine*, p. 60-61.
• *Opera News* 53, 13 (March 18, 1989): 45, by Harvey E. Phillips.
+ *Ovation* 10, 8 (September 1989): 64, by Robert Levine.

92. THE MEDIUM by Gian Carlo Menotti.
1951. Video Artists International

Film version, 80 min., mono, black and white, sung in the original English.
Producer, Walter Lowendahl; director, Gian Carlo Menotti; art director, Georges Wakhevitch; photography, Enzo Serafin. A Transfilm Production recorded at the studios of RAI-Radio Italiana.

CAST:

Madame Flora . . . . Marie Powers
Monica . . . . Anna Maria Alberghetti
Toby, a Mute Boy . . . . Leo Coleman
Mrs. Nolan . . . . Belva Kibler
Mrs. Gobineau . . . . Beverly Dame
Mr. Gobineau . . . . Donald Morgan

Thomas Schippers, Symphony Orchestra of Radio Italiana, Rome.

+ *EFLA* (1965), p. 273. [No. 1955.2485]
+ *Motion Picture Guide*.
+ *Opera News* 49, 14 (March 30, 1985): 26, by Richard Hornak.
++ *Opera Quarterly* 3, 2 (Summer 1985): 133-134, Christopher J. Thomas.
  • technical aspects of the sound track

93. MEFISTOFELE by Arrigo Boito.
1989. Home Vision

Stage production, San Francisco Opera, California, videotaped in September 1989, 159 min., stereo hi-fi, color, sung in Italian with English subtitles.
Director, Robert Carsen; designer, Michael Levine; television director, Brian Large.

CAST:

Mefistofele	Samuel Ramey
Margherita/Helen of Troy	Gabriela Beňačková-Čápová
Faust	Dennis O'Neill
Marta	Judith Christin
Pantalis	Emily Manhart
Wagner	Daniel Harper
Nereo	Douglas Wunsch

Maurizio Arena, Orchestra and Chorus of the San Francisco Opera.

+ *Landers Film and Video Reviews* 35, 4 (Summer 1991): 172.
– *Opera Monthly* 4, 1 (May 1991): 45-47, by Keith Sherburne.
+ *Opera News* 56, 12 (February 29, 1992): 44, by Shirley Fleming.
++ *Video Librarian* 5, 10 (January 1991): 15.

94.1. DIE MEISTERSINGER VON NÜRNBERG by Richard Wagner.
1984. Philips (PolyGram)

Stage production, Bayreuth Festival, Germany, 269 min., stereo hi-fi, color, sung in German with English subtitles.
Director and designer, Wolfgang Wagner; costumes, Reinhard Heinrich; video director, Brian Large; artistic supervision, Wolfgang Wagner.

CAST:

Hans Sachs	Bernd Weikl
Eva	Mari Anne Häggander
Walther von Stolzing	Siegfried Jerusalem
David	Graham Clark
Sixtus Beckmesser	Hermann Prey
Veit Pogner	Manfred Schenk
Fritz Kothner	Jef Vermeersch
Augustin Moser	Helmut Pampuch
Hermann Ortel	Sándor Solyom-Nagý
Hans Schwarz	Heinz Klaus Ecker
Hans Foltz	Dieter Schweikart
Konrad Nachtigall	Martin Egel
Kunz Vogelgesang	András Molnár
Night Watchman	Matthias Hölle
Balthasar Zorn	Udo Holdorf
Ulrich Eisslinger	Peter Maus
Magdalene	Marga Schiml

Horst Stein, Orchestra and Chorus of the Bayreuth Festival.

- *Opera News* 56, 14 (March 28, 1992): 45, by Harvey E. Phillips.

94.2. DIE MEISTERSINGER VON NÜRNBERG by Richard Wagner. **1990**. Home Vision

Stage production, Australian Opera, Sydney, 278 min., stereo hi-fi, color, sung in German with English subtitles.
Stage director, Michael Hampe; sets, John Gunter; costumes, Reinhard Heinrich; television directors, Peter Butler, Virginia Lumsden.

CAST:

Hans Sachs	Donald McIntyre
Eva	Helena Döse
Walther von Stolzing	Paul Frey
David	Christopher Doig
Sixtus Beckmesser	John Pringle
Veit Pogner	Donald Shanks
Fritz Kothner	Robert Allman
Augustin Moser	Christopher Dawes
Hermann Ortel	Stephen Bennett
Hans Schwarz	Arend Baumann
Hans Foltz	David Hibbard
Konrad Nachtigall	Neville Wilkie
Kunz Vogelgesang	Gerald Sword
Night Watchman	John Wegner
Balthasar Zorn	Lawrence Allen
Ulrich Eisslinger	John Miley
Magdalene	Rosemary Gunn
Apprentices	Anne Fish
	Christine Logan
	Lisa Nolan
	Gail Robertson
	Greg Brown
	Brian Evans
	Scott Hannigan
	David Leavis
	Alan Maddox
	Michael Martin
	Stephen Matthews
	Jeffrey Ward

Sir Charles Mackerras, Elizabethan Philharmonic Orchestra, Australian Opera Chorus.

– *Opera News* 56, 12 (February 29, 1992): 44, by Harvey E. Phillips.
+ conducting

The Merry Widow
SEE Die Lustige Witwe, 83.1.—83.2.

The Merry Wives of Windsor
SEE Die Lustigen Weiber von Windsor, 84.1.—84.2.

95. A MIDSUMMER NIGHT'S DREAM by Benjamin Britten.
1982. Home Vision

Stage production, Glyndebourne Festival, England, 156 min., stereo hi-fi, color, sung in the original English.
Producer, Peter Hall; designed by John Bury; television producer, Dave Heather.

CAST:

Fairy Queen (Tytania)	Ileana Cotrubas
Oberon	James Bowman
Bottom	Curt Appelgren
Hermia	Cynthia Buchan
Helena	Felicity Lott
Lysander	Ryland Davies
Demetrius	Dale Duesing
Puck	Damien Nash
Quince	Roger Bryson
Snug	Andrew Gallacher
Starveling	Donald Bell
Flute	Patrick Power
Snout	Adrian Thompson
Theseus	Lieuwe Visser
Hippolyta	Claire Powell
Cobweb	Martin Warr
Mustardseed	Jonathan Whiting
Peaseblossom	Stephen Jones
Moth	Stuart King

Bernard Haitink, London Philharmonic Orchestra, Glyndebourne Festival Chorus.

\+ *Levine*, p. 62-63.
\+ *Opera News* 53, 1 (July 1988): 45, by Harvey E. Phillips.

96. **MIGNON** by Ambroise Thomas.
1982. German Language Video Center, Division of Heidelburg Haus Imports, 7625 Pendleton Pike, Indianapolis, IN 46226-5298
800-252-0957, fax 317-547-1257

Television production (ZDF German Television), Salzburger Marionettentheater, 59 min., stereo hi-fi, color, sung in German.
Also known as *Kennst du das Land*. This video uses puppets and live actors to tell the story of Mignon. In the puppet sequences, Peter Lühr reads from Wilhelm Meister's *Lehrjahre*. The operatic sequences are sung by the performers listed below accompanied by the Munich Philharmonic Orchestra.

CAST:

Mignon . . . . Trudeliese Schmidt
Wilhelm Meister . . . . Adolf Dallapozza
Philine . . . . Sylvia Greenberg
Lothario . . . . Günter Wewel
Laertes . . . . Jürgen Rohe
Jarno . . . . Thomas Schüler
Baron . . . . Will van Deeg
Ballerina (non-singing) . . . . Heidrunk Schwaarz

97.1. **MIKADO** by W.S. Gilbert & Sir Arthur Sullivan.
1939. Home Vision

Film version, D'Oyly Carte Opera Company, 93 min., mono, color, sung in the original English.
Producers, Geoffrey Toye, Josef Somlo; director, Victor Schertzinger; photographers, Bernard Knowles, William Skall (Technicolor); costumes, Marcel Vertes. Originally issued as a motion picture.

CAST:

Mikado . . . . John Barclay
Ko-Ko . . . . Martyn Green
Pooh-Bah . . . . Sydney Granville
Nanki-Poo . . . . Kenny Baker
Yum-Yum . . . . Jean Colin
Katisha . . . . Constance Willis
Pish-Tush . . . . Gregory Stroud
Peep-Bo . . . . Kathleen Naylor
Pitti-Sing . . . . Elizabeth Paynter

Geoffrey Toye, London Symphony Orchestra.

\+ *Motion Picture Guide*.

97.2. MIKADO by W.S. Gilbert & Sir Arthur Sullivan.
1967. Video purchase, Opera Dubs, Inc.; Film rental: Films, Inc., 5547 N. Ravenswood Ave., Chicago, IL 60650-1199 800-323-4222, extension 42

Film version, D'Oyly Carte Opera Company, 125 min., mono, color, sung in the original English.
Producers, Anthony Havelock-Allan, John Brabourne; director, Stuart Burge; photographer, Gerry Fisher (Technicolor); set designer, Disley Jones; costumes, Charles Ricketts, Disley Jones. Conductor, Isidore Godfrey. Filmed at the Savoy Theatre in London. Originally issued as a motion picture by British Home Entertainment (Great Britain).

CAST:
Mikado . . . . Donald Adams
Ko-Ko . . . . John Reed
Pooh-Bah . . . . Kenneth Sandford
Nanki-Poo . . . . Philip Potter
Yum-Yum . . . . Valerie Masterson
Katisha . . . . Christene Palmer
Pish-Tush . . . . Thomas Lawlor
Peep-Bo . . . . Pauline Wales
Pitti-Sing . . . . Peggy Ann Jones
Go-To . . . . George Cook

\+ *Motion Picture Guide*.

97.3. MIKADO by W.S. Gilbert & Sir Arthur Sullivan.
1974. 16mm film rental available prior to June 1993 from the University of Illinois Film Center

Film version, 50 min., abridged, mono, color, sung in the original English.
Producer, John Seabourne; director, Trevor Evans; script, David Maverovitch; photography, Adrian Jenkins; narrators, Johnny Wayne, Frank Shuster. Part of the *World of Gilbert and Sullivan* series.

CAST:
Mikado . . . . Donald Adams
Ko-Ko . . . . John Cartier
Pooh-Bah . . . . Lawrence Richard
Nanki-Poo . . . . Thomas Round
Yum-Yum . . . . Valerie Masterson
Katisha . . . . Helen Landis
Pish-Tush . . . . Michael Wakeham
Pitti-Sing . . . . Anna Cooper

Gilbert & Sullivan Festival Orchestra and Chorus of England.

\+ *Booklist* 74, 13 (March 1, 1978): 1125, by J. Braun.

97.4. MIKADO by W.S. Gilbert & Sir Arthur Sullivan.
1982. Pioneer

Film version, 113 min., stereo hi-fi, color, sung in the original English.
Producer, Judith de Paul; stage producer, Michael Geliot; designer, Allan Cameron; costume coordinator, Jenny Beavan; executive producer, George Walker.

CAST:

Mikado .... William Conrad
Ko-Ko .... Clive Revill
Pooh-Bah .... Stafford Dean
Nanki-Poo .... John Stewart
Yum-Yum .... Kate Flowers
Katisha .... Anne Collins
Pish-Tush .... Gordon Sandison
Peep-Bo .... Fiona Dobie
Pitti-Sing .... Cynthia Buchan

Alexander Faris, London Symphony Orchestra, Ambrosian Opera Chorus.

97.5. MIKADO by W.S. Gilbert & Sir Arthur Sullivan.
1982. Home Vision

Stage production, Stratford Festival of Canada, Avon Theatre, 141 min., stereo-hi-fi, color, sung in the original English.
Produced and directed by Norman Campbell; sets, Susan Benson and Douglas McLean; costumes, Susan Benson. Musical director and additional music arranged by Berthold Carrière. Original Stratford production directed and choreographed by Brian Macdonald.

CAST:

Mikado .... Gidon Saks
Ko-Ko .... Eric Donkin
Pooh-Bah .... Richard McMillan
Nanki-Poo .... Henry Ingram
Yum-Yum .... Marie Baron
Katisha .... Christina James
Pish-Tush .... Allen Stewart-Coates
Peep-Bo .... Karen Skidmore
Pitti-Sing .... Karen Wood

Berthold Carrière, Orchestra and Chorus of the Stratford Festival (Canada).

– *Levine*, p. 63-65.
+ *Opera Canada* 29, 3 (Fall 1988): 52, by Ruby Mercer.

97.6. MIKADO by W.S. Gilbert & Sir Arthur Sullivan.
1987. HBO Video

Stage production, English National Opera at the London Coliseum, England, 131 min., stereo hi-fi, color, sung in the original English.
Producer, Jonathan Miller; television producer and director, John Michael Phillips; choreographer, Anthony van Laast. The action is moved from Japan and re-set in 1920s England.

CAST:

Mikado of Japan .... Richard Angas
Nanki-Poo .... Bonaventura Bottone
Poo-Bah .... Richard Van Allan
Peep-Bo .... Susan Bullock
Yum-Yum .... Leslie Garrett
Ko-Ko .... Eric Idle
Katisha .... Felicity Palmer
Pish-Tush .... Mark Richardson
Pitti-Sing .... Ethna Robinson
Katisha's Pilot and Accompanist (non-singing) ....
Findlay Wilson

Peter Robinson, Orchestra and Chorus of the English National Opera.

98. MITRIDATE, RE DI PONTO by Wolfgang Amadeus Mozart.
1986. London (PolyGram)

Film version, 124 min., stereo hi-fi, sung in Italian with English subtitles.
Director, Jean-Pierre Ponnelle; photography, Xaver Schwarzenberger. Filmed at the Teatro Olimpico in Vincenza, March 1986.

CAST:

Mitridate .... Gösta Winbergh
Aspasia .... Yvonne Kenny
Sifare .... Ann Murray
Farnace .... Anne Gjevang
Ismene .... Joan Rodgers
Marzio .... Peter Straka
Abbate .... Massimiliano Roncato

Nikolaus Harnoncourt, Concentus Musicus Wien.

\+ *Fanfare* 16, 2 (November/December 1992): 485-486, by James Reel.

99. MOSES UND AARON by Arnold Schoenberg.
1975. Video purchase, Opera Dubs, Inc.; formerly available as a film rental from: New Yorker Films, 16 West 61st Street, New York, NY 212-247-6110

Film version, 105 min., hi-fi, color, sung in German with English subtitles.
Directors and writers, Jean-Marie Straub, Daniele Huillet; costumes, Renata Morroni, Guerrino Todero; photographers, Ugo Piccone, Saverio Diamanti, Gianni Canfarelli, Renato Berta. Musical director, Michael Gielen.

CAST:
Moses .... Günter Reich
Aaron .... Louis Devos
Young Man .... Roger Lucas
Young Woman .... Eva Csapó
Other Man .... Richard Salter
Priest .... Werner Mann
Sick Woman .... Friedl Obrowsky
Ephraimite .... Ladislav Illavsky

\+ *Motion Picture Guide*.

100.1. NABUCCO by Giuseppe Verdi.
1981. HBO Video

Stage production, Arena di Verona, Italy, 132 min., stereo hi-fi, color, sung in Italian. This video was initially released without English subtitles; later issues may have subtitles.
Producer, Renzo Giacchieri; designs and costumes, Luciano Minguzzi; video director, Brian Large.

CAST:
Nabucco .... Renato Bruson
Abigaille .... Gena Macheva Dimitrova
Zaccaria .... Dimitur Petkov
Fenena .... Bruna Baglioni
Ismaele .... Ottavio Garaventa
High Priest .... Francesco Ellero D'Artegna
Abdallo .... Aronne Ceroni
Anna .... Giovanna di Rocco

Maurizio Arena, Orchestra and Chorus of the Arena di Verona.

++ *Levine*, p. 65-66. – costumes
\+ *Opera News* 50, 4 (October 1985): 60, by Richard Hornak.
\+ *Opera News* 52, 17 (June 1988): 44, by C.J. Luten.
– Petkov, costumes
\+ *Opera Quarterly* 5, 2-3 (Summer/Autumn 1987): 147, by Robert Levine.
• *Opern Welt* (August 1986): 61, by Gerhard Persché.
\+ *Ovation* 9, 2 (March 1988): 36, by Dick Adler.

100.2. NABUCCO by Giuseppe Verdi.
1986. Home Vision

Stage production, Teatro alla Scala, Milan, Italy, 140 min., stereo hi-fi, color, sung in Italian with English subtitles.
Director, Roberto De Simone; sets, Mauro Carosi; costumes, Odette Nicoletti; video director, Brian Large.

CAST:
Nabucco . . . . Renato Bruson
Abigaille . . . . Gena Macheva Dimitrova
Zaccaria . . . . Paata Burchuladze
Fenena . . . . Raquel Pierotti
Ismaele . . . . Bruno Beccaria

Riccardo Muti, Orchestra and Chorus of Teatro alla Scala.

+ *Landers Film Reviews* 32, 4 (Summer 1988): 172.
+ *Opera News* 52, 13 (March 12, 1988): 44, by Harvey E. Phillips.

101.1. LE NOZZE DI FIGARO by Wolfgang Amadeus Mozart.
1945. Lyric Distribution, Inc.

Film version, about 106 min., mono, black and white, sung in German, no subtitles on the Lyric release; there were English subtitles on the original film release issued by Brandon Films.
Actresses play the Countess and Susanna on screen. All performers lip sync to a prerecorded sound track. The singers are listed below.

CAST:
Figaro . . . . Willi Domgraf-Fassbaender
Susanna . . . . Erna Berger
Countess Almaviva . . . . Tiana Lemnitz
Count Almaviva . . . . Mathieu Ahlersmeyer
Cherubino . . . . Annelies Müller
Doctor Bartolo . . . . Eugen Fuchs
Marcellina . . . . Margarete Klose
Don Basilio . . . . Paul Schmidtmann
Barbarina . . . . Elfriede Hingst

Artur Rother, Berlin State Chamber Orchestra.

+ *EFLA* (1965), p. 269. [No. 1953, 1751] (16mm review, Brandon Films)
+ *Opera Quarterly* 8, 3 (Autumn 1991): 128-129, by William Albright. (video review)

101.2. LE NOZZE DI FIGARO by Wolfgang Amadeus Mozart.
1948. Video Yesteryear

Film version, about 23 min., abridged, mono, black and white, sung in Italian with a commentator, Olin Downes, explaining the plot in English, no subtitles.
Produced by George Richfield; musical arrangement and script, Raffaele Gervasio. Filmed on stage at the Rome Opera House, Italy. Part of the *First Opera Film Festival* series. Giulio Tomei and Gino Conti are singers who also appear as actors.

CAST:
Singers are listed first; actors and actresses are listed second.

Figaro	Piero Brasini
Susanna	Gianna Perea Zabia/Pina Malgharini
Countess Almaviva	Gabriella Gatti/Lidia Melasei
Count Almaviva	Luciano Neroni/Giulio Tomei
Cherubino	Cleo Elmo
Doctor Bartolo	Giulio Tomei/Gino Conti

Angelo Questa, Orchestra and Chorus of the Rome Opera House.

+ *EFLA* (1965), p. 265. [No. 1950.715]

101.3. LE NOZZE DI FIGARO by Wolfgang Amadeus Mozart.
1970.

Feature film, Hamburg State Opera, Germany, 189 min., mono, color, sung in German, no subtitles.
Producer, Rolf Liebermann; director, Joachim Hess; photographer, Hannes Schindler; art director, Ita Maximovna. Made for German television and released theatrically in the United States by Polytel International.

CAST:

Figaro	Heinz Blankenburg
Susanna	Edith Mathis
Countess Almaviva	Arlene Saunders
Count Almaviva	Tom Krause
Cherubino	Elisabeth Steiner
Doctor Bartolo	Noël Mangin
Marcellina	Maria von Ilosvay
Don Basilio	Kurt Marschner
Don Curzio	Jurgen Forster
Antonio	Karl Otto
Barbarina	Natalie Usselmann

Hans Schmidt-Isserstedt, Orchestra and Choir of the Hamburg State Opera.

- *Motion Picture Guide.*

101.4. LE NOZZE DI FIGARO by Wolfgang Amadeus Mozart.
1973. Video Artists International

Stage production, Glyndebourne Festival, England, 169 min., mono hi-fi, color, sung in Italian with English subtitles.
Producer, Peter Hall; sets, John Bury; television producer, Humphrey Burton; television director, Dave Heather; harpsichord continuo, Martin Isepp. Marcellina's and Basilio's arias are cut.

CAST:

Figaro	Knut Skram
Susanna	Ileana Cotrubas
Countess Almaviva	Kiri Te Kanawa
Count Almaviva	Benjamin Luxon
Cherubino	Frederica Von Stade
Doctor Bartolo	Marius Rintzler
Marcellina	Nucci Condò
Don Basilio	John Fryatt
Don Curzio	Bernard Dickerson
Antonio	Thomas Lawlor
Barbarina	Elizabeth Gale

John Pritchard, London Philharmonic Orchestra, Glyndebourne Festival Chorus.

+– *Opera (England)* 39, 8 (August 1988): 1016-1017, by Richard Law.
– technical aspects of the sound track
\+ *Opera News* 50, 2 (August 1985): 36, by Richard Hornak.
– *Opera Quarterly* 3, 4 (Winter 1985/86): 122-125, by William Huck.
\+ *Opera Quarterly* 8, 3 (Autumn 1991): 129-130, by David McKee.

101.5. LE NOZZE DI FIGARO by Wolfgang Amadeus Mozart.
1976. Deutsche Grammophon (PolyGram)

Film version, 181 min., stereo hi-fi, color, sung in Italian with English subtitles.
Production, Jean-Pierre Ponnelle. Marcellina's and Basilio's arias are cut.

CAST:

Figaro	Hermann Prey
Susanna	Mirella Freni
Countess Almaviva	Kiri Te Kanawa
Count Almaviva	Dietrich Fischer-Dieskau
Cherubino	Maria Ewing
Doctor Bartolo	Paolo Montarsolo
Marcellina	Heather Begg
Don Basilio	John van Kesteren
Don Curzio	Willy Caron
Antonio	Hans Kraemmer
Barbarina	Janet Perry

Karl Böhm, Vienna Philharmonic Orchestra.

++ *New York* 22, 15 (April 10, 1989): 108, by Peter G. Davis.
+ *Opera News* 53, 13 (March 18, 1989): 44, by C.J. Luten.
+ *Opera News* 56, 2 (August 1991): 44-45, "The Basics," by Harvey E. Phillips.
++ *Opera Quarterly* 8, 3 (Autumn 1991): 128-129, by William Albright.
+ *Ovation* 9, 12 (January 1989): 47, by David Hurwitz.

101.6. LE NOZZE DI FIGARO by Wolfgang Amadeus Mozart.
1990. London (PolyGram)

Film version, 193 min., stereo hi-fi, color, sung in Italian with English subtitles.
Director, Peter Sellars; sets, Adrianne Lobel; costumes, Dunya Ramicova; continuo: Myron Lutzke, cello, Suzanne Cleverdon, fortepiano. Action takes place in the Trump Tower.

CAST:

Figaro	Sanford Sylvan
Susanna	Jeanne Ommerle
Countess Almaviva	Jayne West
Count Almaviva	James Maddalena
Cherubino	Susan Larson
Doctor Bartolo	David Evitts
Marcellina	Sue Ellen Kuzma
Don Basilio	Frank Kelly
Don Curzio	William Cotton
Antonio	Herman Hildebrand
Barbarina	Lynn Torgow
Dancers	Michael Ing
	Nathaniel Lee
	Bettina Escano

Craig Smith, Vienna Symphonic Orchestra, Arnold-Schoenberg-Choir.

•– *Fanfare* 16, 2 (November/December 1992): 482-485, by James Reel.
+ Maddalena, Sylvan
+ *New York* 25, 22 (June 1, 1992): 62-63, by Peter G. Davis.
+ Sellars, • singing, + Maddalena, Sylvan
– *Opera News* 56, 1 (July 1991): 42-43, by Patrick J. Smith.
++ *Video Magazine* 16, 5 (August 1992): 42, "Editor's Choice," by Kenneth Korman.

102.1. OEDIPUS REX by Igor Stravinsky.
1973. Kultur

Stage production, Harvard University, Massachusetts, about 55 min., (117 min. for the entire lecture on volume 6), stereo hi-fi, color, sung in Latin with English narration, no subtitles.

Producer, Robert Saudek Associates. This performance of *Oedipus Rex* is a segment on volume 6, "The Poetry of Earth," in Leonard Bernstein's lecture series *The Unanswered Question*. The six volumes comprising the complete lecture series at Harvard have been issued as a set by Kultur.

CAST:

Oedipus . . . . René Kollo
Jocasta . . . . Tatiana Troyanos
Creon . . . . Tom Krause
Tiresias . . . . Ezio Flagello
Shepherd . . . . Frank Hoffmeister
Speaker . . . . Michael Wager
Messenger . . . . David Evitts

Leonard Bernstein, Boston Symphony Orchestra, Harvard Glee Club.

+ *Video Rating Guide* 4, 2 (Spring 1993): 115, by Sharon Almquist. A review of the entire lecture series.

102.2. OEDIPUS REX by Igor Stravinsky.
1984. Home Vision (issued with *The Flood*, 50.)

Stage production, Carre Theater, Amsterdam, 58 min. (83 min., total timing), stereo hi-fi, color, sung in Latin with English narration, no subtitles.
Producer and designer, Harry Wich; television director, Hans Hulscher.

CAST:

Oedipus . . . . Neil Rosenshein
Jocasta . . . . Felicity Palmer
Creon . . . . Claudio Desderi
Tiresias . . . . Anton Scharinger
Shepherd . . . . Justin Lavender
Speaker . . . . Alan Howard
Messenger . . . . Anton Scharinger

Bernard Haitink, Concertgebouw Orchestra, N.O.S. Men's Choir.

Omnibus television series
SEE La Bohème, 18.1.
Die Fledermaus, A13.1.
Die Lustige Witwe, A22.2.
The Medium, A24.
La Périchole, A29.
The Pirates of Penzance, A30.1.
Trial by Jury, A34.

Opera Cameos television series
SEE Il Pagliacci, 107.3.
La Traviata, 136.1.

103. L'ORFEO by Claudio Monteverdi.
1978. London (PolyGram)

Stage production, Monteverdi Ensemble, Zurich Opera, Switzerland, 102 min., stereo hi-fi, color, sung in Italian with English subtitles.
Staged, directed, and designed by Jean-Pierre Ponnelle; producer, Helmut A. Mühle; sets, Gerd Janda; costumes, Pet Halmen.

CAST:
Orfeo . . . . Philippe Huttenlocher
Euridice . . . . Dietlinde Turban
Musica/Speranza . . . . Trudeliese Schmidt
Apollo . . . . Roland Hermann
Plutone . . . . Werner Gröschel
Messagiera/Proserpina . . . . Glenys Linos
Caronte . . . . Hans Franzen
Ninfa . . . . Suzanne Calabro
Pastori . . . . Peter Keller
Francisco Araiza
Rudolf A. Hartmann
Christian Boesch
Jozsef Denè
Spiriti . . . . Francisco Araiza
Rudolf A. Hartmann
Jozsef Denè

Nikolaus Harnoncourt, Monteverdi Ensemble, Chorus and Ballet of the Zurich Opera House.

+ *Opera News* 57, 16 (May 1993): 61, by Harvey E. Phillips.
+ *Ovation* 9, 11 (December 1988): 58, 60, by David Hurwitz.

104.1. ORFEO ED EURIDICE by Christoph Willibald Gluck.
1982. Home Vision

Stage production, Glyndebourne Festival, England, 130 min., stereo hi-fi, color, sung in Italian with English subtitles.
Producer and director, Peter Hall; designer, John Bury; video director, Rodney Greenberg; harpsichord continuo, Jean Mallandaine. Includes an introductory comment by Dame Janet Baker on this, her farewell to the operatic stage.

CAST:
Orfeo . . . . Janet Baker
Euridice . . . . Elisabeth Speiser
Amore . . . . Elizabeth Gale

Raymond Leppard, London Philharmonic Orchestra, Glyndebourne Festival Chorus.

++ *Levine*, p. 66-67.
+ *Opera News* 52, 13 (March 12, 1988): 44, by Harvey E. Phillips.
+ *Opern Welt* 27, 3 (März 1986): 67-68, by Gerhard Persché.

104.2. ORFEO ED EURIDICE by Christoph Willibald Gluck.
1991. Home Vision

Stage production, Royal Opera House, Covent Garden, London, England, 88 min., stereo hi-fi, color, sung in Italian with English subtitles.
Director, Harry Kupfer; designer, Hans Schavernock from the Berlin Komische Oper production. The role of Orfeo is sung by a male alto.

CAST:
Orfeo .... Jochen Kowalski
Euridice .... Gillian Webster
Amore .... Jeremy Budd

Hartmut Haenchen, Orchestra and Chorus of the Royal Opera House, Covent Garden.

+ *Opera News* 57, 10 (January 30, 1993): 45, by Harvey E. Phillips.

105. ORLANDO FURIOSO by Antonio Vivaldi.
1989. Home Vision

Stage production, San Francisco Opera, California, 130 min., stereo hi-fi, color, sung in Italian with English subtitles.
Sets and designs, Pier Luigi Pizzi; costumes, Jennifer Green; video director, Brian Large. The role of Ruggiero is sung by a countertenor.

CAST:
Orlando .... Marilyn Horne
Angelica .... Susan Patterson
Bradamante .... Sandra Walker
Ruggiero .... Jeffrey Gall
Alcine .... Kathleen Kuhlmann
Medoro .... William Matteuzzi
Astolfo .... Kevin Langan

Randall Behr, Orchestra and Chorus of the San Francisco Opera.

+ *Landers Film and Video Reviews* 36, 1 (Fall 1991): 30.
+ *Opera News* 56, 6 (December 7, 1991): 58, by Harvey E. Phillips.

106.1. OTELLO by Giuseppe Verdi.
1958. Lyric Distribution, Inc.

Television production (Italian television), 136 min., mono, black and white, sung in Italian, no subtitles.
Director, Franco Enriquez; sets, Mariano Mercuri; costumes, Veniero Colasanti. The singers lip sync to a prerecorded sound track of their own voices.

CAST:

Otello	Mario Del Monaco
Desdemona	Rosanna Carteri
Iago	Renato Capecchi
Cassio	Gino Mattera
Roderigo	Athos Cesarini
Montano	Nestore Catalani
Emilia	Luisella Ciaffi
A Herald	Bruno Cioni
Lodovico	Plinio Clabassi

Tullio Serafin, Orchestra and Chorus di Milano della Radiotelevisione Italiana.

+ *Levine*, p. 94.
+– *Opera News* 51, 9 (January 17, 1987): 42, by Thor Eckert, Jr.
 – technical aspects
+– *Opera Quarterly* 5, 2-3 (Summer/Autumn 1987): 159-160, by Robert Levine.
 – technical aspects

106.2. OTELLO by Giuseppe Verdi.
1969. V.I.E.W. Video

Feature Film, Komische Oper Berlin, Germany, 121 min., mono, color, sung in German, no subtitles.
Director, Walter Felsenstein; sets, Alfred Talle; costumes, Helga Scherff. Adapted by Walter Felsenstein and Georg Mielke.

CAST:

Otello	Hanns Nocker
Desdemona	Christa Noack-Von Kamptz
Iago	Vladimir Bauer
Cassio	Hans-Otto Rogge
Roderigo	Peter Seuffert
Montano	Horst-Erich Blasberg
Emilia	Hanna Schmook
A Herald	Horst-Dieter Kaschel
Lodovico	Herbert Rossler

Kurt Masur, Orchestra and Chorus of the Komische Oper Berlin.

– *Levine*, p. 68.
+– *Opera Quarterly* 4, 4 (Winter 1986/87): 118-121, by Peter Symcox.
+ the three principals, – technical aspects
– *Opera Quarterly* 5, 2-3 (Summer/Autumn 1987): 159, by Robert Levine.

106.3. OTELLO by Giuseppe Verdi.
1974. Deutsche Grammophon (PolyGram)

Film version, 145 min., stereo hi-fi, color, sung in Italian with English subtitles.
Director, Herbert von Karajan. Singers lip sync to a prerecorded sound track; the sound track was recorded in the Philharmonic Hall, Berlin, May 1973.

CAST:
Otello .... Jon Vickers
Desdemona .... Mirella Freni
Iago .... Peter Glossop
Cassio .... Aldo Bottion
Roderigo .... Michel Sénéchal
Montano .... Mario Machì
Emilia .... Stefania Malagù
A Herald .... Hans Helm
Lodovico .... José van Dam

Herbert von Karajan, Berlin Philharmonic, Chorus of the Deutsche Oper, Berlin.

106.4. OTELLO by Giuseppe Verdi.
1982. HBO Video

Stage production, Arena di Verona, Italy, 145 min., stereo hi-fi, color, sung in Italian with English subtitles.
Production, Gianfranco de Bosio; sets and costumes, Vittorio Rossi; television director, Preben Montell.

CAST:
Otello .... Vladimir Atlantov
Desdemona .... Kiri Te Kanawa
Iago .... Piero Cappuccilli
Cassio .... Antonio Bevacqua
Roderigo .... Gianfranco Manganotti
Montano .... Orazio Mori
Emilia .... Flora Rafanelli
A Herald .... Gianni Brunelli
Lodovico .... Gianfranco Casarini

Zoltán Peskó, Orchestra and Chorus of the Arena di Verona.

- *Levine*, p. 67-68. + Te Kanawa
- *Opera Quarterly* 5, 2-3 (Summer/Autumn 1987): 160, by Robert Levine. + Te Kanawa
- • *Opera News* 48, 13 (March 17, 1984): 45, by John W. Freeman.
- *Opera News* 52, 6 (December 5, 1987): 56, by Thor Eckert, Jr.

106.5. OTELLO by Giuseppe Verdi.

1986. Video purchase, Kultur; film rental, Swank Motion Pictures (Chicago office, 800-876-3330; New York office, 800-876-3344; St. Louis office, 800-876-5577)

Feature film, 123 min., stereo hi-fi, color, sung in Italian with English subtitles.

Producers, Menahem Golan and Yoram Globus; film by Franco Zeffirelli; costumes, Anna Anni and Maurizio Millenotti; photography, Ennio Guarnieri. Performers lip sync to a prerecorded sound track. The opera is heavily cut and re-arranged. Originally issued as a motion picture.

CAST:

Otello .... Plácido Domingo
Desdemona .... Katia Ricciarelli
Iago .... Justino Díaz
Cassio ...... Ezio Di Cesare/Urbano Barberini (actor)
Roderigo .... Sergio Nicolai
Montano .... Edwin Francis
Emilia .... Petra Malakova
Lodovico .... Massimo Foschi
Brabanio .... Remo Remotti
Doge .... Antonio Pierfederici

Lorin Maazel, Orchestra and Chorus of Teatro alla Scala.

•– *Levine*, p. 93-94. – Zeffirelli
– *Opera (England)* 37, 11 (November 1986): 1318-1320, by Max Loppert. Film review
+ *Opera News* 51, 6 (December 6, 1986): 62, John W. Freeman. Film review
•– *Opera Quarterly* 5, 2-3 (Summer/Autumn 1987): 160-161, by Robert Levine. – Zeffirelli
+ *Ovation* 9, 10 (November 1988): 45, by Robert Levine. – Zeffirelli
+ *Video Review* 8, 3 (June 1987): 118, by Roy Hemming and G.P. Fagan.
+– *Video Review* 8, 5 (August 1987): 68, by Christie Barter.

107.1. IL PAGLIACCI by Ruggiero Leoncavallo.
1936. Lyric Distribution, Inc.; Video Yesteryear

Feature film, 92 min., mono, color sequences in the original film release, black and white in the video releases, sung and spoken in English.
Producer, Max Schach; director, Karl Grune; contributions, Hans Eisler; photography, Otto Kanturek (Chemicolor was used to color two sequences on the original release); story adaptation and dialogue, Monckton Hoffe and Robert Gurford; lyrics, John Drinkwater. Originally issued as a motion picture by Trafalgar/UA Films in Great Britain as *A Clown Must Laugh*. Tauber is the only singer; he sings Canio's music and prologue as well as Tonio's music.

CAST:

Canio Tonini .... Richard Tauber
Nedda Tonini .... Steffi Duna
Trina .... Diana Napier
Tonio .... Arthur Margetson
Silvio .... Esmond Knight
Beppo .... Jerry Verno

Albert Coates, conductor; music director, Hans Eisler.

- • *Levine*, p. 95.
- – *Motion Picture Guide*.
- + *Opera Quarterly* 4, 2 (Summer 1986): 166-167, by London Green.

107.2. IL PAGLIACCI by Ruggiero Leoncavallo.
1950. Video purchase with English subtitles, Bel Canto Society; 16mm rental, Budget Films

Feature film, 68 min., mono, black and white, sung in Italian.
Director, Mario Costa. Originally issued as a motion picture titled *Love of a Clown*.

CAST:
Singers are listed first; actors and actresses are listed second.

Canio .... Galliano Masini/Afro Poli
Nedda .... Onelia Fineschi/Gina Lollobrigida
Tonio .... Tito Gobbi
Beppe .... Gino Sinimberghi/Filippo Morucci
Silvio .... Tito Gobbi

Giuseppe Morelli, Orchestra and Chorus of the Rome Opera House.

++ *Opera (England)* 39, 11 (November 1988): 1386-1387, by Max Loppert.

107.3. IL PAGLIACCI by Ruggiero Leoncavallo.
1953. Lyric Distribution, Inc. (issued with *Cavalleria Rusticana*, 23.1.)

Television production, 28 min., abridged, mono, black and white, sung in Italian, no subtitles.
Producer, Carlo Vinti; stage director, Fausto Bozza; director, Lou Ames; script, Joseph Vinti; announcer, David Ross; host, Robert McBrian. Includes commercials for Progresso Food Products. This program was part of the television series *Opera Cameos* that ran for five years on WABD-TV in New York and occasionally on the Dumont network. The opera is fully staged. Musical director and conductor, Salvatore Dell'Isola.

CAST:

Canio . . . . Mario Del Monaco
Nedda . . . . Mildred Ellar
Tonio . . . . Paolo Silveri

107.4. IL PAGLIACCI by Ruggiero Leoncavallo.
1974. 16mm rental, Iowa State University

Film version, 61 min., abridged, mono, color, sung in English.
Translation and musical direction, Peter Murray. Filmed at Knebworth House, Hertfordshire, England. Part of the *Focus on Opera* series directed by Peter Seabourne. Originally released by Chatsworth Film Distributors; U.S. distributor, Centron Educational Films.

CAST:

Canio . . . . Kenneth Woollam
Nedda . . . . Valerie Masterson
Tonio . . . . Malcolm Rivers
Beppe . . . . David Young
Silvio . . . . Michael Wakeham

John J. Davies, the Classical Orchestra.

+ *Landers Film Reviews* 26, 1 (September/October 1981): 23.

107.5. IL PAGLIACCI by Ruggiero Leoncavallo.
1982. Philips (PolyGram)

Film version, 70 min., stereo hi-fi, color, sung in Italian with English subtitles.
Director, Franco Zeffirelli; sets, Gianni Quaranta; costumes, Anna Anni; photography, Armando Nannuzzi. This production is set in the 1930s.

CAST:

Canio . . . . Plácido Domingo
Nedda . . . . Teresa Stratas
Tonio . . . . Juan Pons
Beppe . . . . Florindo Andreolli

Silvio . . . . Alberto Rinaldi
Peasants . . . . Alfredo Pistone, Ivan Del Manto

Georges Prêtre, Orchestra and Chorus of Teatro alla Scala.

\+ *New York* 22, 15 (April 10, 1989): 108-109, by Peter G. Davis.
– *Opera Monthly* 4, 1 (May 1991): 44, by David McKee.
\+ *Opera News* 53, 13 (March 18, 1989): 44, by C.J. Luten.
\+ *Opera Quarterly* 6, 3 (Spring 1989): 120-124, by Thor Eckert, Jr.
– *Ovation* 9, 10 (November 1988): 44, by David Hurwitz.

108.1. PARSIFAL by Richard Wagner.
1981. Philips (PolyGram)

Stage production, Bayreuth Festival, Germany, 233 min., stereo hi-fi, color, sung in German with English subtitles.
Artistic supervision, production, and stage design, Wolfgang Wagner; costumes, Reinhard Heinrich; video director, Brian Large.

CAST:
Amfortas . . . . Bernd Weikl
Titurel . . . . Matti Salminen
Gurnemanz . . . . Hans Sotin
Parsifal . . . . Siegfried Jerusalem
Klingsor . . . . Leif Roar
Kundry . . . . Eva Randova
Knights of the Grail . Toni Krämer, Heinz Klaus Ecker
Squires . . . . Marga Schiml
Hanna Schwarz
Helmut Pampuch
Martin Egel
Flower Maidens . . . . Norma Sharp
Carol Richardson
Hanna Schwarz
Mari Anne Häggander
Marga Schiml
Margit Neubauer
A Voice . . . . Hanna Schwarz

Horst Stein, Orchestra and Chorus of the Bayreuth Festival.

+– *Fanfare* 16, 1 (September/October 1992): 468-469, by James Reel.
\+ singing, – production
+– *Opera News* 57, 8 (January 2, 1993): 44, by Harvey E. Phillips.
\+ singing, – visuals

108.2. PARSIFAL by Richard Wagner.
1983. Kultur; Corinth/Image Entertainment

Feature film, 255 min., stereo hi-fi, color, sung in German with English subtitles.
Producers, Henry Nap, Annie Nap-Oleon; director, Hans-Jürgen Syberberg; photography, Igor Luther; music director, Armin Jordan; sets, Werner Achmann; costumes, Veronicka Dorn, Hella Wolter. Filmed in Bavaria.

CAST:
Singers are listed first; actors and actresses are listed second.

Amfortas . . . . Wolfgang Schöne/Armin Jordan
Titurel . . . . Hans Tschammer/Martin Sperr
Gurnemanz . . . . Robert Lloyd
Parsifal . . . . Reiner Goldberg/
Michael Kutter and Karen Krick
Klingsor . . . . Aage Haugland
Kundry . . . . Yvonne Minton/Edith Clever
Knights of the Grail (singers) . . . . . Gilles Cachemaille
Paul Frey
Knights of the Grail (actors) . . . . Rudolph Gabler
Urban von Klebelsberg
Bruno Romani-Versteeg
Squires (singers) . . . . Christer Cladin
Tamara Herz
Michael Roider
Hanna Schaer
Squires (actors) . . . . Monika Gaetner
Thomas Fink
David Meyer
Judith Schmidt
Bearer of the Grail (non-singing) . . . Amelie Syberberg
Young Parsifal . . Gertrud Lahusen-Oertel/David Luther
Flowermaidens . . . . Britt-Marie Aruhn
Jocelyne Chamonin
Tamara Herz
Gertrud Lahusen-Oertel
Eva Saurova
Hanna Schaer

Armin Jordan, Monte Carlo Philharmonic Orchestra, Prague Philharmonic Choir.

•– *Motion Picture Guide.*
+– *Opera Canada* 32, 2 (Summer 1991): 55, by Neil Crory.
+ singing, – production
• *Opera (England)* 34, 6 (June 1983): 686-688, by Bryan Magee.
• *Opera News* 47, 13 (March 12, 1983): 42-43, by Glenn Loney.
+– *Video Review* 11, 6 (September 1990): 41, by G. Kenny.

109. THE PERFUMED HANDKERCHIEF.
1981. Kultur

Film version, a Chinese comic opera (*Hsiang lo pa*) performed by members of the Peking Opera Troupe of Peking, China, 70 min., stereo hi-fi, color, sung in Mandarin Chinese with English and Chinese subtitles.
Hosted by Steve Allen and Jayne Meadows; produced by the China TV Service and Lee Productions; photography, Wang Congqiu. Filmed on location at the Imperial Summer Palace of Peking.

CAST:

Bride to be	Liu Xiuyong
Young Scholar	Zhang Chunxiao
Mother	Ko Yinying
Aunt	Sun Wanhua
Maid	Li Hua
Servant	Zhang Huasen

\+ *Booklist* 82, 5 (November 1, 1985): 424, by B.A. Herbert.
\+ *Opera News* 50, 4 (October 1985): 60, by Richard Hornak.

110. PETER GRIMES by Benjamin Britten.
1981. HBO Video

Stage production, Royal Opera House, Covent Garden, London, England, videotaped on June 30, 1982, 160 min., stereo hi-fi, color, sung in the original English.
Director, Elijah Moshinsky; designers, Timothy O'Brien, Tazeena Firth; television director, John Vernon.

CAST:

Peter Grimes	Jon Vickers
Ellen Orford	Heather Harper
Captain Balstrode	Norman Bailey
Auntie	Elizabeth Bainbridge
Auntie's nieces	Marilyn Hill Smith, Anne Pashley
Mrs. Sedley	Patricia Payne
Boy (John)	Andrew Wilson
Hobson	John Tomlinson
Swallow	Forbes Robinson
Ned Keene	Philip Gelling
Rev. Horace Adams	John Lanigan
Bob Boles	John Dobson
Dr. Crabbe	Ignatius McFadyen

Colin Davis, Orchestra and Chorus of the Royal Opera House, Covent Garden.

\+ *Levine*, p. 68-70.

Pique Dame
SEE The Queen of Spades, 113.1.—113.2.

111.1. THE PIRATES OF PENZANCE by W.S. Gilbert & Sir Arthur Sullivan.
1974. 16mm film rental available prior to June 1993 from the University of Illinois Film Center

Film version, 50 min., abridged, mono, color, sung in the original English.
Producer, John Seabourne; director, Trevor Evans; script, David Maverovitch; photography, Adrian Jenkins; narrators, Johnny Wayne, Frank Shuster. Part of the *World of Gilbert and Sullivan* series.

CAST:

Mabel	Valerie Masterson
Pirate King	Donald Adams
Frederic	Thomas Round
Ruth	Helen Landis
Major-General	John Cartier
Sergeant of Police	Lawrence Richard
Isabel	Elizabeth Lowry
Samuel	Michael Wakeham
Edith	Anna Cooper
Kate	Vera Ryan

Gilbert and Sullivan Festival Orchestra and Chorus of England.

111.2. THE PIRATES OF PENZANCE by W.S. Gilbert & Sir Arthur Sullivan.
1982. CBS/FOX Video

Feature film, 112 min. (timing on videocassette release), 94 min. (timing on laser disc release), stereo hi-fi, color, sung in the original English.
Producer, Judith De Paul; director, Rodney Greenberg; stage producer, Michael Geliot; designer, Allan Cameron; costume coordinator, Jenny Beavan; executive producer, George Walker.

CAST:

Ruth	Gillian Knight
Pirate King	Peter Allen
Major-General	Keith Michell
Frederic	Alexander Oliver
Mabel	Janis Kelly
Sergeant of Police	Paul Hudson
Edith	Kate Flowers
Kate	Jenny Wren

Alexander Faris, London Symphony Orchestra, Ambrosian Opera Chorus.

- *Opera News* 49, 14 (March 30, 1985): 26, by Richard Hornak.
– *Opera Now* (January 1992): 56, by Richard Fawkes.

111.3. THE PIRATES OF PENZANCE by W.S. Gilbert & Sir Arthur Sullivan.
1983. Video purchase, MCA Home Video; film rental, Swank Motion Pictures (Chicago office, 800-876-3330; New York office, 800-876-3344; St. Louis office, 800-876-5577)

Feature film, 112 min., stereo hi-fi, color, sung in the original English.
Producer, Joseph Papp; director, Wilford Leach; sets, Peter Howitt; costumes, Tom Rand; music produced by Peter Asher; music adapted, orchestrated, and conducted by William Elliott; screenplay, Wilford Leach.

CAST:
The principal singers are listed first; actors and actresses are listed second.

Mabel .... Linda Ronstadt
Pirate King .... Kevin Kline
Frederic .... Rex Smith
Ruth .... Angela Lansbury
Major-General .... George Rose
Sergeant of Police .... Tony Azito
Samuel .... Stephen Hanan/David Hatton
Edith .... Alexandra Korey/Louis Gold
Kate .... Marcia Shaw/Teresa Codling
plus more daughters, pirates, and policemen.

+ *Motion Picture Guide.*
+ *Opera News* 49, 14 (March 30, 1985): 26, by Richard Hornak.

112. PRINCE IGOR by Aleksandr Borodin.
1969. Kultur; Corinth/Image Entertainment

Feature film, Kirov Opera, Russia/Soviet Union, about 105 min., abridged, mono, color, sung in Russian with English subtitles.
Producer, A. Nesterov; director, Roman Tikhomirov; production design, V. Zechinayaev, A. Fedotov; screenplay, Isaak Glikman, R. Tikhomirov. Orchestration completed by Nikolay Rimsky-Korsakov and Aleksandr Glazunov. Actors and actresses lip sync to a prerecorded sound track. Originally issued as a motion picture. A Lenfilm.

CAST:
Singers are listed first; actors and actresses are listed second.

Prince Igor .... V. Kiniayev/Boris Khmelnitsky
Princess Yaroslavna .... Tamara Milashkina/ Nelly Pshennaya
Vladimir Igorevitch .... Virgilijus Noreika/B. Tokarev

Khan Kontchak . . . . Evgeny Nesterenko/
Bimibulat Vataev
Vladimir Yaroslavitch, Prince Galititzky . . . .
V. Malyshev/A. Slastin
Kontchakovna . . . . I. Bogacheva/I. Murgoyev
Skoula . . . . N. Morozov/M. Sidorkin
Gzak . . . . M. Ikayev
Yeroshka . . . . S. Strezhnev/P. Merkuryev
Ovlour . . . . G. Vilkhovetsky/M. Akhunbayev

Gennady Provatorov, Orchestra, Chorus and Ballet of the Kirov Opera.

++ *Classical* 2, 4 (April 1990): 34, by Robert Levine.
\+ *Levine*, p. 96-97.
\+ *Opera News* 50, 13 (March 15, 1986): 40, by Richard Hornak.
+– *Opera Quarterly* 9, 2 (Winter 1992): 136-137, by Harlow Robinson.
– technical aspects

113.1. THE QUEEN OF SPADES by Peter Ilich Tchaikovsky.
1960. Kultur; Corinth/Image Entertainment

Feature film, Bolshoi Theatre, Russia/Soviet Union, 102 min., abridged, mono hi-fi, color, sung in Russian with English subtitles.
Director, Roman Tikhomirov. Actors and actresses lip sync to a prerecorded sound track. Originally issued as a motion picture. A Lenfilm.

CAST:
Singers are listed first; actors and actresses are listed second.

Lisa . . . . Tamara Milashkina/Olga Krassina
Pauline . . . . Larissa Avdeeva/I. Gubanova-Gurzo
The Countess . . . . . . Sofia Petrovna Preobrazhenskaya/
Yelena Polevetskaya
Herman . . . . Zurab Andzhaparidze/Oleg Strizhenov
Prince Yeletsky . . Evgeny Gavrilovich Kibkalo/V. Kulik
Count Tomsky . . . . Viktor Nechipailo/Vadim Medvedev
Additional singers . . . . V. Volodin
V. Kirpalov
Mark Reshetin
Vitaly Vlasov
G. Shulgin
L. Maslov
Valeri Yaroslavtsev
Additional actors and actresses . . . . A. Gustavson
I. Daryalov
V. Kosarev
A. Olevanov
D. Radlov
Yury Solovyov
V. Tsitta

Evgeny Fedorovich Svetlanov, Orchestra and Chorus of the Bolshoi Theatre.

+ *Levine*, p. 95-96.
+ *Motion Picture Guide.*
+ *Opera News* 50, 2 (August 1985): 37, by Richard Hornak.
– *Opera News* 55, 17 (June 1991): 52-53, by Harvey E. Phillips.
+– *Opera Quarterly* 3, 4 (Winter 1985/86): 125-128, by Christopher J. Thomas.

113.2. THE QUEEN OF SPADES by Peter Ilich Tchaikovsky.
1983. Kultur

Stage production, Bolshoi Theatre, Russia/Soviet Union, 174 min., mono hi-fi, color, sung in Russian with English subtitles.

CAST:

Lisa .... Tamara Milashkina
Pauline .... Ludmilla Semtschuk
The Countess .... Elena Obrazstova
Herman .... Vladimir Atlantov
Prince Yeletsky .... Yuri Mazurok
Tchekalinsky .... Konstantin Pustovoy
Sourin .... Valeri Yaroslavtsev
Governess .... Nina Grigorieva
Masha .... M. Migpau
Narumov .... V. Lashinsky
Tchaplitsky .... Alexander Arkhipov
Master of Ceremonies .... K. Vaskov
Prilepa [sic] .... Nelya Lebedeva

Yuri Simonov, Orchestra and Chorus of the Bolshoi Theatre.

+ *Billboard* (April 23, 1988): 38, by Is Horowitz.
– *Library Journal* 113, 16 (October 1, 1988): 78, by Adrienne Fischier.
• *Opera News* 53, 15 (April 15, 1989): 22, by Harvey E. Phillips.
• *Opera Quarterly* 6, 2 (Winter 1988/89): 111-112, by London Green.

114. THE RAKE'S PROGRESS by Igor Stravinsky.
1977. Video Artists International

Stage production, Glyndebourne Festival, England, 146 min., mono hi-fi, color, sung in the original English.
Director, John Cox; sets, David Hockney; television producer and director, Dave Heather.

CAST:

Anne Trulove .... Felicity Lott
Tom Rakewell .... Leo Goeke
Trulove .... Richard Van Allan
Nick Shadow .... Samuel Ramey

Mother Goose . . . . Nuala Willis
Baba the Turk . . . . Rosalind Elias
Sellem . . . . John Fryatt
Keeper of the Madhouse . . . . Thomas Lawlor

Bernard Haitink, London Symphony Orchestra, Glyndebourne Festival Chorus.

+ *Levine*, p. 70-71.
+ *Opera Quarterly* 4, 2 (Summer 1986): 167-169, by London Green.

115. IL RE PASTORE by Wolfgang Amadeus Mozart.
1989. Philips (PolyGram)

Stage production, Salzburg Festival, Austria, 116 min., stereo hi-fi, color, sung in Italian with English subtitles.
Director, John Cox; design and costumes, Elisabeth Dalton; video director, Brian Large. Presented by the International Mozarteum Foundation, Salzburg, in association with the Landestheater, Salzburg.

CAST:
Aminta . . . . Angela Maria Blasi
Elisa . . . . Silvia McNair
Tamiri . . . . Iris Vermillion
King Alessandro . . . . Jerry Hadley
Agenore . . . . Claes-Håkan Ahnsjö

Neville Marriner, Academy of St. Martin in the Fields.

• *Opera News* 56, 16 (May 1992): 54, by Patrick J. Smith.

The Return of Ulysses to his Homeland
SEE Il Ritorno d'Ulisse in Patria, 118.1.—118.2.

116.1. DAS RHEINGOLD by Richard Wagner.
1978. Deutsche Grammophon (PolyGram)

Film version, 145 min., stereo hi-fi, color, sung in German.
Director and artistic supervision, Herbert von Karajan; sets and costumes, Georges Wakhevitch, Jean Forestier; video director, Ernst Wild. This film was a studio production produced in 1978 in Munich; the sound track was recorded during a 1974 Salzburg Easter Festival performance. Performers lip sync to a prerecorded sound track.

CAST:
Wotan . . . . Thomas Stewart
Donner . . . . Leif Roar/Vladimir De Kanel (actor)
Froh . . . . Hermin Esser
Fricka . . . . Brigitte Fassbaender
Freia . . . . Jeannine Altmeyer
Alberich . . . . Zoltan Kelemen

Mime .... Gerhard Stolze
Fasolt ...... Karl Ridderbusch/Gerd Nienstedt (actor)
Loge .... Peter Schreier
Fafner .... Louis Hendrikx
Erda .... Birgit Finnilä
Woglinde .... Eva Randova
Wellgunde .... Edda Moser
Flosshilde .... Liselotte Rebmann

Herbert von Karajan, Berlin Philharmonic Orchestra.

- *Fanfare* 16, 5 (May/June 1993): 436, by James Reel.

116.2. DAS RHEINGOLD by Richard Wagner.
1980. Philips (PolyGram)

Stage production, Bayreuth Festival, Germany, 150 min., stereo hi-fi, color, sung in German with English subtitles.
Modern version by Pierre Boulez and director Patrice Chéreau; design, Richard Peduzzi; costumes, Jacques Schmidt; video director, Brian Large.

CAST:
Wotan .... Donald McIntyre
Donner .... Martin Egel
Froh .... Siegfried Jerusalem
Fricka .... Hanna Schwarz
Freia .... Carmen Reppel
Alberich .... Hermann Becht
Mime .... Helmut Pampuch
Fasolt .... Matti Salminen
Loge .... Heinz Zednik
Fafner .... Fritz Hübner
Erda .... Ortrun Wenkel
Wogline .... Norma Sharp
Wellgunde .... Ilse Gramatzki
Flosshilde .... Marga Schiml

Pierre Boulez, Orchestra and Chorus of the Bayreuth Festival.

\+ *Booklist* 80, 13 (March 1, 1984): 1001, by William Ward.
\+ *Classical* 14, 5 (November 1991): 43-44, by Neil Crory.
++ *New York* 25, 20 (May 18, 1992): 65-66, by Peter G. Davis.

116.3. DAS RHEINGOLD by Richard Wagner.
1990. Deutsche Grammophon (PolyGram)

Stage production, Metropolitan Opera, New York City, 162 min., stereo hi-fi, color, sung in German with English subtitles.
Production, Otto Schenk; sets and projections, Günther Schneider-Siemssen; costumes, Rolf Langenfass; television director, Brian Large.

CAST:

Wotan . . . . James Morris
Donner . . . . Alan Held
Froh . . . . Mark Baker
Fricka . . . . Christa Ludwig
Freia . . . . Mari Anne Häggander
Alberich . . . . Ekkehard Wlaschiha
Mime . . . . Heinz Zednik
Fasolt . . . . Jan-Hendrik Rootering
Loge . . . . Siegfried Jerusalem
Fafner . . . . Matti Salminen
Erda . . . . Birgitta Svendén
Wogline . . . . Kaaren Erickson
Wellgunde . . . . Diane Kesling
Flosshilde . . . . Meredith Parsons

James Levine, Orchestra and Chorus of the Metropolitan Opera.

– *New York* 25, 20 (May 18, 1992): 65-66, by Peter G. Davis.

117.1. RIGOLETTO by Giuseppe Verdi.
1947. Lyric Distribution, Inc.

Film version, about 100 min., mono, black and white, sung in Italian, no subtitles.
Producer, Giulio Fiaschi; director, Carmine Gallone; photographer, Anchise Brizzi; writer, Gentilumini Alabardiera. Gilda is played by actress Marcella Govoni.

CAST:

Rigoletto . . . . Tito Gobbi
Duke of Mantua . . . . Mario Filippeschi
Gilda . . . . . . Lina Pagliughi/Marcella Govoni (actress)
Sparafucile . . . . Giulio Neri
Maddalena . . . . Anna Maria Canali
Count Monterone . . . . Marcello Giorda
Borsa . . . . Roberto Brani
Marullo . . . . Virgilio Gottardi
Count Ceprano . . . . Giuseppe Varni

Tullio Serafin, Orchestra and Chorus of the Rome Opera House.

- *Levine*, p. 97. + Gobbi
- *Motion Picture Guide.*
- *Opera (England)* 39, 11 (November 1988): 1386-1387, by Max Loppert.
- *Opera Quarterly* 5, 2-3 (Summer/Autumn 1987): 151, by Robert Levine. + Gobbi

117.2. RIGOLETTO by Giuseppe Verdi.
1954. V.I.E.W. Video

Feature film, 90 min., abridged, mono, black and white for introductory credits, color throughout, sung in Italian, spoken dialogue between arias is dubbed into English.
Director, Flavio Calzavara; photography, Adalberto Albertini. Originally issued as a motion picture titled *Rigoletto e la sua Tragedia* by Telecine Italia. Actors and actresses lip sync to a prerecorded sound track.

CAST:
Singers are listed first; actors and actresses are listed second.

Rigoletto . . . . Tito Gobbi/Aldo Silvani
Duke of Mantua . . . . Mario Del Monaco/Gerard Landry
Gilda . . . . Giuseppina Arnaldi/Janet Vidor
The credits do not identify the following individuals as actors and/or singers.
Sparafucile . . . . Cesare Polacco
Maddalena . . . . Franca Tamantini
Count Monterone . . . . Gualtiero Tumiati
Giovanna . . . . Nietta Zocchi
Borsa . . . . Mario Terribile
Marullo . . . . Vittorio Vaser
Count Ceprano . . . . Loris Gizzi
Il Poeta . . . . Renato Chiantoni

Oliviero De Fabritiis, Orchestra of the Rome Opera House.

– *Opera News* 55, 3 (September 1990): 50-51, by Harvey E. Phillips.
– *Video Rating Guide* 1, 1 (Winter 1990): 145, by F.W. Lancaster.

117.3. RIGOLETTO by Giuseppe Verdi.
1974. 16mm rental, Iowa State University; University of North Texas, Media Library, Box 12898, Denton, TX 76203 817-565-2484

Film version, 54 min., abridged, mono, color, sung in English.
Translation and musical direction, Peter Murray. Filmed at Knebworth House, Hertfordshire, England. Part of the *Focus on Opera* series directed by Peter Seabourne. Originally released by Chatsworth Film Distributors; U.S. distributor, Centron Educational Films.

CAST:
Rigoletto . . . . Malcolm Rivers
Duke of Mantua . . . . John Brecknock
Gilda . . . . Lillian Watson
Sparafucile . . . . Thomas Lawlor
Maddalena . . . . Antonia Butler
Count Monterone . . . . Philip Summerscales

Giovanna	Elizabeth Mynett
Borsa	Michael Clarke
Marullo	Alan Grant

John J. Davies, the Classical Orchestra.

\+ *Landers Film Reviews* 26, 1 (September/October 1981): 26.

117.4. RIGOLETTO by Giuseppe Verdi.
1981. Mastervision (initial release); Applause Video (85 Longview Rd., Port Washington, NY 11050)

Stage production, Arena di Verona, Italy, 115 min., stereo hi-fi, color, sung in Italian. This video was initially released without English subtitles; later issues may have subtitles.
Production, Carlo Lizzani; designed by Carlo Savi; television director, Brian Large.

CAST:

Rigoletto	Garbis Boyagian
Duke of Mantua	Vincenzo Bello
Gilda	Alida Ferrarini
Sparafucile	Antonio Zerbini
Maddalena	Franca Mattiucci
Count Monterone	Orazio Mori
Giovanna	Gigliola Caputi
Borsa	Gianfranco Manganotti
Marullo	Bruno Grella
Count Ceprano	Carlo Meliciani
Countess Ceprano	Rina Pallini
Usher	Vincenzo Sagona
The Page	Mara Farra

Donato Renzetti, Orchestra and Chorus of the Arena di Verona.

117.5. RIGOLETTO by Giuseppe Verdi.
1982. HBO Video

Stage production, English National Opera at the London Coliseum, England, 140 min., stereo hi-fi, color, sung in English, English version by James Fenton.
Production, Jonathan Miller; director and producer, John Michael Philips. The action is re-set in New York City's mob-controlled Little Italy in the 1950s.

CAST:

Rigoletto	John Rawnsley
Duke of Mantua	Arthur Davies
Gilda	Marie McLaughlin
Sparafucile	John Tomlinson
Maddalena	Jean Rigby

Count Monterone	Sean Rea
Giovanna	Myrna Moreno
Borsa	Terry Jenkins
Marullo	Malcolm Rivers
Count Ceprano	Mark Richardson
Countess Ceprano	Susan Underwood
Secretary	Linda Rands
Henchman	Maurice Brown

Mark Elder, Orchestra and Chorus of the English National Opera.

+– *Opera News* 54, 14 (March 31, 1990): 34, by Harvey E. Phillips.
+ singing, – technical aspects
+ *Opern Welt* 27, 8 (August 1986): 61, by Gerhard Persché.

117.6. RIGOLETTO by Giuseppe Verdi.
1983. London (PolyGram)

Film version, 116 min., stereo hi-fi, color, sung in Italian with English subtitles.
Production, Jean-Pierre Ponnelle; costumes, Martin Schlumpf; photography, Pasqualino De Santis. Filmed on location in Mantua.

CAST:

Rigoletto	Ingvar Wixell
Duke of Mantua	Luciano Pavarotti
Gilda	Edita Gruberova
Sparafucile	Ferruccio Furlanetto
Maddalena	Victoria Vergara
Count Monterone	Ingvar Wixell
Giovanna	Fedora Barbieri
Borsa	Rémy Corazza
Marullo	Bernd Weikl/Louis Otey (actor)
Count Ceprano	Roland Bracht
Countess Ceprano	Kathleen Kuhlmann

Riccardo Chailly, Vienna Philharmonic Orchestra, Concert Association of the Vienna State Opera Chorus.

+– *Opera Quarterly* 6, 3 (Spring 1989): 120-124, by Thor Eckert, Jr.
+ singing, – Ponnelle production
+– *Ovation* 9, 10 (November 1988): 44, by David Hurwitz.
+ Gruberova, – Ponnelle production
•– *Variety* (May 20, 1987): 28. Film reviewed at the Cannes Film Festival.

Der Ring des Nibelungen
SEE Die Götterdämmerung, 63.1.—63.2.
Das Rheingold, 116.1.—116.3.
Siegfried, 127.1.—127.2.
Die Walküre, 149.1.—149.2.

118.1. IL RITORNO D'ULISSE IN PATRIA by Claudio Monteverdi.
1973. Video Artists International

Stage production (Leppard edition), Glyndebourne Festival, England, 152 min., mono hi-fi, color, sung in Italian with English subtitles.
Producer, Peter Hall; designer, John Bury; television producer, Humphrey Burton; television director, Dave Heather. Realized by Raymond Leppard.

CAST:

Ulysses . . . . Benjamin Luxon
Penelope . . . . Janet Baker
Eumete . . . . Richard Lewis
Telemaco . . . . Ian Caley
Antinco . . . . Ugo Trama
Pisandro . . . . John Fryatt
Anfimono . . . . Bernard Dickerson
Eurimaco . . . . John Wakefield
Iro . . . . Alexander Oliver
Melanto . . . . Janet Hughes
Ericlea . . . . Virginia Popova
Minerva . . . . Anne Howells
Neptune . . . . Robert Lloyd
Jove . . . . Brian Burrows
Juno . . . . Rae Woodland
Human Frailty . . . . Annabel Hunt
Time . . . . Ugo Trama
Fortune . . . . Patricia Craig
Love . . . . Laureen Livingstone

Raymond Leppard, London Philharmonic Orchestra, Glyndebourne Festival Chorus.

+ *Levine*, p. 72-73.
– *Opera (England)* 41, 1 (January 1990): 120-121, by Max Loppert.
+ *Opera News* 50, 2 (August 1985): 36, by Richard Hornak.
•– *Opera Quarterly* 4, 1 (Spring 1986): 135-136, by Matthew Gurewitsch.

118.2. IL RITORNO D'ULISSE IN PATRIA by Claudio Monteverdi.
1985. Home Vision

Stage production (Henze edition), Salzburg Festival, Austria, 187 min., stereo hi-fi, color, sung in Italian with English subtitles.
Director, Michael Hampe; sets and costumes, Mauro Pagano; video director, Claus Viller. Presented in a freely adapted version by Hans Werner Henze.

CAST:

Ulysses . . . . Thomas Allen
Penelope . . . . Kathleen Kuhlmann
Eumete . . . . Robert Tear

Telemaco . . . . Alejandro Ramirez
Antinco . . . . Harald Stamm
Pisandro . . . . Josef Protschka
Anfimono . . . . Douglas Ahlstedt
Eurimaco . . . . Vinson Cole
Iro . . . . Curtis Rayam
Melanto . . . . Daphne Evangelatos
Ericlea . . . . Márta Szirmay
Minerva . . . . Delores Ziegler
Neptune . . . . Manfred Schenk
Jove . . . . James King
Human Frailty . . . . Thomas Allen
Time . . . . Kurt Rydl
Fortune . . . . Janice Hall
Love . . . . Allan Bergius

Jeffrey Tate, ÖRF Symphony Orchestra, Tölzer Boy's Choir.

+ *Opera News* 56, 4 (October 1991): 58, by Patrick J. Smith.

119. ROBERTO DEVEREUX by Gaetano Donizetti.
1975. Video Artists International

Stage production, Filene Center Auditorium in Wolf Trap Farm Park for the Performing Arts, Vienna, Virginia, 145 min., mono hi-fi, color, sung in Italian with English subtitles.
Director, Tito Capobianco.

CAST:

Elizabeth, Queen of England . . . . Beverly Sills
Robert Devereux . . . . John Alexander
Sara . . . . Susanne Marsee
Duke of Nottingham . . . . Richard Fredricks
Lord Cecil . . . . John Lankston
Raleigh . . . . David Rae Smith
Page . . . . Allan Glassman
Servant of Nottingham . . . . Donnie Ray Albert

Julius Rudel, Filene Center Orchestra, Wolf Trap Company Chorus.

+ *Opera News* 57, 17 (June 1993): 53, by Harvey E. Phillips.

Romeo und Julia auf dem Dorfe
SEE A Village Romeo and Juliet, 147.

120.1. DER ROSENKAVALIER by Richard Strauss.
1960. Video Artists International; Kultur (issued with subtitles and a remastered sound track)

Stage production, Salzburg Festival, Austria, 190 min., mono hi-fi, color, sung in German. This video was initially released without English subtitles; later issues have subtitles. Printed synopses in English precede each act.
Producer and director, Paul Czinner; stage production, Rudolf Hartmann; sets, Teo Otto; costumes, Erni Kniepert. Made by The Rank Organisation Film Productions, Ltd., England.

CAST:

Feldmarschallin	Elisabeth Schwarzkopf
Octavian	Sena Jurinac
Sophie	Anneliese Rothenberger
Baron Ochs von Lerchenau	Otto Edelmann
Italian Singer	Giuseppe Zampieri
Valzacchi	Renato Ercolani
Herr von Fanial	Erich Kunz
Annina	Hilde Rössl-Majdan
Marianne	Judith Hellweg
Landlord	Fritz Sperlbauer
Police Commissar	Alois Pernerstorfer
Notary	Josef Knapp
Major-domo to Faninal	Siegfried Rudolf Frese
Major-domo to the Feldmarschallin	Erich Majkut
Noble Orphans	Liselotte Maikl
	Ute Frey
	Evelyn Labruce
Milliner	Mary Richards
Animal Seller	Kurt Equiluz
Hairdresser (non-singing)	Hans Kres
Little Black Boy (non-singing)	Wolfgang Kres
Leopold (non-singing)	Hermann Tichavsky
Footmen of the Feldmarschallin	Fritz Mayer
	Rudolf Stumper
	Otto Vaja
	Alois Buchbauer
Waiters	Karl Kolowratnik
	Ludwig Fleck
	Kurt Bernhard
	Norbert Balatsch

Herbert von Karajan, the Mozarteum Orchestra, Vienna Philharmonic Orchestra, Vienna State Opera Chorus.

++ *Levine*, p. 97-98.
+ *Opera News* 49, 14 (March 30, 1985): 26, 43, by Richard Hornak.
+ *Opera Quarterly* 3, 2 (Summer 1985): 135-137, by William Huck.

120.2. DER ROSENKAVALIER by Richard Strauss.
1979. Deutsche Grammophon (PolyGram)

Stage production, Bavarian State Opera, National Theater, Munich, Germany, 186 min., stereo hi-fi, color, sung in German with English subtitles.
Staged and directed by Otto Schenk; sets and costumes, Jürgen Rose; television director, Karlheinz Hundorf.

CAST:

Feldmarschallin	Gwyneth Jones
Octavian	Brigitte Fassbaender
Sophie	Lucia Popp
Baron Ochs von Lerchenau	Manfred Jungwirth
Italian Singer	Francisco Araiza
Valzacchi	David Thaw
Herr von Faninal	Benno Kusche
Annina	Gudrun Wewezow
Marianne	Anneliese Waas
Landlord	Norbert Orth
Police Commissar	Albrecht Peter
Notary	Hans Wilbrink
Major-domo to Faninal	Friedrich Lenz
Major-domo to the Feldmarschallin	Georg Paskuda
Noble Orphans	Dorothea Wirtz
	Maja Hake
	Helena Jungwirth
Milliner	Susanne Sonnenschein
Animal Seller	Osamu Kobayashi
Noble Widow (non-singing)	Elisabeth Von Ihering
Hairdresser (non-singing)	Karl Schrader
Flute Player (non-singing)	Heinz Müller
Leopold (non-singing)	Hans Mursch
Mohammed (non-singing)	Patrick Leppelt
Footmen of the Feldmarschallin	Rudolf Schwab
	Walter Brem
	Werner Liebl
	Artur Horn

Carlos Kleiber, Orchestra and Chorus of the Bavarian State Opera.

+– *Classical* 6, 2 (February 1990): 24-25, by Robert Levine.
+ singers, – production
\+ *New York* 22, 15 (April 10, 1989): 110, by Peter G. Davis.
\+ *Opera Canada* 31, 4 (Winter 1990): 51, by Neil Crory.

120.3. DER ROSENKAVALIER by Richard Strauss.
1985. Home Vision

Stage production, Royal Opera House, Covent Garden, London, England, videotaped on February 14, 1985, 204 min., stereo hi-fi, color, sung in German with English subtitles.
Producer, John Schlesinger; sets, William Dudley; costumes, Maria Bjoernson; television director, Brian Large.

CAST:

Feldmarschallin	Kiri Te Kanawa
Octavian	Anne Howells
Sophie	Barbara Bonney
Baron Ochs von Lerchenau	Aage Haugland
Italian Singer	Dennis O'Neill
Valzacchi	Robert Tear
Herr von Faninal	Jonathan Summers
Annina	Cynthia Buchan
Marianne	Phyllis Cannan
Innkeeper	Paul Crook
Police Commissar	Roderick Earle
Notary	John Gibbs
Major-domo to Faninal	John Dobson
Major-domo to the Feldmarschallin	Kim Begley
Noble Orphans	Linda Kitchen
	Kate McCarney
	Yvonne Lea
Milliner	Susan Maisey
Animal Seller	Alan Duffield
Noble Widow (non-singing)	Nada Pobjoy
Hairdresser (non-singing)	Ray Hatch
Flute Player (non-singing)	Ignatius McFadyen
Leopold (non-singing)	Peter Garvie-Adams
Mohammed (non-singing)	Kevin Mathurin
Footmen of the Feldmarschallin	Paschal Allen
	Donald Bell
	Malcolm Campbell
	Keith Jones
Waiters	Richard Hazell
	John Kerr
	John Killmann
	Anthony Smith
Baron Ochs's Retinue	Kenny Baker
	George Macpherson
	John Parry
	Keith Raggett
	Duncan Reece
	John Roche

Sir Georg Solti, Orchestra and Chorus of the Royal Opera House, Covent Garden.

+ *Levine*, p. 73-75.
+ *Opera Canada* 30, 3 (Fall 1989): 60, by Ruby Mercer.
+ *Opera Monthly* 1, 4 (August 1988): 58-59, by Robert Levine.
+ *Opera News* 52, 17 (June 1988): 44, by C.J. Luten.
– Haugland, Summers

121.1. RUDDIGORE by W.S. Gilbert & Sir Arthur Sullivan.
1972. 16mm film: Rochester Public Library, Reynolds Audio Visual Dept., 115 South Ave., Rochester, NY 14604 716-428-7333

Film version, 50 min., abridged, mono, color, sung in the original English.
Producer, John Seabourne; director, Trevor Evans; script, David Maverovitch; photography, Adrian Jenkins; narrators, Johnny Wayne, Frank Shuster. Part of the *World of Gilbert and Sullivan* series.

CAST:

Sir Despard Murgatroyd .... Lawrence Richard
Rose Maybud .... Gillian Humphreys
Mad Margaret .... Ann Hood
Dame Hannah .... Helen Landis
Richard Dauntless .... Thomas Round
Sir Roderick Murgatroyd .... Donald Adams
Sir Ruthven Murgatroyd .... John Cartier
Old Adam Goodheart .... John Banks
Zorah .... Joy Roberts

121.2. RUDDIGORE by W.S. Gilbert & Sir Arthur Sullivan.
1982. CBS/FOX Video

Television production, 112 min., stereo hi-fi, color, sung in the original English.
Producer, Judith de Paul; director, Barrie Gavin; staged by Christopher Renshaw; designer, Allan Cameron; costume coordinator, Jenny Beavan; executive producer, George Walker.

CAST:

Sir Despard Murgatroyd .... Vincent Price
Robert Oakapple (Robin) .... Keith Michell
Rose Maybud .... Sandra Dugdale
Mad Margaret .... Ann Howard
Dame Hannah .... Johanna Peters
Richard Dauntless .... John Treleaven
Sir Roderick Murgatroyd .... Donald Adams
Old Adam Goodheart .... Paul Hudson
Zorah .... Beryl Korman

Alexander Faris, London Symphony Orchestra, Ambrosian Opera Chorus.

+ *Opera (England)* 38, 12 (December 1987): 1465-1466, by Arthur Jacobs.
+ *Opera News* 50, 2 (August 1985): 37, by Richard Hornak.

122. RUSALKA by Antonín Dvořák.
1986. Home Vision

Stage production, English National Opera at the London Coliseum, England, 160 min., stereo hi-fi, color, sung in English, English translation by Rodney Blumer.
Production, David Pountney; designs and settings, Stefanos Lazaridis; television director, Derek Bailey.

CAST:

Rusalka	Eilene Hannan
Jezibaba	Ann Howard
Water Spirit	Rodney Macann
Prince	John Treleaven
Foreign Princess	Phyllis Cannan
Wood Nymphs	Cathryn Pope
	Eileen Hulse
	Linda McLeod
Gamekeeper	Edward Byles
Kitchen Boy	Fiona Kimm
Huntsman	Christopher Booth-Jones

Mark Elder, Orchestra and Chorus of the English National Opera.

+ *Landers Film Reviews* 32, 3 (Spring 1988): 132-133.
+ *Opera Canada* 31, 4 (Winter 1990): 51, by Ruby Mercer.
+– *Opera (England)* 41, 1 (January 1990): 120-121, by Max Loppert.
  + performance, – video technical aspects
• *Opera News* 53, 15 (April 15, 1989): 40, by Harvey E. Phillips.
+ *Opera Quarterly* 7, 3 (Autumn 1990): 148-150, by Roger Pines.

Rustic Chivalry
SEE Cavalleria Rusticana

123.1. SALOME by Richard Strauss.
1974. Deutsche Grammophon (PolyGram)

Stage production, Vienna State Opera, Austria, 102 min., stereo hi-fi, color, sung in German with English subtitles.
Director, Götz Friedrich; designed by Gerd Staub.

CAST:

Salome	Teresa Stratas
Jokanaan	Bernd Weikl
Herod Antipas	Hans Beirer

Herodias . . . . Astrid Varnay
Narraboth . . . . Wieslaw Ochman
Page of Herodias . . . . Hanna Schwarz

Karl Böhm, Vienna Philharmonic Orchestra.

\+ *New York* 22, 15 (April 10, 1989): 110, by Peter G. Davis.
+– *Opera Canada* 31, 4 (Winter 1990): 52, by Neil Crory.
– sets
\+ *Opera (England)* 42, 11 (November 1991): 1361-1362, by Andrew Clements.

123.2. SALOME by Richard Strauss.
1990. Teldec

Stage production, Deutsche Oper Berlin, Germany, 109 min., stereo hi-fi, color, sung in German with English subtitles.
Production, Peter Weigl; sets, Josef Svoboda; costumes, Josef Jelinek; television director, Brian Large.

CAST:
Salome . . . . Catherine Malfitano
Jokanaan . . . . Simon Estes
Herod Antipas . . . . Horst Hiestermann
Herodias . . . . Leonie Rysanek
Narraboth . . . . Clemens Bieber
Page of Herodias . . . . Camille Capasso
Cappadocian . . . . Klaus Lang
Slave (non-singing) . . . . Aimée Elizabeth Willis
Jews . . . . Uwe Peper
Karl-Ernst Mercker
Peter Maus
Warren Mok
Manfred Röhrl
Nazarenes . . . . Friedrich Molsberger, Ralf Lukas
Soldiers . . . . William Murray, Bengt Rundgern

Giuseppe Sinopoli, Orchestra and Chorus of the Deutsche Oper Berlin.

\+ *Opera News* 56, 15 (April 11, 1992): 58, by Harvey E. Phillips.
• *Opera Now* (February 1992): 56-57, by Richard Fawkes.

124.1. SAMSON ET DALILA by Camille Saint-Saëns.
1980. Home Vision

Stage production, San Francisco Opera, California, videotaped on October 24, 1980, 119 min., stereo hi-fi, color, sung in French with English subtitles.
Producer, John Goberman; director, Nicolas Joel; sets, Douglas Schmidt; costumes, Carrie Robbins; video director, Kirk Browning. Includes a short introduction by Julius Rudel.

CAST:

Dalila	Shirley Verrett
Samson	Plácido Domingo
High Priest of Dagon	Wolfgang Brendel
Abimelech	Arnold Voketaitis
Old Hebrew	Kevin Langan
First Philistine	Michael Ballam
Second Philistine	Stanley Wexler
Philistines' Messenger	Robert Tate
Solo Dancer (non-singing)	Christian Holder

Julius Rudel, Orchestra and Chorus of the San Francisco Opera.

\+ *Landers Film and Video Reviews* 34, 4 (Summer 1990): 180.

124.2. SAMSON ET DALILA by Camille Saint-Saëns.
1981. HBO Video

Stage production, Royal Opera House, Covent Garden, London, England, videotaped on October 15, 1981, 135 min., stereo hi-fi, color, sung in French. This video was initially released without English subtitles; later issues may have subtitles.
Producer, Elijah Moshinsky; scenery and costume designer, Sidney Nolan; video director, John Vernon.

CAST:

Dalila	Shirley Verrett
Samson	Jon Vickers
High Priest of Dagon	Jonathan Summers
Abimelech	John Tomlinson
Old Hebrew	Gwynne Howell
First Philistine	Maldwyn Davies
Second Philistine	Matthew Best
Philistines' Messenger	John Dobson

Colin Davis, Orchestra and Chorus of the Royal Opera House, Covent Garden.

– *Opera News* 51, 2 (August 1986): 30, 50, by Richard Hornak.
– Verrett, + Vickers

125. LA SCALA DI SETA by Gioacchino Rossini.
1990. Teldec

Stage production, Schwetzinger Festival, performed at the Rococo Theater at the Schwetzinger Palace in the small town of Schwetzingen near Heidelberg, 100 min., stereo hi-fi, color, sung in Italian with English subtitles.
Production, Michael Hampe; artistic director, Gerhard Reutter; video director, Claus Viller.

CAST:
Giulia . . . . Luciana Serra
Blansac . . . . Alberto Rinaldi
Germano . . . . Alessandro Corbelli
Lucilla . . . . Jane Bunnell
Dorvil . . . . David Kuebler
Dormont . . . . David Griffith

Gianluigi Gelmetti, Stuttgart Radio Symphony Orchestra.

+ *Fanfare* 16, 1 (September/October 1992): 468, by James Reel.
•– *Opera (England)* 43, 3 (March 1992): 369-370, by Arthur Jacobs.
+ *Opera News* 57, 2 (August 1992): 53, by Shirley Fleming.

The Secret Marriage
SEE Il Matrimonio Segreto, 91.

Serse
SEE Xerxes, 154.

126. LA SERVA PADRONA by Giovanni Battista Pergolesi.
1958. V.I.E.W. Video

Television production, 60 min., mono hi-fi, black and white, sung in Italian, no subtitles.

CAST:
Serpina . . . . Anna Moffo
Uberto . . . . Paolo Montarsolo

Franco Ferrara, Orchestra Filharmonica di Roma.

The Sicilian Vespers
SEE Il Vespri Siciliani, 146.1.—146.2.

127.1. SIEGFRIED by Richard Wagner.
1980. Philips (PolyGram)

Stage production, Bayreuth Festival, Germany, 225 min., stereo hi-fi, color, sung in German with English subtitles.
Modern version by Pierre Boulez and director Patrice Chéreau; design, Richard Peduzzi; costumes, Jacques Schmidt; video director, Brian Large.

CAST:
Siegfried . . . . Manfred Jung
Mime . . . . Heinz Zednik
Wotan, disguised as the Wanderer . . . .
Donald McIntyre
Brünnhilde . . . . Gwyneth Jones
Alberich . . . . Hermann Becht
Fafner . . . . Fritz Hübner
Erda . . . . Ortrun Wenkel
Forest Bird . . . . Norma Sharp

Pierre Boulez, Orchestra and Chorus of the Bayreuth Festival.

\+ *Classical* 14, 5 (November 1991): 43-44, by Neil Crory.
++ *New York* 25, 20 (May 18, 1992): 65-66, by Peter G. Davis.

127.2. SIEGFRIED by Richard Wagner.
1990. Deutsche Grammophon (PolyGram)

Stage production, Metropolitan Opera, New York City, 252 min., stereo hi-fi, color, sung in German with English subtitles.
Production, Otto Schenk; sets, Günther Schneider-Siemssen; costumes, Rolf Langenfass; video director, Brian Large.

CAST:
Siegfried . . . . Siegfried Jerusalem
Mime . . . . Heinz Zednik
Wotan, disguised as the Wanderer . . . .
James Morris
Brünnhilde . . . . Hildegard Behrens
Alberich . . . . Ekkehard Wlaschiha
Fafner . . . . Matti Salminen
Erda . . . . Birgitta Svendén
Forest Bird . . . . Dawn Upshaw

James Levine, Orchestra and Chorus of the Metropolitan Opera.

– *New York* 25, 20 (May 18, 1992): 65-66, by Peter G. Davis.

128. IL SIGNOR BRUSCHINO by Gioacchino Rossini.
1989. Teldec

Stage production, Schwetzinger Festival, performed at the Rococo Theater at the Schwetzinger Palace in the small town of Schwetzingen near Heidelberg, 97 min., stereo hi-fi, color, sung in Italian with English subtitles.
Director, Michael Hampe; artistic director, Gerhard Reutter; sets, Carlo Tommasi; costumes, Carlo Diappi; video director, Claus Viller.

CAST:

Sofia . . . . Amelia Felle
Bruschino, padre . . . . Alberto Rinaldi
Marianna . . . . Janice Hall
Florville . . . . David Kuebler
Gaudenzio . . . . Alessandro Corbelli
Filiberto . . . . Carlos Feller
Delegato di Polizia . . . . Oslavio Di Credico
Bruschino, figlio . . . . Vito Gobbi
Servants . . . . Paul Keppeler
Orazio Romano
Werner Simon

Gianluigi Gelmetti, Stuttgart Radio Symphony Orchestra.

+ *Fanfare* 15, 3 (January/February 1992): 455, by James Reel.
+ *Musical America* 112, 1 (January/February 1992): 54-55, by Robert Levine.
+ *Opera (England)* 42, 9 (September 1991): 1111-1112, by Arthur Jacobs.
• *Opera Now* (December 1991): 56-57, by Richard Fawkes.

129.1. SIMON BOCCANEGRA by Giuseppe Verdi.
1984. Bel Canto/Paramount Home Video

Stage production, Metropolitan Opera, New York City, videotaped on Saturday, December 29, 1984, 153 min., stereo hi-fi, color, sung in Italian with English subtitles.
Production, Tito Capobianco; video director, Brian Large.

CAST:

Simon Boccanegra . . . . Sherrill Milnes
Amelia Boccanegra . . . . Anna Tomowa-Sintow
Jacopo Fiesco . . . . Paul Plishka
Gabriele Adorno . . . . Vasile Moldoveanu
Paolo Albiani . . . . Richard J. Clark
Pietro . . . . James Courtney
Amelia's Lady-in-Waiting . . . . Dawn Upshaw
A Captain . . . . Robert Nagy

James Levine, Orchestra and Chorus of the Metropolitan Opera.

- *Opera News* 53, 15 (April 15, 1989): 22-23, by Harvey E. Phillips.

129.2. SIMON BOCCANEGRA by Giuseppe Verdi.
1991. London (PolyGram)

Stage production, Royal Opera House, Covent Garden, London, England, 135 min., stereo hi-fi, color, sung in Italian with English subtitles.
Production, Elijah Moshinsky; sets, Michael Yeargan; video director, Brian Large.

CAST:

Simon Boccanegra .... Alexandru Agache
Amelia Boccanegra .... Kiri Te Kanawa
Jacopo Fiesco .... Roberto Scandiuzzi
Gabriele Adorno .... Michael Sylvester
Paolo Albiani .... Alan Opie
Pietro .... Mark Beesley
Amelia's Lady-in-Waiting .... Elizabeth Sikora
A Captain .... Rodney Gibson

Sir Georg Solti, Orchestra and Chorus of the Royal Opera House, Covent Garden.

\+ *Opera (England)* 44, 1 (January 1993): 120-121, by Charles Osborne.
\+ *Opera News* 57, 17 (June 1993): 53, by Harvey E. Phillips.

Skazka o tsare Saltane
SEE The Legend of Tsar Saltan, 78.

130. LA SONNAMBULA by Vincenzo Bellini.
1949. V.I.E.W. Video

Film version, Rome Opera, Italy, about 76 min., abridged, mono hi-fi, black and white, sung in Italian with English narration between arias.
Producer, Guglielmo Rosa; director, Cesare Barlacchi; photography, Carlo Carlini. Gino Sinimberghi, tenor, also appears as an actor in other opera films. Actors and actresses lip sync to a prerecorded sound track.

CAST:

Singers are listed first; actors and actresses are listed second.

Amina .... Fiorella Ortis/Paola Bertini
Elvino .... Licinio Francardi/Gino Sinimberghi
Count Rodolpho .... Alfredo Colella
Additional singers .... Franca Tamantini
Rosetta Riscica
Maurizio Lolli
Andrea Mineo

Additional actors and actresses .... Millo Marcucci
Blando Giusti
Lucky Ross

Graziano Mucci, Orchestra of the Rome Opera House.

The Spanish Hour
SEE L'Heure Espagnole, 67.

The Story of Tsar Sultan
SEE The Legend of Tsar Saltan, 78.

Straszny Dwór
SEE The Haunted Manor, 66.

131. SUOR ANGELICA by Giacomo Puccini.
1983. Home Vision (issued with the other operas of *Il Trittico*, *Gianni Schicchi* and *Il Tabarro*)

Stage production, Teatro alla Scala, Milan, Italy, 150 min. (total timing for the three operas in *Il Trittico*), stereo hi-fi, color, sung in Italian with English subtitles.
Producer, Sylvano Bussotti; sets and costumes, Michele Canzoneri; television director, Brian Large.

CAST:
Suor Angelica .... Rosalind Plowright
The Princess .... Dunja Vejzović
The Abbess .... Maria Grazia Allegri
La Suora Zelatrice .... Jole Arno
Mistress of the Novices .... Nella Verri
Suor Genovieffa .... Giovanna Santelli
Suor Osmina .... Maria Della Spezia
Suor Dolcina .... Mildela D'Amico
Alms Collectors .... Patrizia Orciani, Stefania Malagù
A Novice .... Antonella Manotti
Lay Sisters .... Giuditta Poli, Anna Baldasserini

Gianandrea Gavazzeni, Orchestra and Chorus of Teatro alla Scala.

+• *Levine*, p. 78. + Plowright
+• *Ovation* 10, 8 (September 1989): 64, by Robert Levine.
+ Plowright

132. IL TABARRO by Giacomo Puccini.
1983. Home Vision (issued with the other operas of *Il Trittico, Gianni Schicchi* and *Suor Angelica*)

Stage production, Teatro alla Scala, Milan, Italy, 150 min. (total timing for the three operas in *Il Trittico*), stereo hi-fi, color, sung in Italian with English subtitles.
Producer, Sylvano Bussotti; sets and costumes, Silvia Lelli, Roberto Masotti, Luciano Morini; television director, Brian Large.

CAST:

Michele	Piero Cappuccilli
Giorgetta	Sylvia Sass
Luigi	Nicola Martinucci
Tinca	Sergio Bertocchi
Talpa	Aldo Bramante
Frugola	Eleonora Jankovic
Songseller	Ernesto Gavazzi
Lovers	Anna Baldasserini, Bruno Brando

Gianandrea Gavazzeni, Orchestra and Chorus of Teatro alla Scala.

- *Levine*, p. 78. – sets
- *Ovation* 10, 8 (September 1989): 64, by Robert Levine.

The Tales of Hoffmann
SEE Les Contes d'Hoffmann, 27.1.—27.3.

133.1. TANNHÄUSER by Richard Wagner.
1978. Philips (PolyGram)

Stage production, Bayreuth Festival, Germany, 190 min., stereo hi-fi, color, sung in German with English subtitles.
Director, Götz Friedrich; stage design and costumes, Jürgen Rose; choreography and video direction of *Bacchanal*, John Neumeier; artistic supervision, Wolfgang Wagner; video director, Thomas Oloffson. Includes Elisabeth and Tannhäuser scene in Act II.

CAST:

Tannhäuser	Spas Wenkoff
Elisabeth	Gwyneth Jones
Venus	Gwyneth Jones
Hermann, Landgrave of Thuringia	Hans Sotin
Wolfram von Eschenbach	Bernd Weikl
Biterolf	Franz Mazura
Young Shepherd	Klaus Brettschneider
Walter von der Vogelweide	Robert Schunk
Heinrich der Schreiber	John Pickering
Reinmar von Zweter	Heinz Feldhoff

Pages .... Irene Hammann
Angelika Jung-Nowski
Roswitha Korff-Krüger
Natuse von Stegmann
Solo Dancers .... Lynne Charles, Kevin Haigen

Colin Davis, Orchestra and Chorus of the Bayreuth Festival.

+ *Opera News* 56, 3 (September 1991): 48-49, by Harvey E. Phillips.

133.2. TANNHÄUSER by Richard Wagner.
1982. Bel Canto/Paramount Home Video

Stage production, Metropolitan Opera, New York City, videotaped on November 22 and December 20, 1982, 176 min., stereo hi-fi, color, sung in German with English subtitles.
Production, Otto Schenk; sets, Günther Schneider-Siemssen; costumes, Patricia Zipprodt; video director, Brian Large.

CAST:
Tannhäuser .... Richard Cassilly
Elisabeth .... Eva Marton
Venus .... Tatiana Troyanos
Hermann, Landgrave of Thuringia ..... John Macurdy
Wolfram von Eschenbach .... Bernd Weikl
Biterolf .... Richard J. Clark
Young Shepherd .... Bill Blaber
Walter von der Vogelweide .... Robert Nagy
Heinrich der Schreiber .... Charles Anthony
Reinmar von Zweter .... Richard Vernon
Pages .... Charle Coleman
Douglas McDonnell
Erik-Peter Mortensen
David Owen
Jean-Briac Perrette
Victor Ruggiero
Eric Sokolsky
Konstantin Walmsley

James Levine, Orchestra and Chorus of the Metropolitan Opera.

- *Classical* 6, 2 (February 1990): 25, by Robert Levine.
  – Cassilly, + Troyanos, Marton, Weikl
- *Levine*, p. 75. – Cassilly, + Troyanos, Marton, Weikl
- *Opera News* 51, 2 (August 1986): 50, by Richard Hornak.
  – Cassilly, + Troyanos, Marton, Weikl

134. THE TELEPHONE by Gian Carlo Menotti.
1992. London (PolyGram) (issued with *La Voix Humaine*, 148.)

Film version (BBC studio production), 23 min., stereo hi-fi, color, sung in the original English.

CAST:

Lucy . . . . Carole Farley
Ben . . . . Russell Smythe

José Serebrier, Scottish Chamber Orchestra.

+ *Fanfare* 16, 4 (March/April 1993): 419-420, by James Reel.

The Terrible Child
SEE L'Enfant et les Sortilèges

This Wine of Love
SEE L'Elisir d'Amore, 38.1.

The Threepenny Opera
SEE Die Dreigroschenoper

135.1. TOSCA by Giacomo Puccini.
1964. Lyric Distribution, Inc.

Stage production, Royal Opera House, Covent Garden, London, England, Act II only, mono, black and white, sung in Italian, no subtitles.
Producer, Franco Zeffirelli; designer, Tom Lingwood. A BBC telecast from February 9, 1964.

CAST:

Floria Tosca . . . . Maria Callas
Mario Cavaradossi . . . . Renato Cioni
Baron Scarpia . . . . Tito Gobbi
Sciarrone . . . . Dennis Wicks
Spoletta . . . . Robert Bowman

Carlo Felice Cillaro, Orchestra and Chorus of the Royal Opera House, Covent Garden.

Ardoin, John. *The Callas Legacy: A Biography of a Career*. rev. ed. NY: Scribner, 1982, p. 184-185.

135.2. TOSCA by Giacomo Puccini.
1976. London (PolyGram)

Film version, 116 min., stereo hi-fi, color, sung in Italian with English subtitles.
Producer, Kinloch Anderson; director, Gianfranco De Bosio; sets and costumes, Giancarlo Pucci. Singers lip sync to a prerecorded sound track of their own voices. Filmed on location in Rome.

CAST:
Floria Tosca . . . . Raina Kabaivanska
Mario Cavaradossi . . . . Plácido Domingo
Baron Scarpia . . . . Sherrill Milnes
Sacristan . . . . Alfredo Mariotti
Cesare Angelotti . . . . Giancarlo Luccardi
Spoletta . . . . Mario Ferrara
Sciarrone . . . . Bruno Grella
A Shepherd Boy . . . . Plácido Domingo, Jr.
A Jailer . . . . Domenico Medici

Bruno Bartoletti, New Philharmonia Orchestra, Ambrosian Singers.

+ *Opera Quarterly* 6, 3 (Spring 1989): 120-124, by Thor Eckert, Jr.
+ *Ovation* 9, 10 (November 1988): 44, by David Hurwitz.

135.3. TOSCA by Giacomo Puccini.
1984. HBO Video

Stage production, Arena di Verona, Italy, 126 min., stereo hi-fi, color, sung in Italian. This video was initially released without English subtitles; later issues may have subtitles.
Producer, Sylvano Bussotti; scenery and costumes, Fiorenzo Giorgi; television director, Brian Large.

CAST:
Floria Tosca . . . . Eva Marton
Mario Cavaradossi . . . . Giacomo Aragall
Baron Scarpia . . . . Ingvar Wixell
Sacristan . . . . Graziano Polidori
Cesare Angelotti . . . . Alfredo Giacomotti
Spoletta . . . . Mario Ferrara
Sciarrone . . . . Giuseppe Zecchillo
A Shepherd Boy . . . . Mario Bonizzato
A Jailer . . . . Gianni Brunelli

Daniel Oren, Orchestra and Chorus of the Arena di Verona.

• *Levine*, p. 75-77.
+ *Opera Canada* 28, 4 (Winter 1987): 52, by Ruby Mercer.
• *Opera News* 51, 4 (October 1986): 82, by Richard Hornak.

135.4. TOSCA by Giacomo Puccini.
1985. Bel Canto/Paramount Home Video

Stage production, Metropolitan Opera, New York City, videotaped on March 20 and 27, 1985, 127 min., stereo hi-fi, color, sung in Italian with English subtitles.
Production, Franco Zeffirelli; costumes, Peter Hall; video director, Kirk Browning. The opera is followed by a twenty-two minute segment titled *Tosca, Zeffirelli and Rome* in which Zeffirelli discusses the characters of the opera and the historic sites serving as a backdrop for the story.

CAST:

Floria Tosca . . . . Hildegard Behrens
Mario Cavaradossi . . . . Plácido Domingo
Baron Scarpia . . . . Cornell MacNeil
Sacristan . . . . Italo Tajo
Cesare Angelotti . . . . James Courtney
Spoletta . . . . Anthony Laciura
Sciarrone . . . . Russell Christopher
A Shepherd Boy . . . . Melissa Fogarty
A Jailer . . . . Richard Vernon

Giuseppe Sinopoli, Orchestra and Chorus of the Metropolitan Opera.

+ *Levine*, p. 77.
+ *Opera News* 51, 4 (October 1986): 82, by Richard Hornak.
• *Opera News* 51, 8 (January 3, 1987): 42, by John W. Freeman.

135.5. TOSCA by Giacomo Puccini.
1986. Kultur

Stage production, Australian Opera, Sydney, 123 min., stereo hi-fi, color, sung in Italian with English subtitles.
Director, John Copley.

CAST:

Floria Tosca . . . . Eva Marton
Mario Cavaradossi . . . . Lamberto Furlan
Baron Scarpia . . . . John Shaw
Sacristan . . . . John Germain
Cesare Angelotti . . . . Pieter van der Stolk
Spoletta . . . . Christopher Dawes
Sciarrone . . . . Robert Eddie
A Shepherd Boy . . . . Anthony Phipps
A Jailer . . . . Anthony Warlow

Alberto Erede, Elizabethan Sydney Orchestra, Australian Opera Chorus.

– *Opera News* 54, 13 (March 17, 1990): 38, by Harvey E. Phillips.

136.1. LA TRAVIATA by Giuseppe Verdi.
1955. Lyric Distribution, Inc.; Video Yesteryear

Television production, 53 min., abridged, mono, black and white, sung in Italian, no subtitles.
Producers and directors, Carlo Vinti and Marion Rhodes; staging (full costumes and sets), Anthony Stivanello; script, Joseph Vinti. Host John Ericson introduces each act in English. This program was part of the television series *Opera Cameos* that ran for five years on WABD-TV in New York and occasionally on the Dumont network. Musical director, Giuseppe Bamboschek.

CAST:
Violetta Valery .... Lucia Evangelista
Alfredo Germont .... Giulio Gari
Giorgio Germont .... Frank Valentino
Doctor Grenvil .... Carlo Tomanelli

136.2. LA TRAVIATA by Giuseppe Verdi.
1968. Video Artists International

Film version, 113 min., mono hi-fi, color, sung in Italian, no subtitles. English synopses precede each act.
Director, Mario Lanfranchi; designer, Maurizio Monteverde; photographer, Leonida Barboni; choreographer, Gino Landi. Made at the INCIR-De Paolis Studios and recorded at the NIS Films Studios, Rome, Italy. Singers lip sync to a prerecorded sound track of their own voices. Originally issued as a motion picture.

CAST:
Violetta Valery .... Anna Moffo
Alfredo Germont .... Franco Bonisolli
Giorgio Germont .... Gino Bechi
Flora Bervoix .... Mafalda Micheluzzi
Gastone de Letorières .... Glauco Scarlini
Baron Douphol .... Arturo La Porta
Marquis d'Obigny .... Maurizio Piacenti
Doctor Grenvil .... Afro Poli
Annina .... Gianna Lollini
Giuseppe .... Athos Cesarini

Giuseppe Patanè, Orchestra and Chorus of the Rome Opera House.

- *Motion Picture Guide.*

136.3. LA TRAVIATA by Giuseppe Verdi.
1973. 16mm rental, Iowa State University

Film version, 57 min., abridged, mono, color, sung in English.
Translation and musical direction, Peter Murray. Filmed at Knebworth House, Hertfordshire, England. Part of the *Focus on Opera* series directed by Peter Seabourne. Originally released by Chatsworth Film Distributors; U.S. distributor, Centron Educational Films.

CAST:

Violetta Valery .... Valerie Masterson
Alfredo Germont .... Kenneth Woollam
Giorgio Germont .... Michael Wakeham
Flora Bervoix .... Ann Hood
Baron Douphol .... Clifford Parkes
Doctor Grenvil .... Glyn Houston
Annina .... Ann Hood

John J. Davies, the Classical Orchestra

\+ *Landers Film Reviews* 26, 3 (January/February 1982): 110.

136.4. LA TRAVIATA by Giuseppe Verdi.
1976. Video Artists International

Stage production, Filene Center Auditorium in Wolf Trap Farm Park for the Performing Arts, Vienna, Virginia, 145 min., mono hi-fi, color, sung in Italian with English subtitles.
Producer, Tito Capobianco; video director, Kirk Browning.

CAST:

Violetta Valery .... Beverly Sills
Alfredo Germont .... Henry Price
Giorgio Germont .... Richard Fredricks
Flora Bervoix .... Fredda Rakusin
Gastone de Letorières .... Neil Rosenshein
Baron Douphol .... Robert Orth
Marquis d'Obigny .... Keith Kibler
Doctor Grenvil .... John Cheek
Annina .... Evelyn Petros
Giuseppe .... Roger Lucas
Gardener .... Christopher Deane

Julius Rudel, Filene Center Orchestra, Wolf Trap Company Chorus.

\+ *Opera News* 57, 13 (March 13, 1993): 44, by Harvey E. Phillips.

136.5. LA TRAVIATA by Giuseppe Verdi.
1982. MCA Home Video

Film version, 105 min., stereo hi-fi, color, sung in Italian with English subtitles.
Producer, Tarak Ben Ammar; written, designed, and directed by Franco Zeffirelli; costumes, Piero Tosi; choreographer, Alberto Testa; photography, Ennio Guarnieri. Singers, actors, and actresses lip sync to a prerecorded sound track; Stratas, Domingo, MacNeil, and Monk act and sing.

CAST:
Singers are listed first; actors and actresses are listed second.

Violetta Valery	Teresa Stratas
Alfredo Germont	Plácido Domingo
Giorgio Germont	Cornell MacNeil
Flora Bervoix	Geraldine Decker/Axelle Gall
Gastone de Letorières	Michael Best/ Maurizio Barbacini
Baron Douphol	Allan Monk
Marquis d'Obigny	Russell Christopher/ Richard Oneto
Doctor Grenvil	Ferruccio Furlanetto/ Robert Sommer
Annina	Ariel Bybee/Pina Cei
Giuseppe	Charles Anthony/Luciano Brizi
Messenger	Richard Vernon/Tony Ammariti
Young Porter (non-singing)	Renato Cestie
Alfredo's Sister (non-singing)	Dominique Journet

James Levine, Orchestra and Chorus of the Metropolitan Opera.

+ *Levine*, p. 98-99.
+ *Motion Picture Guide.*
+ *Opera Canada* 24, 3 (Fall 1983): 52, by Aldo Maggiorotti.
– *Opera (England)* 34, 12 (December 1983): 1372-1374, by Harold Rosenthal.
• *Opera News* 49, 14 (March 30, 1985): 43, by Richard Hornak.
+ *Opera News*, 56, 2 (August 1991): 44-45, "The Basics," by Harvey E. Phillips.
+ *Opera Quarterly* 5, 2-3 (Summer/Autumn 1987): 153-154, by Robert Levine.
+– *Variety* 309, 7 (December 15, 1982): 20.

Solomon, Roxanne Elizabeth. *A Critical Study of Franco Zeffirelli's La Traviata*. Dissertation, EDD (Columbia University Teachers College), 1987.

136.6. LA TRAVIATA by Giuseppe Verdi.
1987. Home Vision

Film version, made at Glyndebourne, England, 135 min., stereo hi-fi, color, sung in Italian with English subtitles.
Production, Peter Hall; sets and costumes, John Gunter; video producer, Derek Bailey. Blue Ribbon winner, American Film and Video Festival, 1989.

CAST:
Violetta Valery . . . . Marie McLaughlin
Alfredo Germont . . . . Walter MacNeil
Giorgio Germont . . . . Brent Ellis
Flora Bervoix . . . . Jane Turner
Gastone de Letorières . . . . David Hillman
Baron Douphol . . . . Gordon Sandison
Marquis d'Obigny . . . . . Christopher Thornton-Holmes
Doctor Grenvil . . . . John Hall
Annina . . . . Enid Hartle
Giuseppe . . . . Martyn Harrison
Messenger . . . . Charles Kerry

Bernard Haitink, London Philharmonic Orchestra, Glyndebourne Festival Chorus.

+– *Classical* 2, 3 (March 1990): 35, by Robert Levine.
+ *Landers Film Reviews* 33, 3 (Spring 1989): 122.
+ *Opera Canada* 30, 4 (Winter 1989): 52, by Ruby Mercer.
+ *Opera News* 54, 2 (August 1989): 35, by Harvey E. Phillips.

137. TREEMONISHA by Scott Joplin.
1982. Kultur

Stage production, Houston Grand Opera, Texas, 86 min., stereo hi-fi, color, sung in the original English.
Director, Sydney Smith; sets and costumes, Franco Colavecchia; staging, Frank Cosaro; orchestration by Gunther Schuller. Filmed at the Miller Outdoor Theater, Houston, Texas.

CAST:
Treemonisha . . . . Carmen Balthrop
Zodzetrick . . . . Obba Babatunde
Monisha . . . . Delores Ivory
Remus . . . . Curtis Rayam
Ned . . . . Dorceal Duckens
Andy . . . . Kenn Hicks
Lucy . . . . Cora Johnson
Simon . . . . Raymond Bazemore
Cephus . . . . Michael Grey
Luddud . . . . Cleveland Williams
Parson Alltalk . . . . Ray Jacobs

John DeMain, Orchestra of the Houston Grand Opera.

\+ *Library Journal* 115, 9 (May 15, 1990): 110, by Adrienne Fischier.
\+ *Opera Canada* 29, 3 (Fall 1988): 52, by Ruby Mercer.
++ *Video Librarian* 5, 4 (June 1990): 15.

138. TRIAL BY JURY by W.S. Gilbert & Sir Arthur Sullivan.
1974. 16mm film: Rochester Public Library, Reynolds Audio Visual Dept., 115 South Ave., Rochester, NY 14604 716-428-7333

Film version, 50 min., abridged, mono, color, sung in the original English.
Producer, John Seabourne; director, Trevor Evans; script, David Maverovitch; photography, Adrian Jenkins; narrators, Johnny Wayne, Frank Shuster. Part of the *World of Gilbert and Sullivan* series.

CAST:
Learned Judge . . . . Lawrence Richard
Counsel for the Plaintiff . . . . Michael Wakeham
Defendant . . . . Thomas Round
Foreman of the Jury . . . . John Banks
Usher . . . . Donald Adams
Associate . . . . Norman Meadmore
Plaintiff . . . . Gillian Humphreys

139. TRISTAN UND ISOLDE by Richard Wagner.
1983. Philips (PolyGram)

Stage production, Bayreuth Festival, Germany, 245 min., stereo hi-fi, color, sung in German with English subtitles.
Set design, costumes, staging, and direction, Jean-Pierre Ponnelle; artistic supervision, Wolfgang Wagner.

CAST:
Tristan . . . . René Kollo
Isolde . . . . Johanna Meier
Brangäne . . . . Hanna Schwarz
Melot . . . . Robert Schunk
Kurwenal . . . . Hermann Becht
King Marke . . . . Matti Salminen
A Shepherd . . . . Helmut Pampuch
A Helmsman . . . . Martin Egel
Young Sailor . . . . Robert Schunk

Daniel Barenboim, Orchestra and Chorus of the Bayreuth Festival.

– *Fanfare* 16, 2 (November/December 1992): 486, by James Reel.
• *Opera News* 57, 8 (January 2, 1993): 44, by Harvey E. Phillips.

Il Trittico
    SEE Gianni Schicchi, 57.
        Suor Angelica, 131.
        Il Tabarro, 132.

The Trojans
    SEE Les Troyens, 142.

140. TROUBLE IN TAHITI: An Opera in Seven Scenes by Leonard Bernstein.
1973. Kultur

Television production, 46 min., stereo hi-fi, color, sung in the original English.
Producer, David Griffiths, WNET NY; director, Billy Hays; designer, Eileen Diss; graphic sequences designer, Pat Gavin.

CAST:

Dinah	Nancy Williams
Sam	Julian Patrick
Trio	Antonia Butler
	Michael Clark
	Mark Brown

Leonard Bernstein, London Symphonic Wind Band.

141.1. IL TROVATORE by Giuseppe Verdi.
1957. Lyric Distribution, Inc.; Bel Canto Society

Television production (Italian television), about 125 min., mono, black and white, sung in Italian, no subtitles.

CAST:

Leonora	Leyla Gencer
Manrico	Mario Del Monaco
Count di Luna	Ettore Bastianini
Azucena	Fedora Barbieri
Ferrando	Plinio Clabassi
Ines	Laura Londi
Ruiz	Athos Cesarini
An Old Gypsy	Sergio Liliani
A Messenger	Walter Artioli

Fernando Previtali, Orchestra and Chorus of Radio Italiana Televisione.

+ *Opera News* 51, 9 (January 17, 1987): 42, by Thor Eckert, Jr.
  – technical aspects
+ *Opera Quarterly* 5, 2-3 (Summer/Autumn 1987): 151-152, by Robert Levine.
  – technical aspects

141.2. IL TROVATORE by Giuseppe Verdi.
1983. SVS, Inc. (SONY)

Stage production, Australian Opera, Sydney, videotaped on July 2, 1983, 138 min., stereo hi-fi, color, sung in Italian with English subtitles.
Producer, Elijah Moshinsky; director, Riccardo Pellizzeri; sets, Sidney Nolan; costumes, Luciana Arrighi; television producer, Brian Adams.

CAST:

Leonora	Joan Sutherland
Manrico	Kenneth Collins
Count di Luna	Jonathan Summers
Azucena	Lauris Elms
Ferrando	Donald Shanks
Ines	Cynthia Johnston
Ruiz	Robin Donald
An Old Gypsy	John Durham

Richard Bonynge, Elizabethan Sydney Orchestra, Australian Opera Chorus.

+– *Levine*, p. 80. + Sutherland, Elms
\+ *Opera Canada* 29, 1 (Spring 1988): 52, by Ruby Mercer.
\+ *Opera (England)* 42, 12 (December 1991): 1493-1494, by Charles Osborne.
– *Opera News* 50, 13 (March 15, 1986): 41, by Richard Hornak.
+– *Opera Quarterly* 5, 2-3 (Summer/Autumn 1987): 152, by Robert Levine. + Sutherland, Elms

141.3. IL TROVATORE by Giuseppe Verdi.
1985. Home Vision

Stage production, Arena di Verona, Italy, 145 min., stereo hi-fi, color, sung in Italian with English subtitles.
Costumes, Gabriella Pescussi; video director, Brian Large.

CAST:

Leonora	Rosalind Plowright
Manrico	Franco Bonisolli
Count di Luna	Giorgio Zancanaro
Azucena	Fiorenza Cossotto
Ferrando	Paolo Washington
Ines	Giuliana Matteini
Ruiz	Gian Paolo Corradi
An Old Gypsy	Bruno Grella
A Messenger	Bruno Balbo

Reynald Giovaninetti, Orchestra and Chorus of the Arena di Verona.

\+ *Levine*, p. 79-80.
• *Opera News* 52, 6 (December 5, 1987): 57, by Harvey E. Phillips.
\+ *Opera Quarterly* 5, 2-3 (Summer/Autumn 1987): 152, by Robert Levine.

141.4. IL TROVATORE by Giuseppe Verdi.
1988. Deutsche Grammophon (PolyGram)

Stage production, Metropolitan Opera, New York City, 133 min., stereo hi-fi, color, sung in Italian with English subtitles.
Production, Fabrizio Melano; sets, Ezio Frigerio; costumes, Franca Squarciapino; video director, Brian Large.

CAST:

Leonora	Eva Marton
Manrico	Luciano Pavarotti
Count di Luna	Sherrill Milnes
Azucena	Dolora Zajic
Ferrando	Jeffrey Wells
Ines	Loretta Di Franco
Ruiz	Mark Baker
An Old Gypsy	Ray Morrison
A Messenger	John Bills

James Levine, Orchestra and Chorus of the Metropolitan Opera.

+– *Opera (England)* 43, 12 (December 1992): 1446-1447, by Noël Goodwin. + singing, – staging

142. LES TROYENS by Hector Berlioz.
1983. Bel Canto/Paramount Home Video

Stage production, Metropolitan Opera, New York City, videotaped on October 8, 1983, 253 min., stereo hi-fi, color, sung in French with English subtitles.
Staging, Fabrizio Melano; sets, costumes, and visual effects, Peter Wexler; television director, Brian Large.

CAST:

Dido, Queen of Carthage	Tatiana Troyanos
Cassandre	Jessye Norman
Enée (Aeneas)	Plácido Domingo
Chorèbe	Allan Monk
Narbal	Paul Plishka
A Trojan Soldier	Vernon Hartman
Helenus, Son of Priam	Robert Nagy
Ascagne	Claudia Catania
Hécube	Barbara Conrad
Panthée	John Cheek
Priam, King of Troy	John Macurdy
Ghost of Hector	Morley Meredith
Anna	Jocelyne Taillon
Iopas	Douglas Ahlstedt
The God Mercury	Julien Robbins
Hylas	Philip Creech

First Soldier .... John Darrenkamp
Second Soldier .... James Courtney
Ghost of Priam .... James Courtney
Ghost of Chorèbe .... Allan Glassman
Ghost of Cassandre .... Jean Kraft
Andromaque, Widow of Hector (non-singing) ....
Jane White
Astryanax, Her Son (non-singing) .... Robert Sanchez

James Levine, Orchestra and Chorus of the Metropolitan Opera.

•– *Opera News* 50, 17 (June 1986): 49, by John W. Freeman.
– *Opera News* 52, 1 (July 1987): 50, by Thor Eckert, Jr.
+ Norman

143. THE TSAR'S BRIDE by Nikolay Rimsky-Korsakov.
1966. Kultur

Feature film, Bolshoi Theatre, Russia/Soviet Union, 95 min., abridged, mono hi-fi, black and white, sung in Russian with English subtitles.
Director, Vladimir Gorikker; art director, G. Balodis; screenplay, Vladimir Gorikker and A. Donatov based on Rimsky-Korsakov's opera. Actors and actresses lip sync to a prerecorded sound track. Originally issued as a motion picture in the Soviet Union by Riga Film Studio/Artkino.

CAST:
Singers are listed first; actors and actresses are listed second.

Marfa ... Galina Oleinichenko/Raisa Nedashkovskaya
Lyubasha .... Larissa Avdeeva/Natalya Rudnaya
Grigori Gryaznoy .... Evgeny Gavrilovich Kibkalo/
Otar Koberidze
Malyuta Skuratov .... Aleksei Geleva/G. Shevtsov
Bomeliy .... P. Chekin/V. Zeldin
Sobakin .... Aleksandr Vedernikov/Nikolay Timofeyev
Dunyasha .... Valentina Klepatskaya/M. Maltseva
Saburova .... Tatiana Tugarinova/T. Loginova
Ivan Lykov .... Evgeny Raikov/Viktor Nuzhny
Ivan the Terrible (non-singing) .... Pyotr Glebov

Evgeny Fedorovich Svetlanov, Orchestra and Chorus of the Bolshoi Theatre.

+ *Classical* 2, 11 (November 1990): 53, by Robert Levine.
+ *Levine*, p. 99-100.
+ *Motion Picture Guide*.
+ *Opera News* 50, 13 (March 15, 1986): 40, by Richard Hornak.
+ *Opera Quarterly* 8, 4 (Winter 1991/92): 112-114, by Harlow Robinson.

Tsarskaya Nevesta
SEE The Tsar's Bride, 143.

144.1. TURANDOT by Giacomo Puccini.
1983. HBO Video

Stage production, Arena di Verona, Italy, 116 min., stereo hi-fi, color, sung in Italian with English subtitles.
Producer, Giuliano Montaldo; scenery, Luciano Ricceri; costumes, Nana Cecchi; television director, Brian Large.

CAST:

Princess Turandot . . . . Gena Macheva Dimitrova
Calaf . . . . Nicola Martinucci
Liù . . . . Cecilia Gasdia
Timur . . . . Ivo Vinco
Ping . . . . Graziano Polidori
Pang . . . . Pier Francesco Poli
Pong . . . . Antonio Bevacqua
Emperor Altoum . . . . Gianfranco Manganotti
A Mandarin . . . . Orazio Mori
Prince of Persia . . . . Ivan Del Manto

Maurizio Arena, Orchestra and Chorus of the Arena di Verona.

+ *Levine*, p. 81-82.
• *Opera News* 53, 13 (March 18, 1989): 44, by C.J. Luten.
  + Dimitrova
+ *Opera Quarterly* 6, 1 (August 1988): 107-109, by Thor Eckert, Jr.
  + Dimitrova
+ *Ovation* 9, 2 (March 1988): 36, by Dick Adler.

144.2. TURANDOT by Giacomo Puccini.
1983. MGM/UA Home Video

Stage production, Vienna State Opera, Austria, 138 min., stereo hi-fi, color, sung in Italian with English subtitles.
Director, Hal Prince; designer, Timothy O'Brien and Tazeena Firth.

CAST:

Princess Turandot . . . . Eva Marton
Calaf . . . . José Carreras
Liù . . . . Katia Ricciarelli
Timur . . . . John Paul Bogart
Ping . . . . Robert Kerns
Pang . . . . Helmut Wildhaber
Pong . . . . Heinz Zednik
Emperor Altoum . . . . Waldemar Kmentt
A Mandarin . . . . Kurt Rydl
Prince of Persia . . . . Bela Perencz

Lorin Maazel, Orchestra and Chorus of the Vienna State Opera, Vienna Boy's Choir.

++ *Levine*, p. 81-82.
•– *Opera News* 49, 14 (March 30, 1985): 43, by Richard Hornak.

144.3. TURANDOT by Giacomo Puccini.
1987. Deutsche Grammophon (PolyGram)

Stage production, Metropolitan Opera, New York City, 134 min., stereo hi-fi, color, sung in Italian with English subtitles.
Production, Franco Zeffirelli; video director, Kirk Browning.

CAST:

Princess Turandot	Eva Marton
Calaf	Plácido Domingo
Liù	Leona Mitchell
Timur	Paul Plishka
Ping	Brian Schexnayder
Pang	Allan Glassman
Pong	Anthony Laciura
Emperor Altoum	Hugues Cuénod
A Mandarin	Arthur Thompson
Prince of Persia	Scott Forest
Girls (non-singing)	Pauline Andrey
	Linda Gelinas
	Suzanne Laurence
	Ellen Rievman
Maschere (non-singing)	Gary Cordial
	Christophe Stocker
	Joseph Fritz
Il Carnefice (non-singing)	Roger Koch
Due Ancelle di Turn	Suzanne Der Derian
	Beverly Hulse

James Levine, Orchestra and Chorus of the Metropolitan Opera.

+ *Classical* 2, 8 (August 1990): 31, by Tom Di Nardo.
+ *New York* 22, 39 (October 2, 1989): 80, by Peter G. Davis.
+ *Opera News*, 56, 2 (August 1991): 44-45, "The Basics," by Harvey E. Phillips.
++ *Video Review* 11, 1 (April 1990): 98, by Christie Barter.

145. THE TURN OF THE SCREW by Benjamin Britten.
1982. Philips (PolyGram)

Film version, 116 min., stereo hi-fi, color, sung in the original English.
Producers, Zdeňek Oves, Hans-Günter Herbertz; director, Petr Weigl; scenery, Miloš Červinka; costumes, Milan Čorba. Actors and actresses lip sync to a prerecorded sound track.

CAST:
Singers are listed first; actors and actresses are listed second.

Governess . . . . . . Helen Donath/Magdalena Vášáryová
Miss Jessel . . . . Heather Harper/Emilia Vášáryová
Quint . . . . Robert Tear/Juraj Kukura
Mrs. Grose . . . . Ava June/Dana Medřická
Miles . . . . Michael Ginn/Michael Gulyás
Prologue (Tenor) . . . . Philip Langridge
Flora . . . . Lillian Watson/Beata Blažičková
Guardian (non-singing) . . . . Vladimir Müller

Colin Davis, Orchestra and Chorus of the Royal Opera House, Covent Garden.

\+ *New York* 21, 38 (September 26, 1988): 127, by Peter G. Davis.

Twilight of the Gods
SEE Die Götterdämmerung, 63.1.—63.2.

The Valkyrie
SEE Die Walküre, 149.1.—149.2.

Les Vêpres Siciliennes
SEE I Vespri Siciliani, 146.1.—146.2.

146.1. I VESPRI SICILIANI by Giuseppe Verdi.
1986. Home Vision

Stage production, Teatro comunale di Bologna, Italy, 155 min., stereo hi-fi, color, sung in Italian with English subtitles.
Producer and television director, Luca Ronconi; sets and costumes, Pasquale Grossi.

CAST:

Duchess Elena . . . . Susan Dunn
Guido di Monforte . . . . Leo Nucci
Arrigo . . . . Veriano Luchetti
Giovanni da Procida . . . . Bonaldo Giaiotti
di Bethune . . . . Gianfranco Casarini
Count Vaudemont . . . . Sergio Fontana
Tebaldo . . . . Bruno Lazzaretti
Roberto . . . . Giuseppe Morresi

Ninetta . . . . Anna Caterina Antonacci
Danieli . . . . Sergio Bertocchi
Manfredo . . . . Walter Brighi

Riccardo Chailly, Orchestra and Chorus of the Teatro comunale di Bologna.

\+ *Landers Film Reviews* 32, 3 (Spring 1988): 119.

146.2. I VESPRI SICILIANI by Giuseppe Verdi.
1989. Home Vision

Stage production, Teatro alla Scala, Milan, Italy, 210 min., stereo hi-fi, color, sung in Italian with English subtitles.
Stage director, sets and costumes, Pierluigi Pizzi; video director, Christopher Swann. The third act ballet is performed.

CAST:

Duchess Elena . . . . Cheryl Studer
Guido di Monforte . . . . Giorgio Zancanaro
Arrigo . . . . Chris Merritt
Giovanni da Procida . . . . Ferruccio Furlanetto
di Bethune . . . . Enzo Capuano
Count Vaudemont . . . . Francesco Musinu
Tebaldo . . . . Paolo Barbacini
Roberto . . . . Marco Chingari
Ninetta . . . . Gloria Banditelli
Danieli . . . . Ernesto Gavazzi
Manfredo . . . . Ferreo Poggi
Dancers . . . . Carla Fracci, Wayne Eagling

Riccardo Muti, Orchestra and Chorus of Teatro alla Scala.

147. A VILLAGE ROMEO AND JULIET by Frederick Delius.
1989. London (PolyGram)

Film version, 113 min., stereo hi-fi, color, sung in the original English.
Director, Petr Weigl. Actors and actresses lip sync to a prerecorded sound track.

CAST:

Singers are listed first; actors and actresses are listed second.

Vreli . . . . Helen Field/Dana Moravkova
Sali . . . . Arthur Davies/Michal Dlouhy
Dark Fiddler . . . . Thomas Hampson
Manz . . . . Barry Mora/Leopold Haverl
Marti . . . . Stafford Dean/Pavel Mikulik
Vreli as a Child . . . . Pamela Mildehall/
Katerina Svobodova
Sala as a Child . . . . Samuel Linay/Jan Kalous

Sir Charles Mackerras, the ÖRF Symphony, Arnold-Schoenberg-Choir.

\+ *Fanfare* 16, 2 (November/December 1992): 487, by James Reel.

148. LA VOIX HUMAINE by Francis Poulenc.
1992. London (PolyGram) (issued with *The Telephone*, 134.)

Film version (BBC studio production), 43 min., color, sung in French with English subtitles.

CAST:
The Woman . . . . Carole Farley

José Serebrier, Scottish Chamber Orchestra.

\+ *Fanfare* 16, 4 (March/April 1993): 419-420, by James Reel.

149.1. DIE WALKÜRE by Richard Wagner.
1980. Philips (PolyGram)

Stage production, Bayreuth Festival, Germany, 216 min., stereo hi-fi, color, sung in German with English subtitles.
Modern version by Pierre Boulez and director Patrice Chéreau; design, Richard Peduzzi; costumes, Jacques Schmidt; video director, Brian Large.

CAST:
Siegmund . . . . Peter Hofmann
Hunding . . . . Matti Salminen
Wotan . . . . Donald McIntyre
Brünnhilde . . . . Gwyneth Jones
Sieglinde . . . . Jeannine Altmeyer
Fricka . . . . Hanna Schwarz
Gerhilde . . . . Carmen Reppel
Ortlinde . . . . Karen Middleton
Helmwige . . . . Katie Clarke
Waltraute . . . . Gabriele Schnaut
Siegrune . . . . Marga Schiml
Grimgerde . . . . Ilse Gramatzki
Schwertleite . . . . Gwendolyn Killebrew
Rossweisse . . . . Elisabeth Glauser

Pierre Boulez, Orchestra and Chorus of the Bayreuth Festival.

\+ *Classical* 14, 5 (November 1991): 43-44, by Neil Crory.
++ *New York* 25, 20 (May 18, 1992): 65-66, by Peter G. Davis.

149.2. DIE WALKÜRE by Richard Wagner.
1989. Deutsche Grammophon (PolyGram)

Stage production, Metropolitan Opera, New York City, 244 min., stereo hi-fi, color, sung in German with English subtitles.
Production, Otto Schenk; sets, Günther Schneider-Siemssen; costumes, Rolf Langenfass; video director, Brian Large.

CAST:
Siegmund .... Gary Lakes
Hunding .... Kurt Moll
Wotan .... James Morris
Brünnhilde .... Hildegard Behrens
Sieglinde .... Jessye Norman
Fricka .... Christa Ludwig
Gerhilde .... Pyramid Sellers
Ortlinde .... Martha Thigpen
Helmwige .... Katarina Ikonomu
Waltraute .... Joyce Castle
Siegrune .... Diane Kesling
Grimgerde .... Wendy Hillhouse
Schwertleite .... Sondra Kelly
Rossweisse .... Jacalyn Bower

James Levine, Orchestra and Chorus of the Metropolitan Opera.

– *New York* 25, 20 (May 18, 1992): 65-66, by Peter G. Davis.

150. WERTHER by Jules Massenet.
1985. European Video Distributors

Film version, 107 min., stereo hi-fi, color, sung in French, no subtitles.
Director, Petr Weigl. Actors and actresses lip sync to a prerecorded sound track; Dvorský and Fassbaender act and sing.

CAST:
Singers are listed first; actors and actresses are listed second.

Charlotte .... Brigitte Fassbaender
Werther .... Peter Dvorský
Albert .... Hans Helm/Michal Dočolomanský
Sophie .. Magdaléna Hajóssyová/Magdalena Vásáryová
Otee .... Peter Mikuláš/František Zvarík
The credits do not identify the following individuals as actors and/or singers ....
Beata Blažičková
Lucie Blažičková
Simona Kolářová
Otto Ohensorg
Jiřina Jelenská

Libor Pešek, Prague Radio Symphony Orchestra.

+ *Levine*, p. 101-102.
– *Opera News* 53, 9 (January 21, 1989): 41, by Harvey E. Phillips. + Fassbaender

151. WHERE THE WILD THINGS ARE by Oliver Knussen.
1985. Home Vision (laser disc issued with *Higglety Pigglety Pop!*, 68.)

Stage production without an audience, filmed at Glyndebourne, England, 40 min., stereo hi-fi, color, sung in the original English.
Director and choreographer, Frank Corsaro; designer, Maurice Sendak; choreographer, Jonathan Wolken; video director, Christopher Swann.

CAST:
Singers are listed first; dancers are listed second.

Max . . . . Karen Beardsley
Mama . . . . Mary King
The Wild Things:
Tzippy . . . . Mary King/Jenny Weston
Moishe . . . . Hugh Hetherington/Perry Davey
Bruno . . . . Jeremy Munro/Cengiz Saner
Emile . . . . Stephen Rhys-Williams/Brian Andro
Bernard . . . . Andrew Gallacher/Bernard Bennet
Goat . . . . Hugh Hetherington/Mike Gallant

Oliver Knussen, the London Sinfonietta.

++ *Levine*, p. 82-83.
+ *Opera News* 52, 10 (January 30, 1988): 40, by Thor Eckert, Jr.
+ *Ovation* 10, 3 (April 1989): 73, 75, by Robert Levine.

152.1.–152.8. WHO'S AFRAID OF OPERA? series.
The eight programs that make up the *Who's Afraid of Opera?* series were originally issued in the early 1970s on 16mm film by Nathan Kroll. The series was re-released on video in the late 1980s, first by MGM/UA Home Video and then by Kultur. The video releases featured two programs per videotape.
Directors, Ted Kotcheff, Herbert Wise; screenplay, Claire Merrill; the Larry Berthelson Puppeteers: Billy (Larry Berthelson), Rudi (Danny Seagren), Sir William (Rod Young).

152.1. WHO'S AFRAID OF OPERA? IL BARBIERE DI SIVIGLIA by Gioacchino Rossini.
1972. *Barbiere* is issued on videotape as volume three with *Lucia di Lammermoor*.

Film version, 30 min., abridged, hi-fi, color, sung in Italian with English dialogue.

CAST:

Rosina .... Joan Sutherland
Count Almaviva .... Ramon Remedios
Figaro .... Tom McDonnell
Doctor Bartolo .... Spiro Malas
Basilio .... Clifford Grant

Richard Bonynge, London Symphony Orchestra.

+ *Opera News* 49, 13 (March 30, 1985): 43, by Richard Hornak. A review of volumes 1, 2, and 3 on videotape.

152.2. WHO'S AFRAID OF OPERA? FAUST by Charles Gounod.
1973. *Faust* is issued on videotape as volume one with *Rigoletto*.

Film version, 30 min., abridged, hi-fi, color, sung in French with English dialogue.

CAST:

Marguérite .... Joan Sutherland
Faust .... Ian Caley
Valentine .... Pieter van der Stolk
Mephistophélès .... Joseph Rouleau
Siebel .... Margreta Elkins

Richard Bonynge, National Philharmonic.

+ *Landers Film Reviews* 20, 2 (November/December 1975): 68-69.

152.3. WHO'S AFRAID OF OPERA? LA FILLE DU RÉGIMENT by Gaetano Donizetti.
1972. *Fille* is issued on videotape as volume two with *La Traviata*.

Film version, 30 min., abridged, hi-fi, color, sung in Italian with English dialogue.

CAST:

Marie .... Joan Sutherland
Tonio .... Ramon Remedios
Sergeant Suplice .... Spiro Malas
Marquise de Birkenfeld .... Monica Sinclair

Richard Bonynge, London Symphony Orchestra.

+ *Landers Film Reviews* 20, 2 (November/December 1975): 63-64.

152.4. WHO'S AFRAID OF OPERA? LUCIA DI LAMMERMOOR by Gaetano Donizetti.
1972. *Lucia* is issued on videotape as volume three with *Il Barbiere di Siviglia*.

Film version, 30 min., abridged, hi-fi, color, sung in Italian with English dialogue.
Director, Piers Haggard; Sutherland's costumes by Franco Zeffirelli.

CAST:

Lucia . . . . Joan Sutherland
Edgardo . . . . John Brecknock
Enrico Ashton . . . . Pieter van der Stolk
Raimondo . . . . Clifford Grant
Alisa . . . . Ailsa Gamley
Lord Arturo Bucklaw . . . . Francis Egerton

Richard Bonynge, London Symphony Orchestra.

152.5. WHO'S AFRAID OF OPERA? MIGNON by Ambroise Thomas.
1973. *Mignon* is issued on videotape as volume four with *La Périchole*.

Film version, 30 min., abridged, hi-fi, color, sung in French with English dialogue.

CAST:

Philine . . . . Joan Sutherland
Mignon . . . . Huguette Turangeau
Wilhelm Meister . . . . Ian Caley
Lothario . . . . Pieter van der Stolk
Laertes . . . . Brian Ralph
Jarno . . . . Gordon Wilcock

Richard Bonynge, London Symphony Orchestra.

+ *Landers Film Reviews* 19, 7 (March 1975): 229.

152.6. WHO'S AFRAID OF OPERA? LA PÉRICHOLE by Jacques Offenbach.
1972. *La Périchole* is issued on videotape as volume four with *Mignon*.

Film version, 30 min., abridged, hi-fi, color, sung in French with English dialogue.

CAST:

La Périchole .... Joan Sutherland
Piquillo .... Pieter van der Stolk
The Viceroy .... Francis Egerton
Don Pedro .... John Fryatt
Panatellas .... Gordon Wilcock
Three Cousins .... Ailsa Gamely
Joy Mammen
Monica Sinclair

Richard Bonynge, London Symphony Orchestra.

152.7. WHO'S AFRAID OF OPERA? RIGOLETTO by Giuseppe Verdi. **1973**. *Rigoletto* is issued on videotape as volume one with *Faust*.

Film version, 30 min., abridged, hi-fi, color, sung in Italian with English dialogue.

CAST:

Rigoletto .... Pieter van der Stolk
Duke of Mantua .... Andre Turp
Gilda .... Joan Sutherland
Sparafucile .... Nilson Taylor
Maddalena .... Huguette Turangeau

Richard Bonynge, London Symphony Orchestra.

\+ *Landers Film Reviews* 19, 7 (March 1975): 233-234.

152.8. WHO'S AFRAID OF OPERA? LA TRAVIATA by Giuseppe Verdi. **1973**. La *Traviata* is issued on videotape as volume two with *La Fille du Régiment*.

Film version, 30 min., abridged, hi-fi, color, sung in Italian with English dialogue.

CAST:

Violetta Valery .... Joan Sutherland
Alfredo Germont .... Ian Caley
Giorgio Germont .... Pieter van der Stolk
Flora Bervoix .... Monica Sinclair
Baron Douphol .... Gordon Wilcock
Annina .... Ailsa Gamley
Doctor Grenvil .... John Gibbs

Richard Bonynge, National Philharmonic.

World of Gilbert and Sullivan series
SEE The Gondoliers, 62.1.
H.M.S. Pinafore, 64.2.
Iolanthe, A19.
The Mikado, 97.3.
The Pirates of Penzance, 111.1.
Ruddigore, 121.1.
Trial by Jury, 138.
Yeomen of the Guard, 155.1.

153. WOZZECK by Alban Berg.
1987. Home Vision

Stage production, Vienna State Opera, Austria, 96 min., stereo hi-fi, color, sung in German with English subtitles.
Director, Adolf Dresen; designer, Herbert Kapplmueller; television director, Brian Large.

CAST:

Wozzeck	Franz Grundheber
Marie	Hildegard Behrens
Marie's Child	Viktoria Lehner
Captain	Heinz Zednik
Doctor	Aage Haugland
Drum-major	Walter Raffeiner
Andres	Philip Langridge
Margret	Anna Gonda
Fool	Peter Jelosits
Apprentices	Alfred Sramek, Alexander Maly
Soldier	Elmar Breneis
Innkeeper	Adolf Tomaschek

Claudio Abbado, Orchestra and Chorus of the Vienna State Opera.

+ *Opera (England)* 43, 7 (July 1992): 871-873, by David Murray.
+ *Opera Quarterly* 8, 1 (Spring 1991): 115-116, by David McKee.

154. XERXES by George Frideric Handel.
1988. Home Vision

Stage production, English National Opera at the London Coliseum, England, 186 min., stereo hi-fi, color, sung in English, translation by Nicholas Hytner.
Director, Nicholas Hytner; sets, David Fielding; video director, John Michael Phillips. Original libretto, Nicolo Minato, revised by Silvio Stampiglia. Edition by Sir Charles Mackerras and Noël Davies.

CAST:

Xerxes	Ann Murray
Romilda	Valerie Masterson

Arsamenes . . . . Christopher Robson
Amastris . . . . Jean Rigby
Atalanta . . . . Leslie Garrett
Elviro . . . . Christopher Booth-Jones
Ariodates . . . . Rodney Macann

Sir Charles Mackerras, Orchestra and Chorus of the English National Opera.

\+ *Opera Monthly* 3, 6 (October 1990): 45-46, by Keith Sherburne.

Yeoman of the Guard
SEE Yeomen of the Guard, 155.1.—155.3.

155.1. YEOMEN OF THE GUARD by W.S. Gilbert & Sir Arthur Sullivan. **1972**. 16mm film: Rochester Public Library, Reynolds Audio Visual Dept., 115 South Ave., Rochester, NY 14604 716-428-7333

Film version, 50 min., abridged, mono, color, sung in the original English.
Producer, John Seabourne; director, Trevor Evans; script, David Maverovitch; photography, Adrian Jenkins; narrators, Johnny Wayne, Frank Shuster. Part of the *World of Gilbert and Sullivan* series.

CAST:

Jack Point . . . . John Cartier
Elsie Maynard . . . . Valerie Masterson
Colonel Fairfax . . . . Thomas Round
Wilfred Shadbolt . . . . Lawrence Richard
Dame Carruthers . . . . Helen Landis
Phoebe Meryll . . . . Sylvia Eaves
Sir Richard Cholmondeley . . . . Michael Wakeham
Sergeant Meryll . . . . Donald Adams
Leonard Meryll . . . . Glyn Adams
First Yeoman . . . . David Young
Second Yeoman . . . . Clifford Parkes

Gilbert and Sullivan Festival Orchestra and Chorus of England.

155.2. YEOMEN OF THE GUARD by W.S. Gilbert & Sir Arthur Sullivan. **1979**. Magnetic Video, a Twentieth Century-Fox Company

Film version, 105 min., hi-fi, color, sung in the original English.
Producer and director, Stanley Doreman; costumes, Peter Rice. Originally produced at the H.M. Towers of London for the Festival of the City of London by Anthony Besch.

CAST:

Jack Point . . . . Tommy Steele
Elsie Maynard . . . . Laureen Livingstone
Colonel Fairfax . . . . Terry Jenkins
Wilfred Shadbolt . . . . Dennis Wicks

Dame Carruthers . . . . Anne Collins
Phoebe Meryll . . . . Della Jones
Sir Richard Cholmondeley . . . . Tom McDonnell
Sergeant Meryll . . . . Paul Hudson
Leonard Meryll . . . . David Fieldsend
Kate . . . . Hilary Western

David Lloyd-Jones, New World Philharmonic Orchestra.

155.3. YEOMEN OF THE GUARD by W.S. Gilbert & Sir Arthur Sullivan.
1982. CBS/Fox Video

Film version, 115 min., stereo hi-fi, color, sung in the original English.
Producer, Judith De Paul; stage producer, Anthony Besch; director, Dave Heather; production designer, Allan Cameron; costume coordinator, Jenny Beavan; executive producer, George Walker.

CAST:

Jack Point . . . . Joel Grey
Elsie Maynard . . . . Elizabeth Gale
Colonel Fairfax . . . . David Hillman
Wilfred Shadbolt . . . . Alfred Marks
Dame Carruthers . . . . Elizabeth Bainbridge
Phoebe Meryll . . . . Claire Powell
Sir Richard Cholmondeley . . . . Peter Savidge
Sergeant Meryll . . . . Geoffrey Chard
Leonard Meryll . . . . Michael Bulman
Kate . . . . Beryl Korman

Alexander Faris, London Symphony Orchestra, Ambrosian Opera Chorus.

- *Opera News* 50, 2 (August 1985): 37, by Richard Hornak.

156.1. DIE ZAUBERFLÖTE by Wolfgang Amadeus Mozart.
1975. Bel Canto/Paramount Home Video

Film version, 134 min., stereo hi-fi, color, sung in Swedish with English subtitles.
Producer and director, Ingmar Bergman; photography, Sven Nykvist. Filmed in the Drottningholm Theatre, Sweden. Originally issued as a motion picture.

CAST:

Tamino . . . . Josef Köstlinger
Pamina . . . . Irma Urrila
Papageno . . . . Haakon Hagegaard
Papagena . . . . Elisabeth Eriksson
The Queen of the Night . . . . Birgit Nordin
Sarastro . . . . Ulrik Cold

Monostatos . . . . Ragnar Ulfung
Three Ladies . . . . Britt-Marie Aruhn
Kirsten Vaupel
Birgitta Smiding
Three Genii . . . . Urban Malmberg
Erland von Haijne
Ansgar Krook
Speaker . . . . Erik Saeden
Two Men in Armor . . . . Hans Johansson
Jerker Arvidson
Two Priests . . . . Gösta Prüzelius, Ulf Johanson

Eric Ericson, Swedish State Broadcasting Network Symphony.

++ *Levine*, p. 92-93.
\+ *Opera News* 51, 15 (April 11, 1987): 52, by John W. Freeman.

156.2. DIE ZAUBERFLÖTE by Wolfgang Amadeus Mozart.
1976. V.I.E.W. Video

Stage production, Gewandhaus zu Leipzig, Germany, 156 min., hi-fi, color, sung in German, no subtitles.
Staging, Joachim Herz; sets and costumes, Rudolf Heinrich; choreography, Marion Schurath.

CAST:
Tamino . . . . Horst Gebhardt
Pamina . . . . Magdalena Falewicz
Papageno . . . . Dieter Scholz
Papagena . . . . Heidrun Halk
The Queen of the Night . . . . Inge Uibel
Sarastro . . . . Hermann Christian Polster
Monostatos . . . . Guntfried Speck
Three Ladies . . . . Jitka Kovarikova
Anne-Kristin Paul
Gertrud Lahusen-Oertel
Three Genii . . . . Gerhild Muller
Renate Schneeweiss
Heike Syhre
Speakers . . . . Rainer Ludeke, Hans-Peter Schwarzbach
Slave . . . . Peter Engelmann
Two Men in Armor . . . . Rolf Apreck, Helmut Eyle

Gert Bahner, Gewandhaus Orchestra of Leipzig.

•– *Video Rating Guide* 1, 1 (Winter 1990): 325, by Glen Kaltenbrun.

156.3. DIE ZAUBERFLÖTE by Wolfgang Amadeus Mozart.
1978. Video Artists International

Stage production, Glyndebourne Festival, England, 164 min., mono hi-fi, color, sung in German with English subtitles.
Producer, John Cox; designer, David Hockney; television production, Dave Heather.

CAST:

Tamino	Leo Goeke
Pamina	Felicity Lott
Papageno	Benjamin Luxon
Papagena	Elizabeth Conquet
The Queen of the Night	May Sandoz
Sarastro	Thomas Thomaschke
Monostatos	John Fryatt
Three Ladies	Teresa Cahill
	Patricia Parker
	Fiona Kimm
Three Genii	Kate Flowers
	Lindsay John
	Elizabeth Stokes
Speaker	Willard White
Two Men in Armor	Neil McKinnon, John Rath
Priest	Richard Berkeley Steele

Bernard Haitink, London Philharmonic Orchestra, Glyndebourne Festival Chorus.

+ *Opera News* 50, 2 (August 1985): 36, by Richard Hornak.
+ *Opera Quarterly* 3, 4 (Winter 1985/1986): 122-125, by William Huck.

156.4. DIE ZAUBERFLÖTE by Wolfgang Amadeus Mozart.
1983. Philips (PolyGram)

Stage production, Bavarian State Opera, National Theater, Munich, Germany, videotaped on September 19 and 20, 1983, at the National Theater in Munich, 160 min., stereo hi-fi, color, sung in German with English subtitles.
Staged and directed by August Everding.

CAST:

Tamino	Francisco Araiza
Pamina	Lucia Popp
Papageno	Wolfgang Brendel
Pagagena	Gudrun Sieber
The Queen of the Night	Edita Gruberova
Sarastro	Kurt Moll
Monostatos	Norbert Orth

Three Ladies	Pamela Coburn
	Daphne Evangelatos
	Cornelia Wulkopf
Three Genii	Cedric Rossdeutscher
	Christian Immler
	Stefan Bandemehr
Speaker	Jan-Hendrik Rootering
Priests	Kurt Böhme
	Franz Klarwein
	Gerhard Auer
	David Thaw
Slaves	Peter Wagner
	Roland Fröhlich
	Abbas Maghfurian

Wolfgang Sawallisch, Orchestra and Chorus of the Bavarian State Opera.

156.5. DIE ZAUBERFLÖTE by Wolfgang Amadeus Mozart.
1986. Kultur

Stage production, Australian Opera, Sydney, 160 min., stereo hi-fi, color, sung in English.
Director, Göran Järvefelt.

CAST:

Tamino	Gran Wilson
Pamina	Yvonne Kenny
Papageno	John Fulford
Papagena	Peta Blyth
The Queen of the Night	Christa Leahmann
Sarastro	Donald Shanks
Monostatos	Graeme Ewer
Three Ladies	Nicola Ferner-White
	Patricia Price
	Rosemary Gunn
Three Genii	Anthony Phipps
	Andrew Wentzel
	Cameron Phipps
Speaker	John Pringle
Priest	Robin Donald

Richard Bonynge, Elizabethan Sydney Orchestra, Australian Opera Chorus.

156.6. DIE ZAUBERFLÖTE by Wolfgang Amadeus Mozart.
1987. Canadian Broadcasting Corporation Enterprises

Stage production, National Arts Centre of Canada, Ottowa, Canada, 160 min., stereo hi-fi, color, sung in English.
Producer and director, John Thomson; sets and costumes, Peter Rice. Host, Lister Sinclair.

CAST:

Tamino	David Rendall
Pamina	Patricia Wells
Papageno	David Holloway
Papagena	Nancy Hermiston
The Queen of the Night	Rita Shane
Sarastro	Don Garrard
Monostatos	Alan Crofoot
Three Ladies	Barbara Collier Diane Loeb Janet Stubbs
Three Genii	John Griffith John Maxwell Kevin Branshell
Two Priests	Donald Bell, Henry Ingram
Two Men in Armor	Paul Frey Christopher Cameron

Mario Bernardi, Orchestra of the National Arts Centre of Canada.

+ *Opera Canada* 29, 2 (Summer 1988): 52, by Ruby Mercer.

156.7. DIE ZAUBERFLÖTE by Wolfgang Amadeus Mozart.
1991. Deutsche Grammophon (PolyGram)

Stage production, Metropolitan Opera, New York City, 169 min., stereo hi-fi, color, sung in German with English subtitles.
Production, John Cox; sets, David Hockney; video director, Brian Large.

CAST:

Tamino	Francisco Araiza
Pamina	Kathleen Battle
Papageno	Manfred Hemm
Papagena	Barbara Kilduff
The Queen of the Night	Luciana Serra
Sarastro	Kurt Moll
Monostatos	Heinz Zednik
Three Ladies	Juliana Gondek Mimi Lerner Judith Christin

Three Genii .... Ted Huffman
Benjamin Schott
Per-Christian Brevig
Speaker .... Andreas Schmidt
Two Priests .... James Courtney, Bernard Fitch
Two Men in Armor ..... Mark Baker, Michael Devlin

James Levine, Orchestra and Chorus of the Metropolitan Opera.

\+ *Fanfare* 16, 5 (May/June 1993): 436, by James Reel.
\+ *Opera (England)* 43, 12 (December 1992): 1448, by Noël Goodwin.

Appendix A: Motion Pictures and Television Productions, Abbreviated Listing

Abbreviated Listing

There are a number of motion pictures and television productions (some out-of-print) included in the *Listing of Operas by Title* section of the mediagraphy. Those titles singled out for entry in this appendix are worthy of mention but because of their relative inaccessibility are not described as fully as the entries in the *Listing of Operas by Title* section. As much information as could be obtained is included in each entry.

Numbering in this appendix is totally independent of that used in the *Listing of Operas by Title* section of the mediagraphy. Numbers in this appendix are prefixed by "A" to indicate entry in Appendix A. Titles listed here are not indexed in any of the indices.

Most of the titles listed below are available either as 16mm film rentals, "private" videocassettes, or video copies available for viewing at the Library of Congress in Washington, D.C. Several are out-of-print either from lack of use (no demand for rentals) or copyright constraints (such as *Porgy and Bess*, A31.). Out-of-print titles will not have a rental or purchase source included in their entries.

All operas are sung in their original language without subtitles unless otherwise noted. All titles are recorded with a monaural sound track.

A1.1. ALEKO by Sergei Rachmaninoff.
1953. Formerly available (1984) as a film rental from Corinth Films.

Film version, 61 min., black and white.

A1.2. ALEKO by Sergei Rachmaninoff.
1989. Lyric Distribution, Inc.

Film version, color.

CAST:

Singers are listed first; actors and actresses are listed in parenthesis.

Evgeny Nesterenko, Volkova (Volshaninova), Matorin (Golovin), Kotowa (Papasjan), Muntjan (Semyonov); Kitajenko, conductor.

A2. ANDREA CHÉNIER by Umberto Giordano.
1970. Lyric Distribution, Inc.

Television production, 110 min., color.

CAST:

Andrea Chénier .... Franco Corelli
Maddalena di Coigny .... Celestina Casapietra
Carlo Gérard .... Piero Cappuccilli
Bersi .... Giovanna Di Rocco
Contess di Coigny .... Gabriella Carturan
Madelon .... Cristina Anghelakova
Roucher .... Luigi Roni
Novelist Pietro Fléville .... Leonardo Monreale
Fouquier-Tinville .... Mario Chiappi
Sans-Culotte Mathieu .... Giorgio Giorgetti
Spy (L'Incroyable) .... Ermanno Lorenzi
Abbé .... Florindo Andreolli

Bruno Bartoletti, Orchestra Sinfonica e coro di Radiotelevisione Italiana.

Le Barbier de Séville
SEE Il Barbiere di Siviglia, A3.1.

A3.1. IL BARBIERE DI SIVIGLIA by Gioacchino Rossini.
1934. Video Yesteryear

Feature film, originally released as *Le Barbier de Séville*, 42 min., abridged, black and white, sung and spoken in French.
A compilation of scenes and music from Rossini's *Barbiere di Siviglia* including "Ecco Ridente," "Largo al Factotum," the tenor/baritone duet "L'Oro," "La Calunnia," "Una voce poco fà," with the addition of Chérubin and Suzanne. The film ends with the overture to Mozart's *Le Nozze di Figaro*. Musical director, Louis Masson.

CAST:

Rosine . . . . Hélène Robert
Count Almaviva . . . . Jean Galland
Figaro . . . . André Baugé
Bazile . . . . Charpin
Doctor Bartholo . . . . Pierre Juvenet
Fanchette . . . . Nane Germon
Marcelline . . . . Yhvonne Yma
Chérubin . . . . Monique Rolland
Suzanne . . . . Josette Day

A3.2. IL BARBIERE DI SIVIGLIA by Gioacchino Rossini.
1949.

Feature film photographed like a stage production, 98 min., black and white, sung in French.
Producer, Claude Dolbert; director, Jean Loubignac. With music by Rossini and Castil-Blaise. Musical director, Louis Musy.

CAST:

Rosina . . . . Lucienne Jourfier
Count Almaviva . . . . Raymond Amade
Figaro . . . . Roger Bussonet
Doctor Bartolo . . . . Louis Musy
Basilio . . . . Roger Bourdin
Berta/Marceline . . . . Renee Gilly

– *Motion Picture Guide.*

A3.3. IL BARBIERE DI SIVIGLIA by Gioacchino Rossini.
1954. Lyric Distribution, Inc.; Bel Canto Society

Film version, color. An abridgement with German dialogue in place of the recitatives.

CAST:

Tito Gobbi as Figaro, with the voices of Giulietta Simionato as Rosina, Nicola Monti, Giulio Neri.

A4. THE BARTERED BRIDE by Bedřich Smetana.
1932. Lyric Distribution, Inc.; Bel Canto Society

Feature film, released as *Die Verkäufte Braut*, about 74 min., black and white, sung and spoken in German, no subtitles.
Director, Max Ophüls.

CAST:

Jarmila Novotna, Willi Domgraf-Fassbaender, Kner, Janowika, Kemp, Valentin, Karlstadt, Sörensen.

A5. THE BEGGAR'S OPERA music by Sir Arthur Bliss.
1953. Lyric Distribution, Inc.

Feature film, 94 min., color, sung and spoken in English.
Producers, Laurence Olivier, Herbert Wilcox; director, Peter Brook; writer, Dennis Cannan, Christopher Fry (based on John Gay's comic opera); photography (technicolor), Guy Green.

CAST:
Olivier and Hollaway did their own singing; others were dubbed.

Captain MacHeath . . . . Laurence Olivier
Lockit . . . . Stanley Holloway
Peachum . . . . George Devine
Mrs. Peachum . . . . Mary Clare
Mrs. Trapes . . . . Athene Seyler
Polly Peachum . . . . Dorothy Tutin
Lucy Lockit . . . . Daphne Anderson
The Beggar . . . . Hugh Griffith
Jenny Diver . . . . Yvonne Furneaux

A6.1. DER BETTELSTUDENT by Carl Millöcker.
1931.

Feature film, 66 min., black and white.
Producer, John Harvel; directors, John Harvel, Victor Hanbury; writers, John Stafford, Hans Zerlett. Originally issued as a motion picture in England by Amalgamated.

CAST:
Countess Novalska . . . . Margaret Halstan
Jan Janitzky . . . . Jerry Verno
Colonel Ollendorf . . . . Frederick Lloyd
Tania . . . . Shirley Dale
Carl Romaine . . . . Lance Fairfax
Sergeant . . . . Mark Daly
Broni . . . . Jill Hands
Nicki . . . . Ashley Cooper

– *Motion Picture Guide*.

A6.2. DER BETTELSTUDENT by Carl Millöcker.
1958. German Language Video Center, Division of Heidelburg Haus Imports, 7625 Pendleton Pike, Indianapolis, IN 46226-5298
800-252-0957, fax 317-547-1257

Feature film, about 97 min., color
Director, Werner Jacobs; writer, Fritz Boetiger. Originally issued as a motion picture in Germany.

CAST:

Symon Rymanowisz	Gerhard Riedmann
Countess Laura	Waltraut Haas
Countess Bronislawa	Elma Karlowa
Count Kaminsky	Dick Price
Palmatica	Fita Benkhoff
Jan Janitzky	Günther Philipp
Colonel Ollendorf	Gustav Knuth
Enterich	Rudolf Vogel
Wagenheim	Karl Lieffen
Additional performers	Ellen Kessler
	Alice Kessler

– *Motion Picture Guide.*

A7.1. CARMEN by Georges Bizet.
1931.

Feature film, 79 min., black and white, sung and spoken in English, released as a motion picture in Great Britain titled *Gipsy Blood*.
Director, Cecil Lewis; writers, Cecil Lewis, Walter C. Mycroft.

CAST:

Carmen	Marguerite Namara
Don José	Thomas Burke
Escamillo	Lance Fairfax
Zuniga	Lester Matthews
Factory Girl	Mary Clare
El Dancairo	Dennis Wyndham
Innkeeper	Lewin Mannering
El Remendado	D. Hay Petrie

– *Motion Picture Guide.*

A7.2. CARMEN by Georges Bizet.
1946. 16mm film, non-circulating, Bristol Community College, Learning Resources Center, Fall Fiver, MA 02720

Feature film, 105 min., black and white, sung and spoken in French with English subtitles.
Director, Christian Jaque. This film was adapted from Prosper Mérimée's original novel using some of Bizet's music

CAST:

Carmen	Viviane Romance
Don José	Jean Marais
Pamela	Ellie Parvo
Lucas Escamillo	Julien Bertau
Dorotea	Margarite Moreno

El Remendado .... Bernard Blier
Lillias Pastia .... Jean Rochard

• *Motion Picture Guide.*

A7.3. CARMEN by Georges Bizet.
1949.

Feature film, 102 min., black and white, sung and spoken in Spanish with English subtitles.
Director and writer, Florian Rey.

CAST:
Imperio Argentina, Rafael Rivelles, Manuel Luna, Alberto Romea, Anselmo Fernandez, Pedro Barreto, Margit Symo, José Prada.

A8. CAVALLERIA RUSTICANA by Pietro Mascagni.
1953.

Feature film, released as *Fatal Desire*, originally shot in color (80 min.), US release in 1963 was in black and white (106 min.), sung and spoken in Italian.
Director, Carmine Gallone; producer, Carlo Ponti; based on a novel by Giovanni Verga and the opera by Mascagni. Musical director, Oliviero De Fabritiis.

CAST:
Alfio .... Anthony Quinn
Lola .... Kermia
Santuzza .... May Britt
Turiddu .... Ettore Manni
Mamma Lucia .... Virginia Balestrieri
Voice (off-screen) .... Tito Gobbi

• *Motion Picture Guide.*

The Cool Mikado
See The Mikado, A26.

A9. LES CONTES D'HOFFMANN by Jacques Offenbach.
1965. Lyric Distribution, Inc.

Film version, color, sung in German.

CAST:
Hanns Nocker, Muszely, Asmus, Ender, Kuziemski; Voigtmann, conductor.

A10. DON PASQUALE by Gaetano Donizetti.
1978. Lyric Distribution, Inc.

Film version, color, sung in German.

CAST:
Oskar Czerwenka, Reri Grist, Luigi Alva, Hermann Prey; Silvio Varviso, conductor.

A11. DON QUIXOTE by Jacques Ibert.
1935. French version, *Don Quichotte*. French and English versions, Lyric Distribution, Inc. and the Bel Canto Society

Feature film based on Cervantes's novel with music by Jacques Ibert, 73 min., black and white. French and English versions were filmed simultaneously.
Producer, Nelson Vandor; director, G.W. Pabst.

CAST:
Don Quixote .... Fydor Ivanovich Chaliapin
Sancho Panza .... George Robey
The Niece .... Sidney Fox
The Duke .... Miles Mander
Dulcinea .... Renee Valliers

Aleksandr Sergeevich Dargomisjsky, conductor.

+ *Motion Picture Guide.*
+ *Video Review* 10, 6 (September 1989): 72, by Bert Wechsler.

Fatal Desire
SEE Cavalleria Rusticana, A8.

A12. FAUST by Charles Gounod.
1930s-1940s. 16mm film rental, Budget Films.

Film version, abridgement of first act of Gounod's *Faust*, 10 min., black and white. An "Official Film." Performed on a small stage (most probably at the old Metropolitan Opera House at Broadway and 39th streets), fully costumed and staged intercut with shots of a couple in evening dress viewing the action. No credits appear on the film except for Dr. Hugo Riesenfeld who is credited as "musical director."

First Opera Film Festival series

SEE Il Barbiere di Siviglia, 13.2.
Carmen, 22.1.
Don Pasquale, 34.
Fra Diavolo, 52.
Guglielmo Tell, A15.
Lucia di Lammermoor, 82.1.
Le Nozze di Figaro, 101.2.

A13.1. DIE FLEDERMAUS by Johann Strauss.
1953. Master and viewing copies at the Library of Congress.

Television production, 65 min., black and white, sung and spoken in English.
Television script by John Gutman, translation by Garson Kanin; English lyrics by Howard Dietz; staged for television by Herbert Graf; producer, William Spier; director, Bob Banner. Originally telecast on the *Omnibus* television series, CBS, on January 2, 1953. Host, Alistair Cooke.

CAST:

John Brownlee, Charles Kullman, Brenda Lewis, Lois Hunt, Hugh Thompson; Eugene Ormandy, conductor, the Metropolitan Opera.

A13.2. DIE FLEDERMAUS by Johann Strauss.
1964.

Feature film, 107 min., color, sung and spoken in German, based on Strauss's operetta. Kurt Edelhagen, the Vienna State Opera.
Director and writer, Geza von Cziffra.

CAST:

Roselinde . . . . Marianne Koch
Gabriel von Eisenstein . . . . Pete Alexander
Adele . . . . Marika Rokk
Prince Orlofsky . . . . Boy Gobert
Alfred . . . . Rolf Kutschera
Joseph . . . . Rudolf Carl

A14. LA FORZA DEL DESTINO by Giuseppe Verdi.
1949. Lyric Distribution, Inc.

Film version, abridged, black and white.

CAST:

Voices of Caterina Mancini, Masini, Tito Gobbi, Giulio Neri, Cleo Elmo; Gabriele Santini, conductor.

Gipsy Blood

SEE Carmen, A7.1.

A15. GUGLIELMO TELL by Gioacchino Rossini.
1948. Lyric Distribution, Inc.; Bel Canto Society; 16mm film, San Francisco State University, San Francisco, CA 94132

Film version, released as *William Tell*, 25 min., abridged, black and white, sung in Italian with English narration.
Produced by George Richfield. Filmed on stage at the Rome Opera House, Italy. Part of the *First Opera Film Festival* series.

CAST:
Voices of Tito Gobbi, Gabriella Gatti, Soler; Angelo Questa, conductor.

+ *EFLA* (1965), p. 466 [EFLA No. 1950.892]

The Gypsy Baron
See Der Zigeunerbaron, A37.

A16. H.M.S. PINAFORE by W.S. Gilbert & Sir Arthur Sullivan.
1960.

Film version, 83 min., black and white. Made by Contemporary Productions in association with the Canadian Broadcasting Corporation and originally released as a 16mm film.
The Stratford (Ontario, Canada) Shakespearean Festival Players. Directors, Tyrone Guthrie, Norman Campbell.

CAST:
Eric House, Marion Studholme, Andrew Downie, Harry Mossfield, Irene Byatt, Douglas Campbell; Louis Applebaum, conductor.

A17. KATERINA IZMAILOVA by Dmitri Dmitrievich Shostakovich.
1969.

Film version, 118 min., color.
Director, Mikhail Shapiro; cinematography, Rostislav Davydov, Vladimir Ponomaryov; musical director, Konstantin Simeonov. A Lenfilm released by Artkino in the Soviet Union.

CAST:
Katerina Lvovna Izmailova ..... Galina Vishnevskaya
Sergey .... Artyom Ionzemstsev
Zinoviy Borisovich Ismailov .... Nikolay Boyarsky
Boris Timofeyevich Ismailov ...... Aleksandr Sokolov
Sonyetka .... Tatyana Gavrilova
Village Drunk .... R. Tkachuk

Additional singers . . . . L. Malinovsakaya
K. Adashevsky
I. Bogolyubov
K. Tyagunov
V. Lyubimova
A. Zhila
G. Krasulya
V. Gerasimchuk

A18. IOLANTHA by Peter Ilich Tchaikovsky.
1964.

Film version, 82 min., color.
Director, Vladimir Gorikker; costumes, U. Pauzer; photography, Vadim Mass; special effects, E. August, V. Shildknekht. Originally issued as a motion picture by Riga and released by Artkino in the Soviet Union.

CAST:

Yolanta . . . . Natalya Rudnaya
King Rene . . . . Fyodor Nikitin
Vaudemont . . . . Yuri Perov
Duke Robert . . . . Alexander Belyavsky
Eon-Hakkia . . . . Pyotr Glebov
Martha . . . . Valentina Ushajova
Bertrand . . . . Valdis Sandbert

A19. IOLANTHE by W.S. Gilbert & Sir Arthur Sullivan.
1974.

Film version, 54 min., color.
Producer, John Seabourne. Part of the *World of Gilbert and Sullivan* series. With soloists of the D'Oyly Carte Opera Company and Sadler's Wells.

Lache Bajazzo
SEE Il Pagliacci, A28.

Laugh, Pagliacci
SEE Il Pagliacci, A28.

A20. LUCIA DI LAMMERMOOR by Gaetano Donizetti.
1946. Lyric Distribution, Inc.; Opera Dubs, Inc.

Film version, black and white.

CAST:

Nelly Corradi, Mario Filippeschi, Afro Poli, Italo Tajo; Oliviero De Fabritiis, conductor.

A21. LULU by Alban Berg.
1978.

Feature film, 94 min., color.
Producer, director, and photographer, Ronald Chase. A feature film based on the well-known Pabst film *Pandora's Box* (*Die Büchse der Pandora*, 1929). This American version tells the story silently with music from Alban Berg's opera *Lulu*. The principal actors are listed below.

CAST:
Lulu . . . . Elisa Leonelli
Ludwig Schon . . . . Paul Shenar
Alwa Schon . . . . John Roberdeau
Countess Gerschwitz . . . . Norma Leistiko
Dr. Goll . . . . Warren Pierce
Jack the Ripper . . . . Thomas Roberdeau

– *Motion Picture Guide.*

A22.1. DIE LUSTIGE WITWE by Franz Lehár.
1952. Film rental, Swank Motion Pictures (Chicago office, 800-876-3330; New York office, 800-876-3344; St. Louis office, 800-876-5577)

Feature film, released as *The Merry Widow*, 105 min., sung and spoken in English.
Producer, Joe Pasternak; director, Curtis Bernhardt; lyrics, Paul Francis Webster. Musical director, Jay Blackton. Lamas sings the major numbers from the operetta. Originally produced and released as a motion picture by MGM.

CAST:
Crystal Radek . . . . Lana Turner
Count Danilo . . . . Fernando Lamas
Kitty Riley . . . . Una Merkel
Baron Popoff . . . . Richard Haydn
King of Marshovia . . . . Thomas Gomez
Marshovian Ambassador . . . . John Abbott

• *Motion Picture Guide.*

A22.2. DIE LUSTIGE WITWE by Franz Lehár.
1954. Master and viewing video copies at the Library of Congress.

Television production, 90 min., black and white, sung and spoken in English.
Staged by Cyril Ritchard; choreography, John Butler; script editor, Max Wylie; film supervisor, Boris D. Kaplan; production designer, Henry May. Originally telecast as *The Merry Widow* on the *Omnibus* television series, CBS, on December 26, 1954. Host, Alistair Cooke.

CAST:

Sonia	Patrice Munsel
Danilo	Theodor Uppman
Natalie	Dorothy Coulter
Jolidon	Jim Hawthorne
Nish	Martyn Green
Popoff	Jerome Kilty
St. Brioche	Robert Goss
Khadja	Christopher Hewett
Cascada	Iggie Wolfington
Nova Kovich	Del Horstmann
Frou-Frou	Gloria Hamilton

Eugene Ormandy, conductor.

A23. MARTHA by Friedrich von Flotow.
1935. Lyric Distribution, Inc.

Feature film, black and white. Starring Helge Roswaenge.

A24. THE MEDIUM by Gian Carlo Menotti.
1959. Master and viewing video copies at the Library of Congress.

Television production, 60 min., black and white.
Directors, Gian Carlo Menotti, William A. Graham; production designer, Henry May. Originally telecast on the *Omnibus* television series, NBC, on February 15, 1959. Host, Alistair Cooke.

CAST:

Madame Flora	Claramae Turner
Monica	Lee Venora
Toby, a Mute Boy	Jose Perez
Additional singers	Beverly Dame
	Donald P. Morgan

Werner Torkanowsky, conductor.

A25. THE MERMAID by Wang Fu-ling.
1966.

Feature film, 99 min., color.
Producer, Runme Shaw; director, Kao Li; photography, Tung Shao-yung. This Chinese fantasy opera was originally issued as a motion picture in Hong Kong.

CAST:

Chang Chen	Ivy Ling Po
Fairy Marina/Peony Chin	Li Ching
Lord Pao	Ching Miao
Madam Wang	Au-yang Sha-fei

Chin . . . . Yang Tse-ching
Turtle Fairy . . . . Chiang Kuang-chao
Sorcerer . . . . Li Yuen-chung

The Merry Widow
SEE Die Lustige Witwe, A22.1.-A22.2.

A26. THE MIKADO by W.S. Gilbert & Sir Arthur Sullivan.
1963.

Feature film, 81 min., color.
Producer, Harold Baim; director, Michael Winner; writers, Michael Winner, Maurice Browning, Lew Schwartz. Originally issued as a motion picture by United Artists titled *The Cool Mikado*. The opera is re-set in post-World War II Japan.

CAST:
Hank Mikado . . . . Kevin Scott
Ko-Ko . . . . Frankie Howerd
Judge Mikado/Charlie . . . . Stubby Kaye
Nanki . . . . Lionel Blair
Katie Shaw . . . . Jacqueline Jones
Yum-Yum . . . . Jill Mai Meredith
Peep-Bo . . . . Yvonne Shima
Pitti-Sing . . . . Tsai Chin
Detective . . . . Tommy Cooper
Ronald Fortescue . . . . Dennis Price
Mike and Bernie . . . . Bernie Winters
Harry . . . . Glen Mason
Elmer . . . . Dermot Walsh

• *Motion Picture Guide.*

A27. MOZART AND SALIERI by Nikolay Rimsky-Korsakov.
1961. Formerly available (1984) as a film rental from Corinth Films.

Film version, 46 min., black and white.

Omnibus television series
SEE La Bohème, 18.1.
Die Fledermaus, A13.1.
Die Lustige Witwe, A22.2.
The Medium, A24.
La Périchole, A29.
The Pirates of Penzance, A.30.1.
Trial by Jury, A34.

A28. IL PAGLIACCI by Ruggiero Leoncavallo.
1943. Lyric Distribution, Inc. (Italian, English subtitles); Bel Canto Society (German, no subtitles; Italian, English subtitles)

Feature film, released in Italian as *Ridi Pagliacco* (also known as *Laugh, Pagliacco*) and in German as *Lache Bajazzo*, 84 min., black and white.
Director, Giuseppe Fatigati; production company, Italia Film. With music by Leoncavallo, Bellini, Millöcker, Ricci. Musical director, Luigi Ricci. Starring Beniamino Gigli as a famous tenor named Morelli and Alida Valli as Canio's daughter, tells the story of Canio after he is released from prison. Parts of the opera *Il Pagliacci* are performed on a stage; the cast of that abridged performance is listed below.

CAST:

Canio . . . . Beniamino Gigli
Nedda . . . . Adriana Perris
Tonio . . . . Leone Pacci
Silvio . . . . Mario Boviello
Beppe . . . . Adelio Zagonara

- *Levine*, p. 91-2.
- *Opera News* 52, 16 (May 1988): 49, by Harvey E. Phillips.

A29. LA PÉRICHOLE by Jacques Offenbach.
1958. Master and viewing video copies at the Library of Congress.

Television production, 70 min., black and white (originally telecast in color), sung and spoken in English, English text by Maurice Valency.
Directors, Cyril Ritchard, Richard Dunlap; choreography, Zachary Solov. Originally telecast on the *Omnibus* television series, NBC, on January 26, 1958. Host, Alistair Cooke.

CAST:

Cyril Ritchard, Laurel Hurley, Theodor Uppman, Osie Hawkins, Paul Franke, and members of the Metropolitan Opera company.

A30.1.THE PIRATES OF PENZANCE by W.S. Gilbert & Sir Arthur Sullivan.
1955. Master and viewing video copies at the Library of Congress.

Television production, abridged, The D'Oyly Carte Opera Company directed by Bridget D'Oyly Carte, 35 min., black and white.
Director, Charles S. Dubin; art director, Henry May; film supervisor, Boris D. Kaplan. Originally telecast on the *Omnibus* television series, CBS, on November 13, 1955. Host, Alistair Cooke.

CAST:

Joy Mornay, Joyce Wright, Neville Griffiths; Isidore Godfrey, conductor.

A30.2.THE PIRATES OF PENZANCE by W.S. Gilbert & Sir Arthur Sullivan.
1961.

Film version, 83 min., black and white. Made by Contemporary Productions in association with the Canadian Broadcasting Corporation and released as a 16mm film.
The Stratford (Ontario, Canada) Shakespearean Festival Players. Directors, Tyrone Guthrie, Norman Campbell.

CAST:
Andrew Downie, Eric House, Harry Mossfield, Irene Byatt, Howell Glynne, Marion Studholme; Louis Applebaum, conductor.

A31. PORGY AND BESS by George Gershwin.
1959.

Feature film, 138 min., color.
Producer, Samuel Goldwyn; director, Otto Preminger; photography, Leon Shamroy; musical director, André Previn with Ken Darby; sets, Howard Bristol; costumes, Irene Sharaff. Originally issued as a motion picture by Samuel Goldwyn. Pulled from distribution in the 1980s because of a copyright controversy.

CAST:
Porgy . . . . Sidney Poitier
Bess . . . . Dorothy Dandridge
Sporting Life . . . . Sammy Davis, Jr.
Maria . . . . Pearl Bailey
Crown . . . . Brock Peters
Jake . . . . Leslie Scott
Clara . . . . Diahann Carroll
Serena . . . . Ruth Attaway
Peter . . . . Clarence Muse
Annie . . . . Everdinne Wilson
Robbins . . . . Joel Fluellen
Mingo . . . . Earl Jackson
Nelson . . . . Moses LaMarr
Lily . . . . Margaret Hairston
Jim . . . . Ivan Dixon
Undertaker . . . . William Walker
Frazier . . . . Roy Glenn

++ *Motion Picture Guide.*

Ridi Pagliacco
SEE Il Pagliacci, A28.

A32. SADKO by Nikolay Rimsky-Korsakov.
1952. Formerly available (1984) as a film rental from Corinth Films.

Film version, 88 min., black and white. Rimsky-Korsakov's music is used as a background for the fairy tale by Alexander Ptushko.

A33. TOSCA by Giacomo Puccini.
1956. Lyric Distribution, Inc.; Bel Canto Society

Film version, black and white.

CAST:
Franco Corelli with the voices of Maria Caniglia, Guelfi; Oliviero De Fabritiis, conductor.

A34. TRIAL BY JURY by W.S. Gilbert & Sir Arthur Sullivan.
1953. Master and viewing video copies at the Library of Congress.

Television production, 23 min., abridged, black and white.
Producer, William Spier; director, Andrew McCullough; sets, Henry May. Originally telecast on the *Omnibus* television series, CBS, on April 19, 1953. Host, Alistair Cooke.

CAST:
Martyn Green, Davis Cunningham, Arylne Frank.

A35. IL TROVATORE by Giuseppe Verdi.
1950. Lyric Distribution, Inc.; Bel Canto Society

Film version, black and white.

CAST:
With the voices of Gino Sinimberghi, Colonello, Pederzini, Enzo Mascherini; Gabriele Santini, conductor.

Die Verkäufte Braut
SEE The Bartered Bride, A4.

William Tell
SEE Guglielmo Tell, A15.

World of Gilbert and Sullivan series
SEE: The Gondoliers, 62.1.
H.M.S. Pinafore, 64.2.
Iolanthe, A19.
The Mikado, 97.3.
The Pirates of Penzance, 111.1.
Ruddigore, 121.1.
Trial by Jury, 138.
Yeomen of the Guard, 155.1.

Yolanta

SEE Iolantha, A18.

A36. ZAR UND ZIMMERMANN by Albert Lortzing.
1976. Lyric Distribution, Inc.

Film version, color.

CAST:

Lucia Popp, Hermann Prey, Karl Ridderbusch, Werner Krenn; Heinz Wallberg, conductor.

A37. DER ZIGEUNERBARON by Johann Strauss.
1954. German Language Video Center, Division of Heidelburg Haus Imports, 7625 Pendleton Pike, Indianapolis, IN 46226-5298
800-252-0957, fax 317-547-1257

Feature film, about 101 min., color.
Originally issued as a motion picture in Germany.

CAST:

Paul Hoerbiger, Gerhard Riedmann, Oskar Sima, Margit Saad.

Appendix B: Distributors

This appendix lists primary and secondary distributors of opera videos on VHS videocassette and laser disc (check with individual distributors for availability of titles on Beta and 8mm videocassette) as well as rental sources for 16mm film. Most distributors offer services for personal and institutional (purchase order) orders. Exceptions to this practice are noted under the individual distributor. Most of the distributors publish catalogs, many of which are available free of charge.

Baker & Taylor Video
201 Gladiolus St.
Momence, IL 60954-1799
Orders: 800-435-6111,
Illinois, 800-892-1879
Information/accounts:
800-435-1845,
Illinois, 800-892-1892
No personal orders.

Bel Canto Society, Inc.*
11 Riverside Drive
New York, NY 10023
800-347-5056 (orders)
*Private source for video and audio. Customer service by mail. Personal orders.

Budget Films
4590 Santa Monica Blvd.
Los Angeles, CA 90029
213-660-0187
16mm rentals.

Chambers Record and Video Corp.
61 Bennington Ave.
Freeport, NY 11520
800-892-9338
fax 516-867-6198. Video and Audio. Institutional orders.

Corinth Video
34 Gansevoort Street
New York, NY 10014
800-221-4720

Criterion Collection
See Voyager Company

European Video Distributors
2321 W. Olive Ave.
Burbank, CA 91506
800-423-6752
Catalog in Hungarian. Videos distributed through Baker & Taylor and others.

Facets Multimedia, Inc.
1517 West Fullerton Ave.
Chicago, IL 60614
800-331-6197

Home Vision
5547 N. Ravenswood Ave.
Chicago, IL 60640-1199
800-323-4222, x45
fax 312-878-8648
Home Vision is a division of Public Media, Inc.

Image Entertainment, Inc.
9333 Oso Avenue
Chatsworth, CA 91311
800-473-3475
fax 818-407-9111
Exemplary pressings of laser discs.

Indiana University
Center for Media and Teaching Resources
Bloomington, IN 47405
800-552-8620
16mm archival opera films.

Ingram Video, Div. Ingram Dist. Group
347 Redwood Dr.
Nashville, TN 37217
800-824-4663

Ingram Library Services
1125 Heil Quaker Blvd.
La Vergne, TN 37086
800-937-5300
Laser discs and videos, institutional distributor.

Iowa State University Film/ Video Library
121 Pearson Hall
Ames, IA 50011
515-294-1540
16mm rentals. Holds the *Focus on Opera* series on 16mm film.

Kultur
121 Highway 36
West Long Branch, NY 07764
800-4-KULTUR

Lyric Distribution, Inc.*
18 Madison Avenue
Hicksville, NY 11801
800-325-9742
fax 516-932-5514
Video and Audio. *Private source.

Metropolitan Opera Guild Video Service
70 Lincoln Center Plaza
New York, NY 10133-0259
800-453-2258
No longer distributes filmstrips, video and audio only.

Movies Unlimited
6736 Castor Ave.
Philadelphia, PA 19149
800-523-0823
fax 215-725-3683

Music Video Distributors
Box 1128
Norristown, PA 19404
800-888-0486
fax 215-272-6074

Opera Dubs, Inc.*
P.O. Box 2051
Hillside Manor Branch
New Hyde Park, NY 11040
Video and Audio. *Private source.

Public Media, Inc.
See Home Vision

Reel Images
See Video Yesteryear

Rose Records
214 South Wabash Ave.
Chicago, IL 60604
800-955-ROSE
fax 312-663-3559
Video and Audio.

Video Arts International
See Video Artists International

Video Artists International
(VAI)
Appears on some early releases as *Video Arts International*
158 Linwood Plaza, Suite 301
Fort Lee, NJ 07024-3704
800-477-7146
fax 201-947-8850

The Video Catalog
Box 64428
Saint Paul, MN 55164-0428
800-733-6656
800-458-4535 (institutional)
fax 612-659-4320

Video Images
See Video Yesteryear

Video Opera House
Box 800
Concord, MA 01742
800-262-8600
fax 508-263-8075

Video Yesteryear
P.O. Box C
Sandy Hook, CT 06482
800-243-0987
Personal orders only.
Distributes Reel Images and Video Images.

V.I.E.W. Video
34 East 23rd Street
New York, NY 10010
800-843-9843
fax 212-979-0266

Viewfinders, Inc.
P.O. Box 1665
Evanston, IL 60204
800-342-3342
fax 708-869-1710

Voyager Company
1351 Pacific Coast Highway
Santa Monica, CA 90401
800-446-2001,
in CA 800-443-2001
Laser disc pressings from the *Criterion Collection*, others.

Index of Singers and Conductors

Numbers refer to entries, not pages. Titles precede entry numbers.

Index of Composers

Numbers refer to entries, not pages. Titles precede entry numbers. For three or more sequential entries under the same title, a dash between the first and last entry number is used to indicate inclusion, e.g., 5.1.–5.4., instead of 5.1., 5.2., 5.3., 5.4.

Index of Production Types

Numbers refer to entries, not pages. Titles precede entry numbers. For three or more sequential entries under the same title, a dash between the first and last entry number is used to indicate inclusion, e.g., 5.1.–5.4., instead of 5.1., 5.2., 5.3., 5.4. Three or more non-sequential entries under the same title are separated by commas, e.g., 4.1., 4.3., 4.4., 4.6.

About the Compiler

SHARON G. ALMQUIST is Head of the Media Library at the University of North Texas. She is the author of *Sound Recordings and the Library* (1987) and "Music at the University of Buffalo: The Baird Years," which appeared in *American Music* (1992). She is a reviewer for *Video Rating Guide for Libraries.*